Digital Image Processing with C++

Digital Image Processing with C++: Implementing Reference Algorithms with the CImg Library presents the theory of digital image processing and implementations of algorithms using a dedicated library. Processing a digital image means transforming its content (denoising, stylizing, etc.) or extracting information to solve a given problem (object recognition, measurement, motion estimation, etc.). This book presents the mathematical theories underlying digital image processing as well as their practical implementation through examples of algorithms implemented in the C++ language using the free and easy-to-use CImg library.

Chapters cover the field of digital image processing in a broad way and propose practical and functional implementations of each method theoretically described. The main topics covered include filtering in spatial and frequency domains, mathematical morphology, feature extraction and applications to segmentation, motion estimation, multispectral image processing and 3D visualization.

Students or developers wishing to discover or specialize in this discipline and teachers and researchers hoping to quickly prototype new algorithms or develop courses will all find in this book material to discover image processing or deepen their knowledge in this field.

David Tschumperlé is a permanent CNRS research scientist heading the IMAGE team at the GREYC Laboratory in Caen, France. He's particularly interested in partial differential equations and variational methods for processing multi-valued images in a local or non-local way. He has authored more than 40 papers in journals or conferences and is the project leader of CImg and G'MIC, two open-source software/libraries.

Christophe Tilmant is associate professor in computer science at Clermont-Auvergne University. His research activities include image processing and artificial intelligence, where he has authored more than 30 papers. His teaching includes deep learning, image processing and network security. He participates or leads several French research programs.

Vincent Barra is a full professor in computer science at Clermont-Auvergne University and associate director of the LIMOS Lab. He teaches artificial intelligence and image processing in engineering schools and master's programs. His research activities focus on n-dimensional data analysis with methodological and application aspects in various fields. He has authored more than 90 papers in journals or conferences and participates or leads several French and European research programs.

Digital Image Processing with C++

Implementing Reference Algorithms with the CImg Library

David Tschumperlé
Christophe Tilmant
Vincent Barra

CRC Press
Taylor & Francis Group
Boca Raton London New York

CRC Press is an imprint of the
Taylor & Francis Group, an **informa** business

Contents

Preface

Rachid Deriche is a senior research director at *The Inria center at Université Côte d'Azur* in France where he leads the *Athena* research project-team. His research aims to explore the Central Nervous System (CNS) through mathematical and computational models of medical imaging, with a focus on the recovery of the human brain's structural and functional connectivities. He was awarded the EADS Grand Prize (Computer Science) by the French Academy of Sciences in 2013, a prestigeous ERC Advanced Grant for his project in Computational Brain Connectivity Mapping in 2016, Doctorate Honoris Causa by Sherbrooke University in 2014 and a 3IA *Université Côte d'Azur* Chair in 2019. He has published over 100 journal articles and over 300 conference papers. His extensive scientific career includes three main research areas: i) computational image processing, ii) 3D computer vision, and iii) computational neuroimaging.

It is with great pleasure that I accepted to preface this book, which is the successful outcome of several years of research and experience by a trio of authors who are experts in digital image processing, combining both its theoretical aspects and its software implementations.

I know David Tschumperlé since I had him as a trainee in my project-team at *Inria Sophia Antipolis-Méditerranée*, in March 1999, as part of his Master's degree, from the University of Nice Sophia-Antipolis in which I was teaching a module about image processing based on variational approaches, *PDE*-based and *Level Sets* techniques (*PDE*: Partial Differential Equation).

The internship was about the study and development of *diffusion PDE* methods for multi-valued images (more particularly color images), i.e., images with potentially more than three components per pixel. I selected him among several applicants of the promotion, because he was also a general engineer in computer science, and his double background perfectly met the need for a trainee who could program with ease in *C/C++* while mastering the theoretical aspects and those related to an efficient software implementation of the developed algorithms. PDE-based methods often require several hundreds or even thousands of complex iterations to be applied to images, as you will discover in this book, and the need to optimize the machine's processor resources is therefore all the more pressing.

After promising results, David continued his work in a PhD thesis, under my supervision. And very quickly, it became obvious that we needed to develop a reference $C/C++$ library to process images with more than three channels or volume images with any values (matrices, tensors, ...) to develop our research work.

Through the implemented algorithms, tests, successes and failures, David gradually built his own personal $C++$ library of reusable features, in order to complete his thesis work. The originality of David's research work, the need to optimize and develop software that survives his PhD period and that is "reusable" by the members of the team constitute in my opinion the basis of the *CImg* library's genesis.

At the end of David's thesis, the ease of use of *CImg* had already seduced the new PhD students and permanent members of the team. At the end of 2003, we decided, in agreement with *Inria*'s development department, to distribute *CImg* more widely as free software, naturally using the new French free license *CeCILL*, which had just been created jointly by *Inria*, *CEA* and *CNRS*.

More than 20 years after its first lines of code, *CImg* is now an image processing library used by thousands of people around the world, at the heart of dozens of free projects, and just as importantly, continuously and actively maintained.

At the origin of this remarkable success is, first of all, the nature and the quality of the methodological work carried out throughout the doctoral program, as well as its implementation guided by the development of processing algorithms that must work on images of types and modalities from the field of computer vision (cameras, video, velocity fields) as well as in the satellite or medical fields, in particular neuroimaging, with magnetic resonance diffusion imaging and its well-known model called the diffusion tensor.

This aspect of data genericity was very quickly a central element in the design and success of the library. With a focus on simplicity of design and use, and a constant and coherent development of the library *API*, the authors have clearly succeeded in coupling ease of use with the genericity of the processing that the library allows. The free distribution of the library has allowed the academic world, as well as the research and industrial world, to discover the prototyping and implementation of efficient image processing algorithms in a gentle and enjoyable way.

For teachers, researchers, students or engineers, this book will provide you with an introduction to the vast field of image processing, as well as an introduction to the *CImg* library for the development of state-of-the-art algorithms.

This book is expected to spark new passions for image processing, e.g., for beginners or more experienced *C++* developers who are interested in getting started in this discipline. But this book will also shed new light on the field of image processing for users and readers interested in recent advances in artificial intelligence, deep learning, and neural networks. You will learn, for example, that it is not necessary to have a neural network with 500 million weights, nor a million training images, to extract the edges of an image, to segment it, to detect geometric features as segments and circles, or objects located in it, to estimate displacement vectors in video sequences, etc. And even better, you will be able to study the implementations of corresponding algorithms, disseminated and explained throughout this book, made with the *CImg* library, while testing them on your own data.

Exploring an exciting branch of science like image processing, in a reproducible way, with a free library as good as *CImg*, is a valuable gift that the authors are offering us. I personally dreamed about it. They made it happen ! I would like to thank them because with this book, digital image processing is not only given a new life but also opens new perspectives for a bright future.

Rachid Deriche
Sophia Antipolis, June 22, 2022.

Preamble

WHAT IS IMAGE PROCESSING?

Image processing is a discipline where different scientific fields meet: signal processing, applied mathematics and computer science. As a result, the definition of what image processing is varies according to the background of the person speaking about it. Signal processing is a broader discipline that consists in extracting information from a measurement or an observation that is generally perturbed by noise, distorted and where the information we are looking for is not directly accessible. The word signal, coming from electrical engineering, is a generic term that represents an observable quantity that can be a measurement over time (one dimension = time), an image (two dimensions = two distances), a video sequence (three dimensions = two distances + time), a volume (three dimensions = three distances), a temporal volume (four dimensions = three distances + time), ... The objective of signal processing, and by the way of image processing, is to develop methods that allow to efficiently search for this information by a denoising, reconstruction or estimation process for example. The design of these processing methods calls upon many fields of mathematics (stochastic processes, statistics, probability, linear algebra, ...) and applied mathematics (information theory, optimization, numerical analysis, ...).

The practical realization of these methods depends on the nature of the image. In the vast majority of cases, they are in digital form, i.e., sampled and quantified signals. One carries out *digital image processing* which processes data-processing algorithms on numerical machines (computers or dedicated circuits).

WHAT IS AN IMAGE?

An image is a d dimensional signal. In order to process it, we associate this signal with the notion of abstract signal. In this book we will only consider deterministic signals to which we associate a function. In the context of random or stochastic signals, we can use for example random processes.

To present an image processing method, we can switch between a continuous representation of the image for the theory and its numerical representation for its computer realization (Eq. 1 and Fig. 1).

$$I \; : \quad \underbrace{\begin{array}{ccc} Z \subset \mathbb{R}^d & \rightarrow & \mathbb{R}^c \\ (x_1,\ldots,x_d) & \mapsto & I(x_1,\ldots,x_d) \end{array}}_{\text{Continuous image}} \qquad I \; : \quad \underbrace{\begin{array}{ccc} \Omega \subset \mathbb{N}^d & \rightarrow & \mathbb{Z}^c \\ [i_1,\ldots,i_d] & \mapsto & I[i_1,\ldots,i_d] \end{array}}_{\text{Digital (or numerical) image}} \quad (1)$$

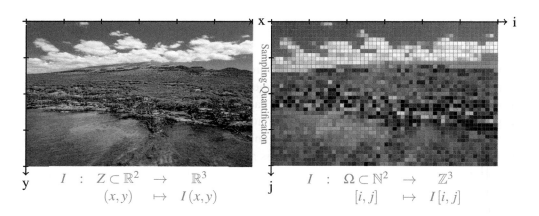

$$\begin{array}{cccc} I \; : & Z \subset \mathbb{R}^2 & \rightarrow & \mathbb{R}^3 \\ & (x,y) & \mapsto & I(x,y) \end{array} \qquad\qquad \begin{array}{cccc} I \; : & \Omega \subset \mathbb{N}^2 & \rightarrow & \mathbb{Z}^3 \\ & [i,j] & \mapsto & I[i,j] \end{array}$$

Figure 1 – Continuous and digital representations of a color image ($d = 2 \; c = 3$).

The conversion of a continuous signal (or image) to a digital (or numerical) signal (or image) is carried out in two stages (Fig. 2):

- Sampling: discretize the evolution parameters (time, distances) ;
- Quantization: discretize the signal values.

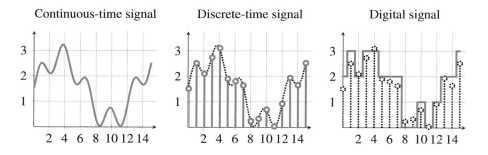

Figure 2 – Principle of sampling and quantization. Example with 16 samples and a quantization on 2 bits ($2^2 = 4$ discrete values).

I- Introduction to CImg

1. Introduction

Whom is this book for?

With this book, we would like to offer you an enchanting, yet pragmatic walk through the wonderful world of image processing:

- *Enchanting*, because image processing is a vast and captivating universe, resting on diversified but solid theoretical bases, which are used as well to model and propose efficient algorithms to solve problems. The number of amusing and/or practical applications that can be imagined and implemented in image processing is potentially infinite.
- *Pragmatic*, because we do not want to make a simple overview of the different formalisms. We will try to make each of the techniques discussed tangible, by systematically "translating" the theoretical points presented in the form of functional and usable C++ programs.

This intertwining of theory and implementation is the essence of this book, and its content is therefore intended for a variety of readers:

- C++ *Programmers, beginners or experts, amateurs of applied mathematics*, wishing to study the discipline of image processing, to eventually develop concrete applications in this field.
- *Mathematicians, image or signal processing makers*, wishing to confront the practical problem of software implementation of the various methods of the domain in *C++*, a language universally recognized as being generic, powerful and fast at execution.
- *Teachers or students in computer science and applied mathematics*, who will find in this book the basic building blocks to develop or perform their practical work.
- *Developers or experienced researchers*, for whom the *CImg* library described in this book will be an ideal companion for rapid and efficient prototyping of new innovative image processing algorithms.

It is important to underline that we will only use simple concepts of the *C++* language and that the proposed programs will therefore be readable enough to be easily transcribed into other languages if necessary. The *CImg* library, on which we rely, has been developed for several years by researchers in computer science and image processing (from CNRS - *French National Centre for Scientific Research*, INRIA - *French National Institute for Research in Digital Science and Technology*, and the University), mainly to allow rapid prototyping of new algorithms. It is also used as a development tool in the practical work of several courses given at the bachelor's, master's or engineering school level. Its use is therefore perfectly adapted to the pedagogical approach that we wish to develop in this book.

The book is structured to allow, on the one hand, a quick appropriation of the concepts of the *CImg* library (which motivates the first part of this book), and on the other hand, its practical use in many fields of image processing, through various workshops (constituting the second part of the book). The set of examples proposed, ranging from the simplest application to more advanced algorithms, helps developing a joint know-how in theory, algorithmic and implementation in the field of image processing. Note that all the source codes published in this book are also available in digital format, on the following repository:
`https://github.com/CImg-Image-Processing-Book`.

WHY STILL DO IMAGE PROCESSING TODAY?

Image is everywhere. It is the medium of many types of information, is used in various applications such as medical diagnosis using *MRI* (*Magnetic Resonance Imaging*), scanner or scintigraphic imaging, the study of deforestation by satellite imagery, the detection of abnormal behaviors in crowds from video acquisitions, photographic retouching and special effects, or handwriting recognition, to name but a few. Today, even without realizing it, we use image processing algorithms on a daily basis: automatic contrast enhancement of our favorite vacation photos, detection of license plates at the entrance of the supermarket parking, automatic detection of faces or places in the photographs that we post on social networks, etc.

Image processing is based on a solid theoretical background, derived from signal processing and Shannon's information theory [38]. Processing an image aims to extract one or several relevant pieces of information for a given problem: the size of an object, its localization, its movement, its color, even its identification. Extracting this information may require some pre-processing steps, if the image is too noisy or badly contrasted.

Image processing took off in the 1960s, with the advent of computers and the development (or rediscovery) of signal processing techniques (the Fourier transform, for example). From then on, in all the domains that this book proposes to approach in its second part, many algorithms have been developed, always more powerful and precise, that are able to process images of increasingly important size and in consequent number.

In parallel to this development, since the 2000s, machine learning, and more particularly deep learning, has achieved unequalled performance in computer vision, even surpassing human capacities in certain areas. A deep neural network is now able to annotate a scene by identifying all the objects, to realistically colorize a grayscale image, or to restore highly noisy images.

So why are we still interested in "classical" image processing ? The shift from image processing to deep learning is accompanied by a paradigm shift in data processing: classical techniques first compute features on the original images (Chapter 6) and then use them for the actual processing (segmentation: Chapter 7, tracking: Chapter 8, ...). The computation of these features is possibly preceded by pre-processing (Chapters 3, 4 and 5) facilitating their extraction. In contrast, deep learning *learns* these features, most often through convolution layers in deep networks, and uses these learned features to perform processing.

And this is where the major difference comes in: to perform its task, the deep network must *learn*. And to do this, it must have a training set made up of several thousands (or even millions) of examples, telling it what it must do. For example, to be able to recognize images of cats and dogs, the network must learn on thousands of pairs (x, y), where x is an image of a cat or a dog and y is the associated label, before being able to decide on an unknown image (Fig. 1.1).

However, obtaining this data is far from being an easy task. If, in some domains (such as object recognition), well-established labeled databases are available (for example, ImageNet[1], composed of more than 14 million different images distributed in 21800 categories), it is most often very difficult, if not impossible, to constitute a sufficiently well-supplied and constituted training set to train a neural network.

Moreover, beyond this problem of training data availability, deep neural networks often require, during their learning phase, significant computing power and hardware resources (via the use of GPUs - *Graphics Processing Units* - and TPUs - *Tensor Processing Units*). Power that the student, or the engineer in search of a quick result, will not necessarily have at his disposal.

---

[1] http://www.image-net.org

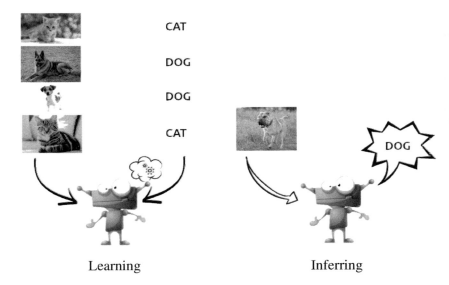

Figure 1.1 – Principle of learning in image processing.

So, even if the field of deep neural network learning has been expanding rapidly for the last twenty years, and provides impressive results, classical image processing has certainly not said its last word!

WHY DO IMAGE PROCESSING IN *C++*?

Among the plethora of existing programming languages, the C++ language has the following advantages:

- It is a *multi-paradigm*, *well-established*, and *popular* language. It is generally taught in universities and engineering schools offering computer science related courses. It therefore reaches a wide audience, who will be able to use it to write programs addressing a wide range of problems, in order to solve various tasks, both at "low-level" and "high-level".
- *C++* is a *compiled* language, which produces highly *optimized* binaries. In image processing, the data to be processed is often large: a standard resolution image has several million values to analyze, and it is therefore important to have programs that are fast enough to iterate on these values within a reasonable time, which is not always possible with interpreted languages. In Python, for example, most of the existing modules for image processing are implemented in *C/C++*, for speed issues (if you have already tested looping over all pixels of an image with a "pure" Python loop, you guess why!).

• The use of *C++* *templates* eases the manipulation of *generic* image data, for example, when the pixel values of images you process have different numerical types (Boolean, integer, floating point, etc.).

WHY USE AN EXTERNAL LIBRARY?

Classically, programming image processing algorithms requires the ability to import/export images in the form of *arrays of values*. Images are usually stored on the disk in standardized file formats (*JPEG, PNG, TIFF, . . .*). Displaying them on the screen is also often desirable. However, no such functionality is present in the standard *C++* library, neither for loading or saving image files, nor for analyzing, processing, and visualizing images.

One has to realize that writing such features from scratch is actually a tedious task. Today, classic file formats have indeed a very complex binary structure: images are mostly stored on disk in *compressed* form, each format uses its own compression method that can be destructive or not. In practice, each image format is associated with an advanced third-party library (e.g., `libjpeg`, `libpng`, `libtiff`, . . .), each being focused on loading and saving image data in its own file format. Similarly, displaying an image in a window is a more complex task than it seems, and is always done through the use of third-party libraries, either specialized in "raw" display (`libX11`, `Wayland` under Unix, or `gdi32` under Windows), or in the display of more advanced graphical interfaces with *widgets* (GTK, Qt, . . .).

Finally, basic processing algorithms themselves are not always trivial to implement, especially when optimized versions are required. For all these reasons, one usually resorts to a high-level third-party library specialized in image processing, to work comfortably in this domain in *C++*.

WHICH *C++* LIBRARIES FOR IMAGE PROCESSING?

A relevant image processing library should allow the reading/writing of image data in the most common file formats, the display of these images, and should propose a few of the most classical algorithms for image processing. Among the dozens of existing choices, we propose this purified list of libraries, verifying these minimal conditions:

CImg, ITK, libvips, Magick++, OpenCV, and *VTK.*

Why only these six libraries? Because they are well-established ones (all of them existing for more than 15 years), widely used in the image processing community and therefore well-proven in terms of performance and robustness. They are also still under active development, free to use, multi-platform, and extensive enough to allow the development of complex and diversified image processing programs. We have voluntarily put aside libraries that are either distributed under a proprietary license, or that are too young, or not actively maintained, or with a too restrictive application domain (for example, libraries that are only capable of reading/writing images in a few file formats, or that propose a too limited panel of image processing algorithms). This diversity of choice actually reflects the various application domains that were initially targeted by the authors of these different libraries.

Our selection can be summarized as follows:

- *CImg* (*Cool Image*) was created in the early 2000s by the French National Institute for Research in Digital Science and Technology (*Inria*), a French public research institute. It is an open source library that was designed in the context of research in image processing algorithms, in order to allow its users (initially, mainly researchers, teachers and PhD students) to conceive, easily implement and test new original image processing algorithms, even from scratch. *CImg* can be downloaded from `http://cimg.eu`.

- *ITK* (*Insight Segmentation and Registration Toolkit*) is a library made available in 2001, initially created for medical image analysis and processing (the project was initiated by the American National Library of Medicine). This medical specialization is still relevant today, and *ITK* is mainly used for visualization, segmentation and registration of medical images. *ITK* can be downloaded from `https://itk.org`.

- *libvips* is a library written mainly in *C*, in the 1990's, specialized in the processing of large images. It is part of a larger framework (named *VIPS*) which also includes a software offering a graphical interface dedicated to image visualization and processing. It is a library well adapted when the images to be analyzed or processed are very large, typically when the set of images is larger than the memory available on the computer. *libvips* can be downloaded from `https://libvips.github.io/libvips`.

- *Magick++* is one of the oldest libraries in our list. It was designed in the late 1980s. Its original purpose was the conversion of formats between 2D images in color or grayscale. However, it is not that easy to use for writing processing algorithms for generic image types (for example, 3D volumetric images or images with more than 4 channels). *Magick++* can be downloaded from `https://imagemagick.org/Magick++`.

- *OpenCV* is a library developed in the early 2000s, which focuses on *computer vision*, a field at the crossroads of image processing and artificial intelligence seeking to imitate human vision. *OpenCV* is a very popular library, and offers a large set of already implemented algorithms, often in a very optimized way. It is ideal for a user wishing to chain together elementary algorithmic blocks in order to build efficient processing pipelines. On the other hand, using *OpenCV* for *prototyping* new algorithms is less convenient: the already implemented algorithms act like "black boxes", which are difficult to modify. The relatively complex *API* of the library does not really facilitate writing new algorithms from scratch. *OpenCV* can be downloaded from `https://opencv.org`.

- *VTK* is a library created in the mid-1990s, specialized in the processing and visualization of 3D meshes. It is therefore focused on the processing and visualization of structured data in the form of graphs or meshes, rather than on the processing of more traditional images defined on regular sampling grids. This library is distributed by the American company *Kitware, Inc.*, which also develops the *ITK* library. *VTK* and *ITK* are often used together, mainly for the analysis and visualization of medical images. *VTK* can be downloaded from `https://vtk.org`.

a) *CImg* b) *ITK* c) *VTK*

d) *OpenCV* e) *Magick++*

Figure 1.2 – Logos of the main opensource *C++* libraries for image processing (note that the *libvips* library does not have an official logo).

WHY DID WE ADOPT *CImg* FOR THIS BOOK?

CImg is a lightweight *C++* library, which has been around for more than 20 years. It is a free library, whose source code is open (distributed under the *CeCILL-C open-source* license), and which runs on various operating systems (*Windows*, *Linux*, *Mac OSX*, *FreeBSD*, etc.). *CImg* gives the programmer access to classes and methods for manipulating images or sequences of images, an image being defined here in the broadest sense of the term, as a volumetric array with up to three spatial coordinates

(x, y, z) and containing vector values of any size and type. The library allows the programmer to be relieved of the usual "low-level" tasks of manipulating images on a computer, such as managing memory allocations and I/O, accessing pixel values, displaying images, user interaction, etc. It also offers a fairly complete range of common processing algorithms, in several areas including:

- Arithmetic operations between images, and applications of usual mathematical functions: *abs(), cos(), exp(), sin(), sqrt(),...*
- Statistical calculation: extraction of the minimum, maximum, mean, variance, median value, ...
- Color space manipulation: *RGB, HSV, YC_bC_r, $L^*a^*b^*$,* ...
- Geometric transformations: rotation, mirror, crop, resize, warp, ...
- Filtering: convolution/correlation, Fourier transform, Gradient and Laplacian computation, recursive filters, morphological filters, anisotropic smoothing, ...
- Feature extraction: interpolated values, connected components labeling, distance function, ...
- Matrix calculus: *SVD* and *LU* decomposition, eigenvalues/eigenvectors, linear system solver, least-square solver, ...
- Graphical primitive drawing: segments, polygons, ellipses, *splines*, text, 3D mesh objects, ...
- Evaluation of mathematical expressions, specified as character strings.

Compared to its competitors, the properties of the *CImg* library make it particularly interesting in a pedagogical context such as the one we want to develop with this book:

- *CImg* is a *lightweight* library, and therefore particularly easy to *install* and *deploy*. *CImg* as a whole is indeed implemented as a single header file `CImg.h`, which you just have to copy on your computer to use the library's features immediately.
- *CImg* is a *generic* library, able to manipulate indifferently 1D (signals), 2D or 3D images, or sequences of images, whose pixel values are of any type (via the use of *C++ templates*). It is therefore adaptable to all kinds of input images and can be used to tackle a wide variety of problems and applications in image processing.
- *CImg* is *simple* to understand and manipulate, since it is entirely structured in only four different classes and two namespaces. Its design does not rely on advanced *C++* concepts, which makes it easy to learn and use, even for *C++* beginners. It also makes it easy to re-read and modify algorithms already implemented in the library. Finally, its syntax, which favors the elaboration of *pipelines*, allows the writing of source codes that are both concise and readable.

- *CImg* is *powerful*. Most of its algorithms can be run in parallel, using the different cores of the available processor(s). Parallelization is done through the use of the *OpenMP* library, which can be optionally activated when compiling a *CImg*-based program.
- *CImg* is an *open source* library, whose development is currently led by the *GREYC* (Research lab in digital science of the *CNRS*), a public research laboratory located in Caen, France. This ensures that the development of *CImg* is scientifically and financially independent from any private interest. The source code of *CImg* is and will remain open, freely accessible, studyable by anyone, and thus favoring the reproducibility and sharing of image processing algorithms. Its permissive free license (*CeCILL-C*) authorizes its use in any type of computer program (including those with closed source code, intended to be distributed under a proprietary license).

All these features make it an excellent library for practicing image processing in *C++*, either to develop and prototype new algorithms from scratch, or to have a complete and powerful collection of image processing algorithms already implemented, immediately usable in one's own programs.

STRUCTURE OF THE *CImg* LIBRARY

The *CImg API* is simple: the library exposes four classes (two of them with a *template* parameter) and two namespaces (Fig. 1.3).

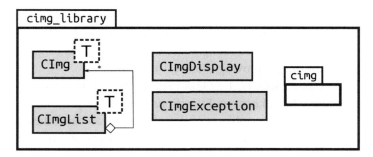

Figure 1.3 – Structure of the *CImg* library.

CImg defines two namespaces:

- `cimg_library`: this namespace includes all the classes and functions of the library. A source code using *CImg* usually starts with the following two lines:

```
#include "CImg.h"
using namespace cimg_library;
```

Thus, the programmer will have direct access to the library classes, without having to prefix them with the namespace identifier `cimg_library::`.

- `cimg`: this namespace contains some utility functions of the library, which are not linked to particular classes, and which can be useful for the developer. For example, functions `cimg::sqr()` (returns the square of a number), `cimg::factorial()` (returns the factorial of a number), `cimg::gcd()` (returns the greatest common divisor between two numbers) or `cimg::maxabs()` (compute the maximum absolute value between two numbers) are some of the functions defined in the `cimg::` namespace.

CImg defines four classes:

- `CImg<T>`: this is the most essential and populated class of the library. An instance of `CImg<T>` represents an "image" that the programmer can manipulate in his *C++* program. The numerical type `T` of the pixel values can be anything. The default type `T` is `float`, so we can write `CImg<>` instead of `CImg<float>`.
- `CImgList<T>`: this class represents a list of `CImg<T>` images. It is used for example to store sequences of images, or sets of images (that may have different sizes). The default type `T` is float, so you can write `CImgList<>` instead of `CImgList<float>`.
- `CImgDisplay`: this class represents a window that can display an image on the screen, and interact through user events. It can be used to display animations or to create applications requiring some user interactions (e.g., placement of key points on an image, moving them, ...).
- `CImgException`: this is the class used to handle library exceptions, i.e., errors that occur when classes and functions of the library are misused. The programmer never instantiates objects of this class, but can catch the corresponding exceptions raised with this class by the library to manage errors.

This concise design of the library makes it easy to learn, even for novice *C++* programmers.

WHY ONLY A SINGLE HEADER FILE?

CImg is a library distributed in a rather particular form, since it is entirely implemented in a single *C++* header file, named `CImg.h`.

At first sight, this conception may seem surprising: in *C/C++*, the libraries that one encounters are generally organized in the form of one or more header files (most often, one header file per different structure or class defined by the library), completed by a binary file (`.a` or `.so` files under Linux, `.lib` or `.dll` files under Windows), which contains the library's functions in compiled form.

Our teaching experience with *CImg* has shown that the first question raised by new users of the library is: *"Why is everything put in one file?"*. Here we answer this frequent question, by listing the technical choices justifying this kind of structuring, and by pointing out the advantages (and disadvantages) of it. The global answer takes into account several different aspects of the *C++* language, and requires consideration of the following points:

1. Why doesn't CImg *propose a pre-compilation of its functions as* `.a`, `.lib`, `.so` *or* `.dll` *binary file(s)?*

Because the library is *generic*. The `CImg<T>` image and `CImgList<T>` image structures exposed by the library have a *template* parameter `T`, which corresponds to the type of pixels considered for these images. However, the types `T` that will be selected by the user of *CImg* classes are a priori *unknown*.

Of course, the most commonly used types `T` are in practice the basic *C++* types for representing numbers, i.e.,: `bool` (Boolean), `unsigned char` (unsigned 8-bit integer), `unsigned short` (unsigned 16-bit integer), `short` (signed 16-bit integer), `unsigned int` (unsigned 32-bit integer), `int` (signed 32-bit integer), `float` (float value, 32-bit), `double` (float value, 64-bit), etc. However, it is not uncommon to see source codes that uses images of other types, such as `CImg<void*>`, `CImg<unsigned long long>` or `CImg<std::complex>`.

One might think that pre-compiling the methods of the two classes `CImg<T>` and `CImgList<T>` for these ten or so most common types `T` would be a good idea. This is to overlook the fact that many of these methods take as arguments values whose types are themselves `CImg<t>` images or `CImgList<t>` image lists, with another *template* parameter `t` potentially different from `T`.

For instance, the method

```
CImg<T>::warp(CImg<t>&, unsigned int, unsigned int, unsigned int)
```

applies an arbitrary deformation field to an image `CImg<T>`. It is common to use this method to deform an image of type `CImg<unsigned char>` (classic color image, with 8 bits/channel), passing as argument a deformation field of type `CImg<float>`, which contains deformation vectors with floating-point precision (sub-pixel).

One can easily see that the multiplicity of possible combinations of types for the arguments of the library's methods makes it unwise to precompile these functions in the form of binary files. The size of the generated file(s) would simply be huge, and the functions actually used by the programmer would in practice only represent a tiny portion of the pre-compiled functions.

The correct approach is therefore to let the compiler instantiate the methods and functions of the *CImg* classes only for those combinations of template types that are actually exploited in the user's program. In this way, lighter and more optimized binary objects or executables are generated, compared to what would be done with a static binding to a large pre-compiled library. The main disadvantage is that the functions of the *CImg* library used in the program must be compiled at the same time as those of the program itself, which leads to an additional compilation overhead.

2. Why isn't CImg subdivided into multiple header files?

If we follow this principle of usage minimality, why doesn't *CImg* propose to include only the classes of the library the user needs in his program? If he only needs objects of type `CImg<T>`, why make him include a header file that also defines `CImgList<T>`? After all, that's what the standard *C++* library provides: if you only want to work with `std::vector`, you just have to include `<vector>`...

First, because unlike the *C++* standard library, *CImg* defines only four different classes, which turn out to be strongly *interdependent*. Moreover, the algorithms operating on these class instances are defined as *methods* of the classes, not as *external* functions acting on "containers". This differs a lot from how the *C++* standard library is designed.

In practice, methods of the `CImg<T>` class need methods of `CImgList<T>` (even if this is sometimes invisible to the user), simply because implementations of `CImg<T>` methods require the functionality of `CImgList<T>` (and vice versa). Similarly, `CImgException` is a ubiquitous class in `CImg`, since it is used to handle errors that occur when library functions are misused. If the programmer does not want to handle these errors, this class might seem useless to include. However, it is required during compilation, since it is obviously used by the library core, which is, after all, compiled at the same time as the user's program.

This class interdependence means that if we wanted to have one header file per *CImg* class, the first thing it would do is probably include the header files for the other classes. From a purely technical point of view, the gain from such a split would be null: the four header files would be systematically included as soon as only one of the classes in the library is used. In consequence, *CImg* proposes only one header file, rather than one per class, without any real consequences on the compilation time.

   3. What are the advantages of a single header file?

But the fact that *CImg* is distributed in the form of a single header file is not only due to the satisfaction of technical constraints bound to the *C++* language. In practice, this is indeed an undeniable advantage for the library user:

• **Easy to install**: copying a single file to a folder to get access to the functions of a complete image processing library is comfortable (a thing that few current libraries actually offer).

• **Lightweight and performance**: on-the-fly compilation of *CImg* functions means more *optimized* output binaries. The library code as well as the program that uses it are compiled as a single entity. As a consequence, some of the library functions can be *inlined* in the final binary, bringing more performance at runtime (typically, the methods for accessing pixel values in images).

• **Fine-tuning of dependencies**: *CImg*'s on-the-fly compilation also allows the user to define specific macros that tell the library to use features from a particular third-party library. For example, writing in your program:

```
#define cimg_use_tiff
#define cimg_use_jpeg
#include <CImg.h>
```

will tell *CImg* to use the functions of the `libtiff` and `libjpeg` libraries when it needs to read or write images in *TIFF* or *JPEG* format (it is then of course necessary to link the generated binary, statically or dynamically, with these two libraries). There are a lot of such *configuration macros* that can be set to activate specific features of *CImg*, when compiling a program.

On the other hand, this means that it is also possible to compile a *CImg*-based program without activating any dependencies on external libraries. This flexibility in the control of dependencies is very important: using *CImg* does not imply an automatic dependency on dozens of "low-level" third-party libraries, whose functionalities might not be used by the programmer. Yet this is what happens with most of the competing image processing libraries!

- **Possibility of internally extending the library**: in a similar way, defining some of these macros allows the library user to insert pieces of code directly into the *CImg* classes, while it is compiling, via an original system of *plug-ins*. Consequently, the library is extensible *from the outside*, without having to explicitly modify its code: a user can, if desired, add his own methods to the `CImg<T>` and `CImgList<T>` classes (for example, new processing algorithms). We will not use this possibility in this book, but it is an interesting approach when one wishes to develop functionalities that integrate harmoniously with the rest of the library *API*.

But one of the great strengths of the *CImg* library is its *ease of use*, and its ability to express image processing algorithms in a clear and concise way in *C++*. This is what we will show you in the rest of this book.

2. Getting Started with the *CImg* Library

As mentioned in Chapter 1, *CImg* is structured with a minimum of classes to represent the relevant and manipulable objects of the library. In practice, the possibilities offered by the library are expressed by the great diversity of methods available in its classes (in particular those of the principal class `CImg<T>`, representing the main "image" object). This chapter illustrates the actual use of *CImg*, by detailing the development of a simple *C++* source code example (about 100 lines), to implement a basic image processing application. This example has been chosen to maximize the use of the different classes and concepts of the library, without actually requiring advanced knowledge in image processing. At the end of this tutorial, you will have sufficient experience with *CImg* to start building your own applications: you will quickly realize that *CImg* is easy to use, not based on complex *C++* concepts, and therefore perfectly suited to discover, learn and teach image processing, as well as to build prototypes or more elaborate applications in this field.

Let us first explain the purpose of the application, then the details of its *C++* implementation.

2.1   Objective: subdivide an image into blocks

A 2D digital image is represented as a 2D array of pixels, usually in grayscale or color. If we want to analyze the global geometry of an image (e.g., to detect its contours or to compress its data), it can be interesting to subdivide the image into several distinct regions of interest, each having its own characteristics (flat areas, texture, contours, etc.). The image decomposition into blocks is one of the simplest ways to achieve this subdivision: we try to split the image into several square (or rectangular) areas of different sizes, such that the large rectangles contain few locally complex structures (rather flat areas), while the small blocks focus on the contours and textures of the various elements present in the image.

Our goal here is thus to implement such a decomposition in blocks of a color image, but also to propose an interactive visualization of this decomposition. The visualization should let the user explore each extracted block, by visualizing its content in the original image, as well as its internal variations (Fig. 2.1b).

 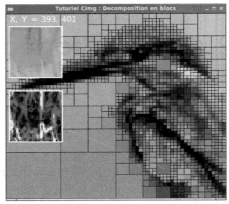

a) Color input image   b) Visualization of the image decomposition
into blocks

Figure 2.1 – Goal of our first *CImg*-based program: decompose an image into blocks
of different sizes, and visualize the result in an interactive way.

The most informed readers will notice a parallel with the so-called *quadtree*
decomposition. The same type of decomposition is proposed here, but by putting
aside the tree structure of the decomposition (so, in practice, we only keep the leaves
of the *quadtree*).

2.2   Setup and first program

Since the *CImg* library is written entirely in a single `CImg.h` header file, it does
not require any special pre-compilation or installation procedure. All you have to do
is copy `CImg.h` to a folder of your choice (e.g., your project's folder), to have the
library ready to be used. Note however that some of the features it provides, such as
displaying images in windows, or reading/writing compressed files (typically in `.png`
or `.jpg` format), may require the use of third-party libraries. To use these functionalities, be sure to have these intermediate libraries installed on your system: `gdi32`
(under Windows) or `X11/pthread` (under Unix) for display capabilities, `libpng`
or `libjpeg` for image format management, etc. *CImg* has many configuration *flags*
allowing you to enable or disable the use of these third-party libraries when compiling
programs, which allows you to fine-tune your dependence on external libraries.

In this tutorial, we need to display images in windows, so we need to enable the
display capability in *CImg*. It is actually enabled by default: being able to display
images when programming in image processing is a feature that indeed seems useful
most of the time !

All the necessary third-party libraries are expected to be installed, so let's write our first code:

Code 2.1 – A first code using _CImg_.

```
// first_code.cpp:
// My first code using CImg.
#include "CImg.h"
using namespace cimg_library;

int main() {
  CImg<unsigned char> img("kingfisher.bmp");
  img.display("Hello World!");

  return 0;
}
```

As you can guess, the purpose of this first program is to instantiate an image object of type `CImg<unsigned char>` (i.e., each pixel channel stored as an 8-bit unsigned integer), by reading the image from the file `kingfisher.bmp` (the bmp format is generally uncompressed, so it doesn't require any additional external dependencies), and displaying this image in a window.

In order to compile this program, we must specify that the program has to be linked with the necessary libraries for display. Under _Linux_, with the _g++_ compiler, we will for instance write the following minimal compilation command:

```
$ g++ -o first_code first_code.cpp -lX11 -lpthread
```

Under _Windows_, with the _Visual C++_ compiler, we will write in a similar way:

```
> cl.exe /EHsc first_code.cpp /link gdi32.lib user32.lib
  shell32.lib
```

Running the corresponding binary does indeed display the image `kingfisher.bmp` in an interactive window, and it allows us to explore the pixel values and zoom in to see the details of the image (Fig. 2.2). At this point, we are ready to use more advanced features of _CImg_ to decompose this image into several blocks.

2.3   Computing the variations

The principle of image decomposition into blocks is based on a statistical analysis of the local variations of pixel values. We try to separate areas that locally have strong

Figure 2.2 – Result of our program `first_code.cpp`.

contrast variations (generally corresponding to contours or textures), from areas that have none (flat areas). Mathematically speaking, the measure of the local geometric variations of a scalar image I (in grayscale) is classically given by $\|\nabla I\|$, the scalar image of the *gradient norm*, which is the vector $\nabla I = \left(\frac{\partial I}{\partial x} \;\; \frac{\partial I}{\partial y} \right)^{\top}$ of the first directional derivatives of the image intensities along the horizontal and vertical axes respectively, estimated on each point (x, y) of the image. For color images, more or less complex extensions of the gradient exist (see Section 9.2.3), but for the sake of simplicity we will not use them here. We will just estimate $\|\nabla I\|$ from an image relative to the color brightness, which is simply computed as the L^2 norm of each vector (R, G, B) composing our input image. More precise definitions of the color brightness exist and could be calculated, but the L^2 norm will be more than sufficient in the context of our tutorial.

With *CImg*, obtaining such an image of smoothed and normalized brightness can be written as:

```
CImg<> lum = img.get_norm().blur(sigma).normalize(0,255);
```

Here, we notice that the calculation of the `lum` image is realized by pipelining three calls to methods of the `CImg<T>` class:

1. First, `CImg<unsigned char>::get_norm()` computes the image whose pixels are the L^2 norms of the colors of the instance image (here, the original image `img`), and returns its result as a new image of type `CImg<float>`. Note the change of pixel type of the returned image: the norm of a vector (here, an *RGB* color) whose components are included in the range $[\![0, 255]\!]$ (since it

is encoded as an `unsigned char`) is indeed a non-integer (floating-point) value that could potentially be greater than 255, and *CImg* therefore adapts the type of the pixels of the returned image to avoid possible arithmetic overflows or truncations of floating-point values into integers.

2. This norm image is then spatially smoothed, using the `CImg<float>::blur()` method, which implements an efficient recursive filter for this task. Smoothing the image with a small standard deviation $\sigma \approx 1$ makes the subsequent calculation of variations more robust and accurate. So why is this method not called `CImg<float>::get_blur()`? Simply because, unlike the previous `CImg<float>::get_norm()` method, `CImg<float>::blur()` directly modifies the pixels of the instance image, instead of returning its result as a new image. In practice, the vast majority of *CImg* methods are thus available in two versions, `get` and non-`get`. Note that it could be possible to use `CImg<float>::get_blur()` here, but it would be less appropriate: the considered image instance (which was the one returned by `CImg<unsigned char>::get_norm()`) is a *temporary* image in our pipeline, which we can then afford to smooth "on the fly". Using the `CImg<float>::get_blur()` version would imply the creation of a new image, with the memory allocation that goes along. In image processing, one deals with large arrays of numbers and not allocating more memory than necessary is a good practice. Here, the `CImg<float>::blur()` method does not return a new image, but a *reference* to the instance that has just been blurred, which allows to continue writing our pipeline by adding other methods afterwards if necessary.

3. The `CImg<float>::normalize()` method concludes our sequence of operators. It allows to linearly normalize the pixel values of the resulting image in the range $[\![0, 255]\!]$ (keeping of course floating-point values). This way, we can control the order of magnitude of the different values of variations expected in the `lum` image, depending on the type of geometry that will be found there. Here again, the non-`get` version of the method is called, acting in place for reasons of memory efficiency.

Thus, with a single line of code, we have defined a processing pipeline that returns an image of type `CImg<>` (i.e., `CImg<float>`), providing information about the luminosity of the colors in the original image (Fig. 2.3). The *CImg* architecture makes it very easy to write this kind of *pipelines*, which are often found in source codes based on this library.

a) Color input image   b) Resulting image `lum`

Figure 2.3 – Computation of the `lum` image of color brightness, from an input image.

Now let's look at the variations of this brightness image. Since the calculation of the gradient ∇I is a basic operation in image processing, it is already implemented in *CImg* via the method `CImg<>::get_gradient()`, that we are going to use here:

```
CImgList<> grad = lum.get_gradient("xy");
```

This method returns an instance of `CImgList<float>`, a *CImg* class that represents a *list of images*. In our case, the returned list contains two distinct images, corresponding to the estimates of the two first derivatives along `x` (`grad[0]` $= \frac{\partial I}{\partial x}$) and `y` (`grad[1]` $= \frac{\partial I}{\partial y}$) of the image `lum`. Computing the gradient norm $\|\nabla I\| = \sqrt{\frac{\partial I}{\partial x}^2 + \frac{\partial I}{\partial y}^2}$ from these two gradients (scalar images) can then be done as follows:

```
CImg<> normGrad = (grad[0].get_sqr() + grad[1].get_sqr()).sqrt();
```

CImg has many methods for applying mathematical functions to pixel values, and the usual arithmetic operators are redefined to allow writing such expressions. Here, calls to the `CImg<float>::get_sqr()` method return images where each pixel value has been squared. These two images are then summed via the *CImg* method `CImg<float>::operator+()` which returns a new image of the same size. Finally, `CImg<float>::sqrt()` replaces each value of this summed image by its square root.

Here again, we chose to use the `get` and non-`get` versions of the methods in order to minimize the number of image copies. With this in mind, we can even use `CImg<float>::operator+=()`, which can be seen as the non-`get` version of `CImg<float>::operator+()`, and which avoids an additional creation of an image in memory:

```
CImg<> normGrad = (grad[0].get_sqr() += grad[1].get_sqr()).sqrt();
```

Figure 2.4 shows a detail of the different images of variations that we obtain. Remember: at any time, in a *CImg* program, the content of an image or a list of images can be displayed by calling the `CImg<T>::display()` and `CImgList<T>::display()` methods, which proves to be very useful for checking the correct step-by-step implementation of a program.

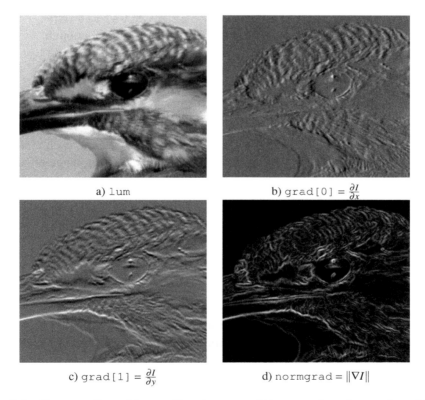

a) `lum`   b) `grad[0]` $= \frac{\partial I}{\partial x}$

c) `grad[1]` $= \frac{\partial I}{\partial y}$ d) `normgrad` $= \|\nabla I\|$

Figure 2.4 – Computation of the gradient image and its norm, from image `lum` *(detail)*.

2.4   Computing the block decomposition

We now have all the image data needed to perform our image decomposition into
blocks. We will adopt a top-down strategy for the decomposition, performing the steps
described in Algorithm 1.

Algorithm 1: Algorithm for image decomposition into blocks.

Input: Input image: $I(x,y)$ of size $W \times H$.
Data: Threshold τ for the variation $\|\nabla I\|$.
Result: List of blocks that compose the image I.
```
/* Algorithm initialization                              */
```
Create a single block of size $W \times H$ corresponding to the whole image domain
While *there are still new blocks to analyze* **Do**
    Find the maximal value M of the variation $\|\nabla I\|$ in the block
    If $M > \tau$ **Then** - if M is high enough
```
            /* this block contains at least one
                significant local geometric variation    */
```
        If *block size* $> 8 \times 8$ *pixels* **Then** - the block is large enough
```
                /* we have arbitrarily chosen a minimal
                    block size of 8×8 pixels              */
```
            we subdivide it then into four smaller blocks of same size

---

To store the whole set of blocks, we use a `CImgList<int>`: each element (of
type `CImg<int>`) of this list will represent a block, stored as an image of size 1×4
containing the coordinates $(x0, y0, x1, y1)$ of the top-left and bottom-right corners of
the block. To initialize our algorithm, we can therefore write:

```
CImgList<int> blocks; // Create an empty list of blocks
// Add the first block of size WxH to the list.
CImg<int>::vector(0,0,img.width() - 1,img.height() - 1).
        move_to(blocks);
```

The function `CImg<T>::vector()` returns a new object of type `CImg<I>` with
size $1 \times N$ (where N is the number of arguments passed to the function) containing
the values passed as arguments. Here we use the `CImg<T>::move_to()` method
to transfer this image into a new image inserted at the end of the list `blocks`.
The definition of this first block tells us that with *Clmg*, the pixel coordinates start
at $(0,0)$ (corresponding to the top left pixel), not at $(1,1)$ (a frequent mistake for
beginners). The last accessible pixel of the image (pixel at the bottom right) has

therefore coordinates $(W - 1, H - 1)$. We could also have written:

```
// Add the first block of WxH to the list.
blocks.insert(CImg<int>::vector(0,0,img.width() - 1,img.height() -
    1));
```

Using `CImg<T>::move_to()` rather than `CImgList<T>::insert()` allows the image instance to be "transferred" directly to the list, without creating an additional copy of the image in memory. In return, the image instance used for `move_to()` becomes an empty image after the call to this method. In our case, this is not an issue since our instance is a temporary image, which can be "cleared" of its content, without any consequences.

In a second step, we iterate over the existing blocks in the list `blocks`, inserting the new blocks resulting from the successive subdivisions at the end of the list (and deleting from the list the blocks that have been subdivided):

Code 2.2 – Computing the block decomposition of the image.

```
for (unsigned int l = 0; l<blocks.size(); ) {
  CImg<int>& block = blocks[l];
  int
    x0 = block[0], y0 = block[1],
    x1 = block[2], y1 = block[3];
  if (std::min(x1 - x0,y1 - y0)>8 &&
      normGrad.get_crop(x0,y0,x1,y1).max()>threshold) {
    int
      xc = (x0 + x1)/2,
      yc = (y0 + y1)/2;
    CImg<int>::vector(x0,y0,xc - 1,yc - 1).move_to(blocks);
    CImg<int>::vector(xc,y0,x1,yc - 1).move_to(blocks);
    CImg<int>::vector(x0,yc,xc - 1,y1).move_to(blocks);
    CImg<int>::vector(xc,yc,x1,y1).move_to(blocks);
    blocks.remove(l);
  } else ++l;
}
```

The central part of this code portion concerns the block subdivision test, where two criteria must be met. On the one hand,

```
std::min(x1 - x0,y1 - y0)>8
```

requires that both the width and height of a block must be greater than 8 pixels.

On the other hand,

```
normGrad.get_crop(x0,y0,x1,y1).max()>threshold
```

selects the blocks whose maximum variation value $\|\nabla I\|$ is greater than the `threshold` (set by the user). Note the chaining of *CImg* methods in this last expression: `CImg<float>::get_crop()` first returns the portion of the `normGrad` image that corresponds only to the considered block (in the form of a new temporary image `CImg<float>`). Then `CImg<float>::max()` returns the maximum value encountered in this sub-image.

The subdivision of a block is done by calculating first the coordinates of its center `(xc,yc)`, then splitting it into four equal parts, which are added to the list of blocks to be further examined.

Now we have a list of blocks and their coordinates. What remains is visualizing them as an image such as the one presented in Fig. 2.1b.

2.5　Rendering of the decomposition

This part will allow us to illustrate another interesting aspect of the *CImg* library: its ability to draw graphical primitives in images. *CImg* defines indeed a complete set of methods to draw points, lines, polygons, ellipses, or even 3D meshes.

The first thing to do is to define an image in which we will draw the blocks we just calculated, let us name it `res`:

```
CImg<unsigned char> res(img.width(),img.height(),1,3,0);
```

Here we have used one of the basic constructors of the library, which takes as arguments the desired dimension of the image to allocate, according to its different axes:

- Its `width`, defining the number of columns of the image (here chosen to be W), i.e., its dimension along the x-axis.
- Its `height`, defining the number of rows of the image (here chosen to be H), i.e., its dimension along the y-axis.
- Its `depth`, defining the number of slices of the image (here chosen to be 1), i.e., its dimension along the z-axis.
  A number of slices greater than 1 is found when storing and manipulating *volumetric* images, composed of voxels (rather than pixels). This type of data is often encountered in medical imaging (*MRI* images for instance). It can also be encountered when processing image sequences, the key images of the animation being stored as a set of slices in a volumetric image. For "conventional" images (in two dimensions), the number of slices is always equal to 1.
- Its number of channels, denoted as `spectrum`, defining its dimension along the c-axis (here chosen to be 3). A scalar image has a single channel, a color image has three, if it is stored in the form of *RGB* pixels (more rarely 4, in the case of images encoded in *CMYK* or *RGBA*, i.e., with an alpha channel). Here,

we wish to draw *RGB* colored blocks in the image `res`, so we provide it with 3 channels.

- And finally, the default value of its pixels (here chosen at 0, corresponding to a default background colored in black).

Keep in mind that a `CImg<T>` image *always* has four dimensions, no more, no less: three of these dimensions have a spatial meaning (*width*, *height* and *depth*), the remaining dimension has a spectral meaning (number of *channels*). Furthermore, *CImg* will never try to store the *meaning* of what the pixel or voxel values represent in an image. Thus, the pixels of a three-channel `CImg<T>` image can represent as well *RGB* colors, as 3D point coordinates (x,y,z), or as probabilities of occurrence of three distinct events. It is up to the user of the library to know the meaning of the pixels he manipulates. The good news is that, he actually knows it 100% of the time! In the case of the image `res`, we decide that the pixels of the image represent colors stored in *RGB*, with 256 possible integer values per component (hence the choice of type `CImg<unsigned char>`, with 3 channels to define this image).

Now that the image `res` is allocated, let's draw in it the different blocks calculated in the previous step, using `CImg<T>::draw_rectangle()`, which is the appropriate method for this task:

Code 2.3 – Rendering of the block decomposition of the image.

```
cimglist_for(blocks,l)
{
  CImg<int>& block = blocks[l];
  int
    x0 = block[0], y0 = block[1],
    x1 = block[2], y1 = block[3];
  CImg<unsigned char> color(1,1,1,3);
  color.rand(0,255);
  res.draw_rectangle(x0,y0,x1,y1,color.data(),1);
}
```

The statement `cimglist_for(blocks,l)`, which may seem strange, simply reflects the use of a loop macro. It comes down to writing:

```
for (int l = 0; l<(int)blocks.size(); ++l)
```

In this way, we will go through all the elements of the list of blocks.

CImg defines many useful macros that simplify the writing of loops iterating over objects of type `CImg<T>` and `CImgList<T>`. The most common loop macros are `cimg_forX()` (loop over image columns), `cimg_forY()` (loop over rows), `cimg_forXY()` (loop over rows and columns), `cimg_forC()` (loop over channels), and `cimglist_for()` (loop over image list items). In practice, more than 300 loop macros are defined in *CImg* and using them helps having a code that looks more concise and readable.

The `CImg<unsigned char>::draw_rectangle()` method takes as arguments the coordinates of the rectangle to be filled, its color and its opacity (a value between 0=*transparent* and 1=*completely opaque*). The color is specified as a pointer to an array containing as many values as there are channels in the image. All the *CImg* primitive drawing methods follow this principle. Here, we therefore store the filling color in a 1×1 image with three channels, filled with random values (using `CImg<unsigned char>::rand()`) before each call to `CImg<unsigned char>::draw_rectangle()`. Each block thus appears filled with a random *RGB* color. The resulting rendering is shown in Fig. 2.5a. The small blocks are indeed concentrated where complex contours and textures of the image are located.

If we now want to define the color of each block as the average color of the input image pixels located below the block, the definition of `color` has to be replaced by:

```
CImg<unsigned char> color = img.get_crop(x0,y0,x1,y1).
                            resize(1,1,1,3,2);
```

Calling `CImg<unsigned char>::get_crop()` retrieves the portion of the image corresponding only to the block being rendered, then `CImg<unsigned char>::resize()` resizes it into a 1×1 color image, averaging the colors to form a single colored pixel whose color is that which interested us.

Adding a black border:

In order to better visualize the different blocks, especially neighboring blocks with similar colors, we now add a one-pixel thick black border around each block. To do that, we want to fill in black all pixels whose direct neighbor to the right or bottom has a different color. This problem can be approached in several ways with *CImg*. We propose here three variations which introduce different concepts of the library.

1. A first method would be to multiply our resulting color image by a *mask image*, whose pixels are either 0 (on the borders) or 1 (elsewhere). This mask image can be calculated in a clever way, from the arithmetic difference between the color image, and its translated version of 1 pixel up, and 1 pixel to the left. All the non-zero vectors of this difference image correspond to the desired border pixels. The norm of this difference image can therefore be calculated as:

```
CImg<unsigned char> mask = (res.get_shift(-1,-1,0,0,0) - res).
                            norm();
```

The `CImg<unsigned char>::cut()` method limits the pixel values within a given range and allows here to obtain a binary-valued image, either with values 1 (on the block borders) or 0 (elsewhere):

```
CImg<unsigned char> mask = (res.get_shift(-1,-1,0,0,0) - res).
                            norm().cut(0,1);
```

In our final rendering, we want the opposite (pixels with value 0 on the border, and 1 elsewhere), so we can multiply the image `1 - mask` to our rendered color image. All can be done in a single line of code:

```
res.mul(1 - (res.get_shift(1,1,0,0,0) - res).norm().cut(0,1));
```

This results in the rendering are shown in Fig. 2.5.

2. A second, even more concise method, uses one of the variants of the `CImg<unsigned char>::fill()` methods, capable of evaluating a mathematical expression, potentially complex, for each pixel of an image. Thus we can write:

```
res.fill("I*(I!=J(1,0) || I!=J(0,1)?0:1)",true);
```

The mathematical expression is passed as a string, which will be parsed and compiled in the form of *bytecode* by *CImg*, before being evaluated for all the image pixels. Here, the variable `I` corresponds to the vector-valued color of each pixel (x, y) of the image `res`. It is compared to the neighboring colors obtained by calls to the functions `J(1,0)` (color on one pixel to the right) and `J(0,1)` (color on one pixel to the bottom), to return a value equal to 0 or 1, which is then multiplied to the current color. Our intention here is not to go into the details of this mathematical expression evaluator, capable of evaluating very complex expressions, but to mention its existence. In some situations, having such an evaluator at hand is really convenient for quick prototyping.

3. The third method introduces a particular type of *CImg* loops: loops on *neighborhoods*. We have already mentioned the existence of simple loop macros, but there are also more sophisticated macros, allowing not only to explore each pixel independently, but also to give access at any time to the values of the neighboring pixels. For instance, we can fill our image `mask` this way:

```
CImg<unsigned char>
  mask(res.width(),res.height(),1,1,1),
  V(3,3);
cimg_forC(res,c) cimg_for3x3(res,x,y,0,c,V,unsigned char)
  if (V[4]!=V[5] || V[4]!=V[7]) mask(x,y) = 0;
```

Here we defined a 3×3 neighborhood as a new image V, which will be passed
as a parameter to the loop macro cimg_for3x3. The role of this macro is
to browse all the coordinates (x, y) of the image res, and to retrieve for each
of these coordinates, all pixel values in the corresponding 3×3 neighborhood
centered at (x, y). Inside the loop, we thus have a direct and fast access to the
values of the neighbors, with the convention:

```
V[0] = res(x-1,y-1); V[1] = res(x,y-1); V[2] = res(x+1,y-1);
V[3] = res(x-1,y);   V[4] = res(x,y);   V[5] = res(x+1,y);
V[6] = res(x-1,y+1); V[7] = res(x,y+1); V[8] = res(x+1,y+1);
```

Once our mask image has been computed, we just have to multiply it point to
point with the res image, obtained by the block decomposition.

```
res.mul(mask);
```

Note that we don't use the multiplication operator ⋆ between two images. This
operator exists in *CImg*, but corresponds to the *matrix multiplication* of two
images (seen as matrices).
Note also that this kind of loop macro cimg_forNxN() exists for a large
number of different *N*. 3D versions of these neighborhood loops are also
available, with macros such as cimg_forNxNxN().

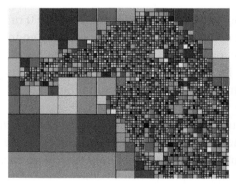 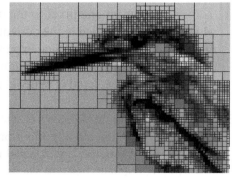

a) Rendering blocks with random colors   b) Rendering blocks with averaged colors

Figure 2.5 – Rendering of the different blocks of the decomposed image.

2.6 **Interactive visualization**

The last part of this tutorial illustrates the use of the third most important class of *CImg*, namely `CImgDisplay`. An instance of this class represents a visualization window, used to display images or lists of images, and to interact with the user via event management: detection of key press or release, mouse buttons, retrieval of the location of the mouse cursor, etc. Here we are going to use some of the methods of `CImgDisplay` to build an interactive display of our block decomposition `res`.

Let us start by declaring an instance of `CImgDisplay`, named `disp`:

```
CImgDisplay disp(res,"CImg Block Decomposition Tutorial",0);
```

The constructor takes as argument the image to be displayed, the desired title appearing in the display window bar, as well as a normalization mode for the values, chosen here to be 0, which indicates that we do not want `CImgDisplay` to manage the normalization of the values before displaying them (because we will take care of it by ourselves).

A brief word on this normalization mode argument, appearing in all `CImgDisplay` constructors: *CImg* being a generic image processing library, it happens very often that the values of the images we manipulate are defined in various numerical ranges, especially when dealing with images of types `CImg<float>` and `CImg<double>`. It is not unusual to analyze and display images whose pixels have values defined in ranges, e.g., $[\![0, 255]\!]$, $[\![0, 65535]\!]$, $[0, 1]$, $[-1, 1]$, or even $]-\infty, +\infty[$. However, computer screens most often have a display capacity limited to 8 bits per component, i.e., three integer values R, G, B included in the range $[\![0, 255]\!]$. It may therefore be necessary to *normalize* the values of the pixels being manipulated before they can be displayed on the screen. Rather than forcing the user to carry out this normalization of the values himself, the `CImgDisplay` class proposes to do it automatically, when required. The normalization argument proposed in all `CImgDisplay` constructors is used to determine the behavior of the class regarding this normalization step.
It can take the following values:

- `normalization=0`: no normalization is applied before the image is displayed in the window. It is therefore up to the user to make sure that all image values provided to a `CImgDisplay` are indeed within the range $[\![0, 255]\!]$. On the other hand, this is also the fastest display mode.
- `normalization=1`: a linear normalization of the image values in the range $[\![0, 255]\!]$ is automatically done before the display. This means that each time the image has to be displayed, its minimum value is brought back to 0, and its maximum value to 255. This ensures we are protected from any outlier value (outside the range $[\![0, 255]\!]$) when displaying the image. Note that this

normalization is done internally to the `CImgDisplay` class and is not really applied to the pixels of the image being displayed (i.e., the values of the `CImg<T>` or `CImgList<T>` instance displayed remain unchanged in practice).

- `normalization=2`: a linear normalization of the values is also performed in this mode, but with normalization parameters calculated at the first display only. The `CImgDisplay` class then reuses these parameters when displaying other images in the same display (even if the min/max values of these images are different). This is useful when one wants to keep a coherence of the gray levels or colors when displaying sequences of images whose minimum and maximum values may change over time.

- `normalization=3`: this is the *automatic* mode (also the *default* mode in `CImgDisplay` constructors). It is equivalent to one of the three previous normalization behaviors, chosen according to the type `T` of the image values. More precisely, in this mode, the display of a `CImg<T>` in a `CImgDisplay` will correspond to the mode:

  - `normalization=0`, if type `T` is an 8-bit unsigned integer (i.e., an `unsigned char`).
  - `normalization=1`, if `T` is a floating-point value type (`float`, `double`, …).
  - `normalization=2`, for other integer types (`char`, `int`, …).

Note that all `CImgDisplay` parameters passed to a constructor can be modified afterwards, by calling the appropriate methods, for example `set_title()` or `set_normalization()`.

Once the `CImgDisplay` instance has been constructed, the image `res` is displayed in a new window that appears on the screen. On the contrary, when the destructor `~CImgDisplay()` is called, this window disappears. Between these two states, we can manage an event loop, which will drive the behavior of the window according to the user actions. The simplest event loop can be written as:

```
while (!disp.is_closed() && !disp.is_keyESC()) {
  disp.wait(); // Wait for an user event
}
```

This loop does nothing but wait for the user to close the window, or press the `Escape` key on his keyboard. The call to `disp.wait()` is blocking, and only succeeds when some event occurs. During this time, it does not consume any resources.

We now detect if the mouse cursor is over a block. The cursor position is retrieved by methods `CImgDisplay::mouse_x()` and `CImgDisplay::mouse_y()`:

```
int
  x = disp.mouse_x(),
  y = disp.mouse_y();
if (x>=0 && y>=0) {
  // Mouse cursor is over the display window.
}
```

If the cursor is above the displayed window, the values of x and y give the coordinates of the cursor (relative to the top-left corner of the displayed image, having coordinates $(0,0)$). If the cursor is outside the window, x and y are both equal to -1.

We want to display the content of the original color image corresponding to the block under which the mouse is positioned, as shown in Fig. 2.6. How can we simply find the coordinates $(x0, y0) - (x1, y1)$ of the block under the mouse cursor? We will slightly modify our block image rendering code, to fill, in addition to the res image, a second image, named coords, defined as follows:

```
CImg<int> coords(img.width(),img.height(),1,4,0);
```

The coords image has four channels, with integer values, which contain for each pixel the coordinates of the decomposed block to which it belongs, namely the values $(x0, y0, x1, y1)$:

Code 2.4 – Rendering of the image decomposition (version 2).

```
cimglist_for(blocks,l)
{
  CImg<int>& block = blocks[l];
  int
    x0 = block[0], y0 = block[1],
    x1 = block[2], y1 = block[3];
  CImg<unsigned char> color(1,1,1,3);
  color.rand(0,255);
  res.draw_rectangle(x0,y0,x1,y1,color.data(),1);
  // Filling image 'coords':
  coords.draw_rectangle(x0,y0,x1,y1,block.data());
}
```

In the event loop, we can now easily retrieve the coordinates $(x0, y0) - (x1, y1)$ of the block pointed by the mouse, as well as the center of this block (xc, yc):

```
if (x>=0 && y>=0)
{
  int
    x0 = coords(x,y,0), y0 = coords(x,y,1), // Bottom-left coords
    x1 = coords(x,y,2), y1 = coords(x,y,3), // Bottom-right coords
    xc = (x0 + x1)/2, yc = (y0 + y1)/2;     // Center coords
}
```

All that remains is to retrieve the portions of the original image img and the image of the variations norm corresponding to the current block, to resize them to a fixed size (here 128×128), and draw them on a copy of the image res, intended to be displayed in the display window disp:

```
CImg<unsigned char>
  pImg = img.get_crop(x0,y0,x1,y1).resize(128,128,1,3,1),
  pGrad = normGrad.get_crop(x0,y0,x1,y1).resize(128,128,1,3,1).
              normalize(0,255).
              map(CImg<unsigned char>::hot_LUT256());
```

Note that in the meantime, the values of the region extracted from the normGrad variation image are normalized, mapped to colors using a hot colormap, i.e., a classic palette of 256 colors ranging from black to white through red and yellow. The pGrad image thus becomes a normalized color image ready to be displayed (whereas the normGrad image was a scalar image, with a different range of values as $[\![0,255]\!]$). We can now create the visual rendering of our image to be displayed:

Code 2.5 – Visual rendering for interactive display.

```
1-  unsigned char white[] = { 255,255,255 }, black[] = { 0,0,0 };
2-  (+res).
3-    draw_text(10,3,"X, Y = %d, %d",white,0,1,24,x,y).
4-    draw_rectangle(x0,y0,x1,y1,black,0.25f).
5-    draw_line(74,109,xc,yc,white,0.75,0xCCCCCCCC).
6-    draw_line(74,264,xc,yc,white,0.75,0xCCCCCCCC).
7-    draw_rectangle(7,32,140,165,white).
8-    draw_rectangle(7,197,140,330,white).
9-    draw_image(10,35,pImg).
10-   draw_image(10,200,pGrad).
11-   display(disp);
```

The unary operator operator+() is used here to make a *copy* of the image res, in which we will draw several graphic elements. A few things to note:

- *Line 4*: the call to draw_rectangle() decreases the luminosity of the block pointed by the mouse, by drawing a black rectangle over it, with a 25% opacity.
- *Lines 5 and 6*: note here the use of an opacity of 0.75 for the drawing of the lines going from the center of the block to the two left-hand thumbnails,

with the specification of a drawing *pattern* (0xCCCCCCCC), in order to draw a dotted segment. This dotted pattern consists of an unsigned integer on 32 bits, whose bits (worth 0 or 1) define the binary pattern of the plot. Thus, a pattern of 0xFFFFFFFF (all bits set to 1) corresponds to a solid line. A pattern of 0xAAAAAAAA is a line with even pixel lit. 0xCCCCCCCC is a line alternating two lit pixels followed by two unlit pixels. This pattern argument is present in many *CImg* drawing methods.

- *Line 11*: the copy of the image res thus decorated is finally displayed in the disp window. Note that the definition of this rendering *pipeline*, from the copy of the image res to the display, did not require the explicit definition of intermediate variables, thanks to *CImg*'s ability to write complex sequences of methods in a concise and efficient way.

Figure 2.6 illustrates the result of the different methods for plotting graphical primitives.

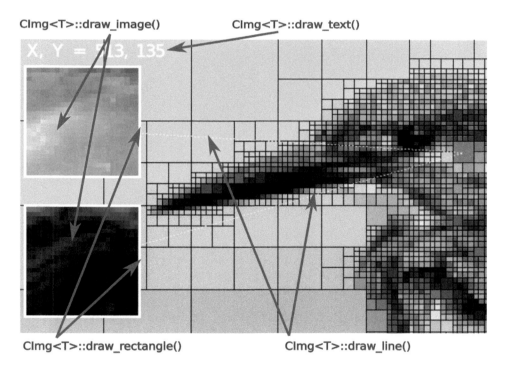

Figure 2.6 – Detail of the role of each methods for drawing graphical primitives.

2.7 Final source code

The whole program (101 lines), which gathers all together, is illustrated in Code 2.6. Compared to the description given in this tutorial, we have added the management of parameter passing on the command line, thanks to the use of the macros `cimg_usage()` and `cimg_option()`. They ease the parsing of options passed to the program, from the command line. The use of these macros also allows to generate and display automatically a help page, reminding the available options, when the program is called with the `-h`, `-help` or `--help` options. The color image given as input is downscaled if necessary to make it appear entirely on the screen (using `img.resize(-50,-50,1,-100,2)`). We also force the window to keep a fixed size, when the user tries to resize it. This size is the one passed to the constructor of `CImgDisplay`, when it has been called.

> **Code 2.6 – Source code of the tutorial on image decomposition.**

```cpp
/*
   File: decompose_blocks.cpp

   Example of image decomposition into rectangular blocks.
*/
#include "CImg.h"
using namespace cimg_library;

int main(int argc, char **argv) {

  // Reading parameters from the command line.
  cimg_usage("Decomposition into blocks of a color image");
  const char *filename = cimg_option("-i","img.bmp","Color image");
  float
    threshold = cimg_option("-t",25.0f,"Gradient threshold"),
    sigma = cimg_option("-s",0.7f,"Gradient smoothness");

  // Initialization of the images and the list of blocks.
  CImg<unsigned char> img(filename);
  while (img.width()>=CImgDisplay::screen_width() ||
         img.height()>=CImgDisplay::screen_height())
    img.resize(-50,-50,1,-100,2);

  CImg<> lum = img.get_norm().blur(sigma).normalize(0,255);
  CImgList<> grad = lum.get_gradient("xy");
  CImg<> normGrad = (grad[0].get_sqr() += grad[1].get_sqr()).sqrt();

  CImgList<int> blocks;
  CImg<int>::vector(0,0,img.width() - 1,img.height() - 1).
    move_to(blocks);
```

```
// Calculation of the decomposition of the image into blocks.
for (unsigned int l = 0; l<blocks.size(); ) {
  CImg<int>& block = blocks[l];
  int
    x0 = block[0], y0 = block[1],
    x1 = block[2], y1 = block[3];
  if (normGrad.get_crop(x0,y0,x1,y1).max()>threshold &&
      std::min(x1 - x0,y1 - y0)>8) {
    int xc = (x0 + x1)/2, yc = (y0 + y1)/2;
    CImg<int>::vector(x0,y0,xc - 1,yc - 1).move_to(blocks);
    CImg<int>::vector(xc,y0,x1,yc - 1).move_to(blocks);
    CImg<int>::vector(x0,yc,xc - 1,y1).move_to(blocks);
    CImg<int>::vector(xc,yc,x1,y1).move_to(blocks);
    blocks.remove(l);
  } else ++l;
}

// Rendering of the decomposition.
CImg<unsigned char> res(img.width(),img.height(),1,3,0);
CImg<int> coords(img.width(),img.height(),1,4,0);
cimglist_for(blocks,l) {
  CImg<int>& block = blocks[l];
  int
    x0 = block[0], y0 = block[1],
    x1 = block[2], y1 = block[3];
  CImg<unsigned char> color = img.get_crop(x0,y0,x1,y1).
    resize(1,1,1,3,2);
  res.draw_rectangle(x0,y0,x1,y1,color.data(),1);
  coords.draw_rectangle(x0,y0,x1,y1,block.data());
}

// Adding black borders.
res.mul(1 - (res.get_shift(1,1,0,0,0) - res).norm().cut(0,1));

// Start the interactive viewer.
CImgDisplay disp(res,"CImg Tutorial: Block Decomposition",0);
unsigned char white[] = { 255,255,255 }, black[] = { 0,0,0 };

while (!disp.is_closed() && !disp.is_keyESC()) {
  int
    x = disp.mouse_x(),
    y = disp.mouse_y();
  if (x>=0 && y>=0) {
    int
      x0 = coords(x,y,0), y0 = coords(x,y,1),
      x1 = coords(x,y,2), y1 = coords(x,y,3),
      xc = (x0 + x1)/2, yc = (y0 + y1)/2;
```

```
CImg<unsigned char>
  pImg = img.get_crop(x0,y0,x1,y1).resize(128,128,1,3,1),
  pGrad = normGrad.get_crop(x0,y0,x1,y1).resize(128,128,1,3,1).
                    normalize(0,255).
                    map(CImg<unsigned char>::hot_LUT256());
  (+res).
    draw_text(10,3,"X, Y = %d, %d",white,0,1,24,x,y).
    draw_rectangle(x0,y0,x1,y1,black,0.25f).
    draw_line(74,109,xc,yc,white,0.75,0xCCCCCCCC).
    draw_line(74,264,xc,yc,white,0.75,0xCCCCCCCC).
    draw_rectangle(7,32,140,165,white).
    draw_rectangle(7,197,140,330,white).
    draw_image(10,35,pImg).
    draw_image(10,200,pGrad).
    display(disp);
  }

  disp.wait(); // Wait for an user event
  if (disp.is_resized()) disp.resize(disp);
}

return 0;
}
```

Now you have a better idea of the features offered by the *CImg* library, as well as the practical use of its classes and their associated methods. The technical reference documentation, available on the *CImg*[1] website, lists all the methods and operators available for each of the four classes `CImg<T>`, `CImgList<T>`, `CImgDisplay` and `CImgException` exposed by the library. Reading it will be useful to dive into the details of all the available methods. So will the developments that follow in this book!

---

[1] http://cimg.eu/reference

II- Image Processing Using *CImg*

Introduction

In this section, we illustrate various aspects of the *CImg* library for image processing, through several workshops.

In the classic workflow of digital image processing, several steps are generally used:

- The *pre-processing* step (i.e., how to improve the image to reach the goal of the processing): it can be a matter of denoising, improving the contrast, transforming the initial image into another image, easier to process ...;
- The *processing* step as such: the objective may be to find objects in the image, to follow objects in a temporal sequence, to classify pixels in different homogeneous groups, to reconstruct a 3D scene, to extract compressed information from an image composed of many channels ...;
- The *quantization* step, which uses the previous step to provide quantitative results to measure the processing (e.g., what is the surface of the isolated object? What is the average speed of the moving object? What is the depth of the object in the image?...).

Without pretending to be exhaustive, we propose here a few workshops, organized in chapters, allowing us to approach classical methods among the wide range of classical algorithms in the field image processing. Each workshop is organized in a short but necessary introduction to its theoretical aspects, followed by the implementation in *CImg* of useful algorithms. The source codes presented allow to make an immediate parallel with the equations described in the theoretical part. The results of the algorithms are illustrated with many figures.

3. Point Processing Transformations

In this chapter, we are interested in grayscale images. A d-dimensional image is considered as a function $I : \Omega \subset \mathbb{N}^d \to [\![0, N-1]\!]$, where N is the number of gray levels that pixel values can take.

The simplest way to process an image is to apply a pointwise operation

$$J(x,y) = T[I(x,y)],$$

where T acts directly on the image I, or on the histogram of I. Gonzalez and Woods [15] propose many examples of *ad hoc* transformations. In the following, we give an overview of some of them.

3.1 Image operations

3.1.1 Mathematical transformations

A natural idea is to define a mathematical transformation T on I. Any "classical" mathematical function can be applied, regarding its definition domain. The `CImg<T>` class has many pre-defined methods allowing to apply pointwise functions on an image (Table 3.1).

Figures 3.1 and. 3.2 show some outputs provided by Code 3.1.

Code 3.1 – Some mathematical transformations applied to an image.

```
CImg<> imgIn("butterfly.bmp");
CImgList<> mathOps(imgIn,
                   imgIn.get_exp()/50,
                   10*imgIn.get_sqrt(),
                   (1 + imgIn.get_abs()).log(),
                   imgIn.get_pow(3));
mathOps.display();
```

It is also possible to apply image transformations directly from a mathematical expression. The image of Figure 3.3 is for example produced by

```
img.fill("(x*y)%255",true);
```

Function	Name
Power	`sqr(), sqrt(), pow(double p),` `pow(CImg<t>& img),` `pow(const char *expression)`
Logarithm	`log(), log2(), log10(), exp()`
Trigonometry	`cos(), sin(), tan(), acos(), asin(),` `sinc(), atan(), atan2(CImg<t>& img)`
Hyperbolic	`cosh(), sinh(), tanh(), acosh(), asinh(),` `atanh()`
Min-Max	`min(T& value), max(T& value),` `minabs(T& value), maxabs(T& value)`
Various	`abs(), sign()`

Table 3.1 – Mathematical functions available as methods of `CImg<T>`. For each method `f()`, there is an equivalent version `get_f()`.

Figure 3.1 – Gamma transform $c.i^\gamma$, $c \in \mathbb{R}$. For $\gamma < 1$, the transformation compresses the dynamic range of I; for $\gamma > 1$, it compresses the high grayscale values, and stretches the range of small values.

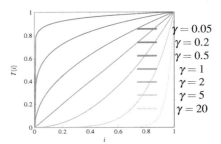

Finally, it can be sometimes useful to transform an image I using another image J. *CImg* provides methods for performing point operations between two images: addition (overloaded operators + and −), multiplication (`mul(CImg<t>& img)`), division (`div(CImg<t>& img)`), or even elevation to power (`pow(CImg<t>& img)`, where each pixel in I being raised to the power of the gray level of the corresponding pixel in J. For example, writing

```
CImg<> C = A.get_pow(B);
```

on A and B in Figure 3.4 produces image C.

3.1.2 Bitwise transformations

Classic bitwise transformation operators (AND, OR, XOR) are also overloaded. They can be applied on images with binary values $\{0, 1\}$ to produce logical combinations, as illustrated in Fig. 3.5, produced by Code 3.2.

Figure 3.2 – Some examples of mathematical transformations. From left to right: Input image I, $exp(I/50)$, $10\sqrt{I}$, $log\,(1 + |I|)$, and I^3.

Figure 3.3 – From a mathematical formula to an image. The image is produced by using `img.fill("(x*y)%255",true);`.

Code 3.2 – Illustration of some binary operations.

```
CImg<unsigned char> A("A.bmp"), B("B.bmp");
CImgList<unsigned char> binOps(A | B,    // OR
                               A & B,    // AND
                               A ^ B);   // XOR
binOps.display();
```

In the case of non-binary images, these operators act at the bit level, encoding the values of the intensities of each pixel.

As an illustration, consider the classic steganography problem, where the objective is to hide a message in an image. The message is encoded in a separate image (Fig. 3.6a), with the text pixels set to 1 on a black background (whose pixels are set to 0). We choose to encode the message on the *Least Significant Bits* (LSB method) of the original image (Fig. 3.6b).

This is done by setting the least significant bits of these images to 0, then applying a bitwise OR between the output and the image of the text to produce an image, visually indistinguishable from the original one, which contains the hidden text (Fig. 3.6c). To decode the message, a bitwise AND is applied with the value 1 to recover the message (Fig. 3.6d). Code 3.3 illustrates how easy this operation is performed with *CImg*.

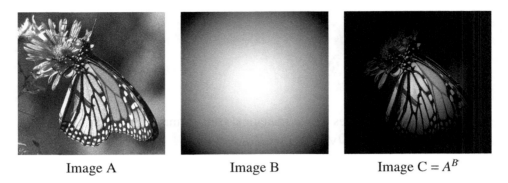

Image A   Image B   Image C = A^B

Figure 3.4 – Example of point processing of an image by another image.

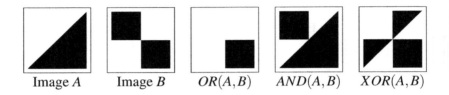

Image A Image B $OR(A,B)$ $AND(A,B)$ $XOR(A,B)$

Figure 3.5 – Illustration of some binary operations.

Code 3.3 – Steganography using LSB method.

```cpp
CImg<unsigned char>
  imgIn("butterfly.bmp"),
  mess("message.bmp");

// The text pixels are set to 1 on a background of 0.
mess.threshold(128);
CImg<unsigned char> imgIn2 = imgIn.get_channel(0);

// Encoding step. We remove the 1's in the least significant bits.
imgIn2 &= 0xFE;

// Encoding of the message in the least significant bit.
CImg<unsigned char> imgOut = imgIn2 | mess;

// Decoding step.
CImg<unsigned char> res = (imgOut&1) *= 255;
```

a) Message   b) Original Image

c) Image with hidden message   d) Decoded message

Figure 3.6 – Steganography using Least Significant Bit coding strategy.

3.1.3 Contrast enhancement

When image I is low contrasted, it can be interesting to increase the dynamics of its gray levels (or its colors in the case of a color image). To do this, the simplest way is to define a piecewise linear function on the interval $[\![0, N-1]\!]$. This interval is subdivided into M subintervals $[g_i, g_{i+1}]$, with $g_0 = 0$, $g_{M-1} = N - 1$, $i \in [\![0, M-2]\!]$ and for each of these intervals, a linear transform is defined:

$$(\forall j \in [g_i, g_{i+1}]) \; T_i(j) = a_i . j + b_i$$

with $T_i(g_{i+1}) = T_{i+1}(g_{i+1}), i \in [\![0, M-2]\!]$.

This set of transformations can be used, for example, to calculate the negative of an image, or to perform thresholding operations. They can be visualized by a

Look-Up Table (LUT) which gives the correspondence between old and new gray levels (Fig. 3.7). Of course, the mathematical transformations previously described also define LUTs, corresponding to the graph of the function on the image intensity domain.

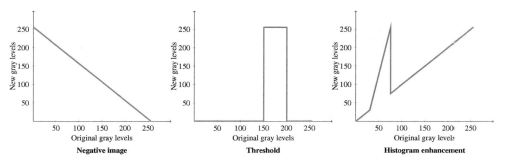

Figure 3.7 – Some Look-Up Tables.

3.2   Histogram operations

An important class of point operations is related to the histogram of the image or part of the image.

3.2.1   Definition

The probability distributions of the gray levels can be estimated by measurements on the histogram of the image. For example, the first order distribution

$$\mathbf{P}\left(I(x,y) = k\right)$$

can be evaluated using a set of D images, D large, representative of a given image class. The estimated distribution is then

$$h(k,x,y) = \frac{Num(k)}{D}$$

where $Num(k)$ is the number of images for which $I(x,y) = k$. Using the ergodicity hypothesis, the measure on D images can be replaced by a spatial measure: the first order probability distribution can then be estimated by

$$H(k) = \frac{Num(k)}{|I|}$$

where $|I|$ is the total number of pixels and $Num(k)$ the number of times in I where $I(x,y) = k$, for all (x,y).

Definition 3.2.1

$$H : [\![0, N-1]\!] \quad \rightarrow \quad \mathbb{N}$$
$$k \mapsto H(k) \quad = \quad \frac{Num(k)}{|I|}$$

is the histogram of image I.

In the case of color images, the histogram generally refers either to the intensity (luminance) of the pixels or to the histograms of the different color channels.

3.2.2 Histogram specification

The histogram of a typical natural image I that has been linearly quantized has a large number of pixels with a lower gray level than the average gray level of I. The details in the darkest regions become hardly perceptible. One way to improve these images is to perform a histogram specification operation, which transforms the histogram so that it approaches a given distribution. This can for example be a uniform distribution, and in this case the operation is called "histogram equalization".

Histogram specification can be thought of as a monotonic transformation $J_j = T(I_i)$ such that the probability distribution $\mathbf{P}(J_j = k_j)$ follows a given constraint for a given probability $\mathbf{P}(I_i = l_i)$, where l_i and k_j are the reconstructed values of the ith and j^{th} gray levels. Since both distributions sum up to 1, then

$$\sum_{i=1}^{N_i} \mathbf{P}(I_i = l_i) = 1 \text{ and } \sum_{j=1}^{N_j} \mathbf{P}(J_j = k_j) = 1$$

Furthermore, if T is monotonic, the probability that the pixels of I have a gray level less than or equal to l_i must be equal to the probability that the pixels of the output image have a gray level less than or equal to k_j, with $k_j = T(l_i)$. Then:

$$\sum_{p=1}^{j} \mathbf{P}(J_p = k_p) = \sum_{q=1}^{i} \mathbf{P}(I_q = l_q)$$

The second term is nothing but the cumulative distribution of I and can thus be replaced by the cumulative histogram: $\sum_{p=1}^{j} \mathbf{P}(J_p = k_p) = \sum_{q=1}^{i} H_I(q)$.

Since J_j must be a function of I_i, this equation has to be inverted. The analytical inversion is sometimes impossible, and T can then be estimated by numerical methods. To approach the solution, it is usual to express the discrete probability distributions with continuous densities. If $\mathbf{p}_j$ is the output density and H_I the cumulative histogram of I, then

$$\mathbf{p}_j(j) = \frac{1}{j_{max} - j_{min}} \Rightarrow j = (j_{max} - j_{min}) H_I(i) + j_{min} \text{ (equalization)}$$

$$\mathbf{p}_j(j) = a.e^{(-a(j-j_{min}))} \Rightarrow j = j_{min} - \frac{1}{a} Ln(1 - H_I(i)) \text{ (exponential output)}$$

Code 3.4 presents a simple version of the histogram equalization. Figure 3.8 illustrates some results. The histograms are plotted using the method:

```
CImg<T>& display_graph(CImgDisplay &disp, unsigned int plot_type=1,
          unsigned int vertex_type=1,
          const char *labelx=0, double xmin=0, double xmax=0,
          const char *labely=0, double ymin=0, double ymax=0)
```

The `CImg<T>` class also proposes a method to directly compute this equalization:

```
CImg<T>& equalize(unsigned int nb_levels, T value_min, T value_max)
```

3.2.3 Local histogram specification

The previous method assigns an identical gray level to all pixels with the same gray level in the input image I. The regions in the transformed image then often have sharp boundaries, which may not follow the original boundaries in I. To overcome this problem, it is possible to compute the histogram only in a neighborhood of a pixel, and to apply the specification to this central pixel only. This simple modification leads to the definition of spatial image processing techniques, which will be illustrated in Section 5.1 in the case of spatial filtering.

Code 3.4 – Histogram equalization.

```
/*
  Histogram equalization

  imgIn : Input image
  nb    : Number of bins
*/
CImg<> equalizeHisto(CImg<>& imgIn, unsigned int nb) {
  CImg<> imgOut(imgIn);
  float vmin, vmax = imgIn.max_min(vmin);
  int size = imgIn.size();

  if (vmin==vmax && vmin==0)
    vmin = imgIn.min_max(vmax);

  int vdiff = vmax - vmin;
```

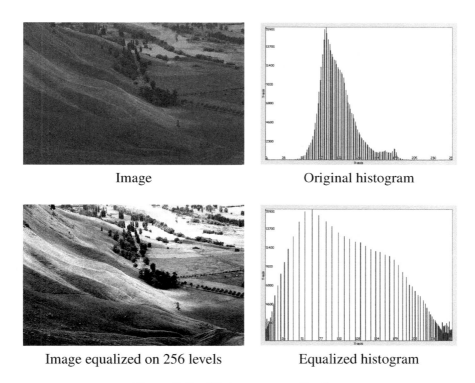

Figure 3.8 – Histogram equalization.

```
CImg<> hist = imgIn.get_histogram(nb,vmin,vmax);
long int cumul = 0;

// Cumulated histogram.
cimg_forX(hist,pos)
{
  cumul += hist[pos];
  hist[pos] = cumul;
}
if (cumul==0) cumul = 1;

// Equalized image.
cimg_for(imgIn,off)
{
  int pos = (int)((imgIn[off] - vmin)*(nb - 1)/vdiff);
  if (pos>=0 && pos<(int)nb)
    imgOut[off] = vmin + vdiff*hist[pos]/size;
}
return imgOut;
}
```

4. Mathematical Morphology

Mathematical morphology [36] is a formalism initially designed to explore the geometrical structure of objects in an image. The development of techniques based on these tools then allowed the application domains to be widened, for example for contrast enhancement or filtering. Seen from the "pattern recognition" point of view, image processing aims to extract geometric information (location, perimeter, area, orientation, ...) from a given image, allowing objects to be distinguished in a scene.

In the context of mathematical morphology and in order to extract a particular geometrical structure, the key point is the design of a *shape operator* which possesses a certain number of expected properties (for example, invariance by translation) and allowing to discriminate a particular object. Several problems then arise, notably the fact that the objects are opaque, and therefore the shape information is not additive. In fact, the objects in a scene are mainly combined in two forms:

- by union of sets (overlapping objects): $X = X_1 \cup X_2$
- by intersection of sets (occlusion): $X = X_2 \setminus X_1 = X_1^C \cap X_2$

The shape operator Ψ to be designed must then be distributed over the set of unions and intersections (equivalent to linearity), that is:

- $\Psi_\delta(X_1 \cup X_2) = \Psi_\delta(X_1) \cup \Psi_\delta(X_2)$
- $\Psi_\varepsilon(X_2 \setminus X_1) = \Psi_\varepsilon(X_1) \cap \Psi_\varepsilon(X_2)$

The first operation will be called *morphological dilation* and the second *morphological erosion*. These two operations are the basis of mathematical morphology, from which more complex morphological operators can be designed.

In the following, we specify the notions of erosion, dilation and various other operations in the context of binary images, and then we extend the discussion to the more general case of grayscale images.

4.1   Binary images

Let $A, B \subset \mathbb{Z}^2$ be two subsets, whose elements are denoted $\mathbf{a} = (a_1, a_2)^\top$ and $\mathbf{b} = (b_1, b_2)^\top$:

- the translation of A by $\mathbf{x} = (x, y)^\top$, denoted $(A)_\mathbf{x}$ is $(A)_\mathbf{x} = \{\mathbf{c} = \mathbf{a} + \mathbf{x}, \mathbf{a} \in A\}$
- the reflection of B, denoted B' is $B' = \{\mathbf{x} = -\mathbf{b}, \mathbf{b} \in B\}$
- the complement of A, denoted A^C is $A^C = \{\mathbf{x}, \mathbf{x} \notin A\}$
- the difference of A and B is $A \setminus B = A \cap B^C = \{\mathbf{x}, \mathbf{x} \in A, \mathbf{x} \notin B\}$

In this section, A is a binary image and B a binary shape operator.

4.1.1   Dilation and erosion

Definition 4.1.1 The *dilation* of A by B, denoted $A \oplus B$ is the set defined by

$$A \oplus B = \{\mathbf{x}, (B')_\mathbf{x} \cap A \neq \varnothing\}$$

Definition 4.1.2 The *erosion* of A by B, denoted $A \ominus B$ is the set defined by

$$A \ominus B = \{\mathbf{x}, (B)_\mathbf{x} \subseteq A\}$$

B is the shape operator, also known as the *structuring element* in mathematical morphology.

To be clear, for a binary object A and a binary and symmetric structuring element B, the simple operations of mathematical morphology consist in going through the image and considering B as a binary mask: if, centered in $\mathbf{x}$, B intersects A, then the value of the dilation of A by B in $\mathbf{x}$ is 1, and 0 otherwise. Similarly if B is not fully enclosed in A, then the value of the erosion of A by B in $\mathbf{x}$ is 0, and 1 otherwise (Fig. 4.1). Thus, erosion shrinks A, and dilation extends it, according to B.

When B is not symmetric, the reflection of the structuring element must be taken into account (Fig. 4.2).

It is easy to show that erosion is the dual transformation of dilation *versus* complementation: $A \ominus B = (A^C \oplus B)^C$. Thus, it is equivalent to erode an object or to dilate its complement.

The implementation in *CImg* uses the dedicated methods `CImg<T>::erode()` and `CImg<T>::dilate()` (code 4.1).

> **Code 4.1 – Erosion and dilation.**

```
CImg<unsigned char> img("yin.png");

// Structuring element. Here a 3*3 square.
```

```
CImg<unsigned char> B = CImg<unsigned char>(3,3).fill(1);

CImg<unsigned char>
  imgErode  = img.get_erode(B),    // Erosion
  imgDilate = img.get_dilate(B);   // Dilation
```

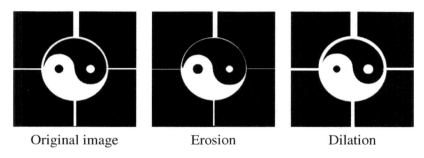

Original image   Erosion   Dilation

Figure 4.1 – Erosion and dilation by a 3×3 square structuring element.

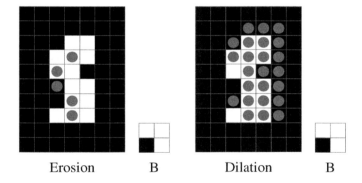

Erosion   B   Dilation   B

Figure 4.2 – Erosion and dilation. The object is in white, the background in black, the erosion and the dilation are represented by the pixels filled with gray disks. The structuring element B, not symmetrical, is centered on the black box.

The size of the structuring element and its shape greatly influence the results of morphological operations (Fig. 4.3). In particular, erosion tends to remove details of object A whose characteristic size is smaller than that of the structuring element (e.g., the thinnest lines, or the white circle that disappears almost entirely). Conversely, dilation enlarges the object.

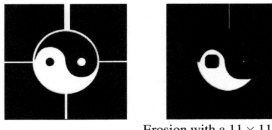

Original image   Erosion with a 11×11 square   Dilation with a 11×11
                      structuring element   square structuring element

Figure 4.3 – Effect of the size of the structuring element (to be compared to Fig. 4.1).

4.1.2 Opening and closing

From the dilation and erosion operators, we can define two new operations: *opening* and *closing*.

> **Definition 4.1.3** The opening of A by B is defined by $A \circ B = (A \ominus B) \oplus B$

> **Definition 4.1.4** The closing of A by B is defined by $A \bullet B = (A \oplus B) \ominus B$

The opening generally smoothes the contours of a binary shape, breaks the closed links between objects (isthmuses), and eliminates "small" isolated objects ("small" in the sense of the structuring element B). The type and the amount of smoothing are determined by the shape and the size of B. Closing also tends to smooth contours, but gathers "close" objects (in the sense of B), eliminates "small" holes (in the sense of B) and connects contours. Figure 4.4 shows the result of opening and closing the previous image, with a square structuring element of size 11×11.

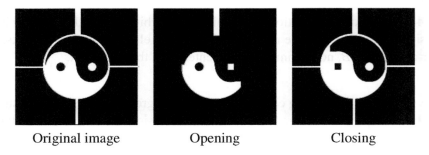

Original image   Opening   Closing

Figure 4.4 – Opening and closing by a structuring element of size 11.

Figure 4.5 presents these same operations with a non-symmetric structuring element.

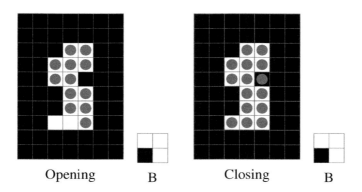

Figure 4.5 – Opening and closing. The object is in white, the background in black, the opening and closing are represented by the pixels filled with gray disks. The structuring element B, not symmetrical, is centered on the black box.

Code 4.2 illustrates the implementation of these operations.

Code 4.2 – Opening and closing.

```cpp
CImg<unsigned char> img("yin.png");

// Structuring element. Here a 3*3 square.
CImg<unsigned char> B = CImg<unsigned char>(3,3).fill(1);

CImg<unsigned char>
  imgErode = img.get_erode(B),          // Erosion
  imgDilate = img.get_dilate(B),        // Dilation
  imgOpening = imgErode.get_dilate(B),  // Opening
  imgClosing = imgDilate.get_erode(B);  // Closing
```

Opening and closing are morphological filters. The notion of filtering becomes important when considering a shape and a size adapted to B: Fig. 4.6a presents a painting by Henri Matisse (Woman with Amphora and Pomegranates, 1953), Fig. 4.6b a noisy version of the original image by a vertical noise, and Fig. 4.6c the restored image, by morphological opening using an adapted structuring element.

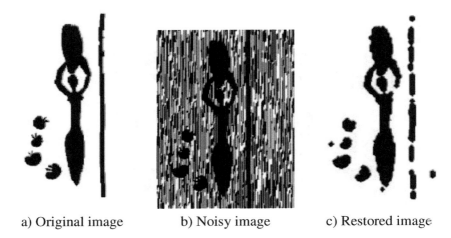

a) Original image   b) Noisy image   c) Restored image

Figure 4.6 – An example of morphological filter.

4.2   Gray-level images

Now $A = I$ is a gray-level image and B is a gray-level structuring element (a function).

Definition 4.2.1 The dilation of A by B is defined by

$$(A \oplus B)(s,t) = \max_{(s-x),(t-y) \in D_I, (x,y) \in D_B} \{I(s-x,t-y) + B(x,y)\}$$

where D_I (resp. D_B) is the image (resp. the structuring element) domain. Serra [36] proposed to illustrate this definition on 1D functions (Fig. 4.7, where $I = f$), for which the previous formula is rewritten

$$(A \oplus B)(s,t) = \max_{(s-x) \in D_I, x \in D_B} \{I(s-x) + B(x)\}$$

One can define as well the gray-level erosion of an image by a gray-level structuring element

Definition 4.2.2 The erosion of A by B is defined by

$$(A \ominus B)(s,t) = \min_{(s+x),(t+y) \in D_I, (x,y) \in D_B} \{I(s+x,t+y) - B(x,y)\}$$

and the corresponding 1D illustration is proposed in Fig. 4.8.

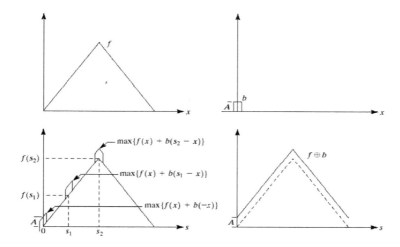

Figure 4.7 – Gray-level dilation in 1D (from [36]).

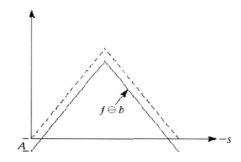

Figure 4.8 – Gray-level erosion in 1D (from [36]).

These two definitions allow to develop more complex operations of mathematical morphology (opening, closing, but also skeletonization, hit-and-miss transformation, filtering ... [15, 36]).

4.3   Some applications

4.3.1   Kramer-Bruckner filter

We are interested here in the application of mathematical morphology to contrast enhancement. Let I be an image and (x, y) the generic position of a pixel. For each

(x, y), a function M is computed as:

$$M(x,y) = \frac{1}{2}\left((f \ominus b)(x,y) + (f \oplus b)(x,y)\right)$$

and the output image J is defined as

$$J(x,y) = \begin{cases} (f \ominus b)(x,y) & \text{if } I(x,y) \leq M(x,y) \\ (f \oplus b)(x,y) & \text{otherwise} \end{cases}$$

Code 4.3 performs this enhancement, and Fig. 4.9 shows the result for two sizes of structuring element.

Code 4.3 – Kramer-Bruckner filter.

```
/*
  Kramer-Bruckner filter.

  imgIn : Input image
  n     : size of the square structuring element
*/
CImg<> KramerBruckner(CImg<>& imgIn, int n)
{
  CImg<>
    imgOut(imgIn),                          // Copy of the input image
    mask = CImg<>(n,n).fill(1),             // Structuring element
    imgErode = imgIn.get_erode(mask),      // Erosion
    imgDilate = imgIn.get_dilate(mask);    // Dilation

  cimg_forXY(imgOut,x,y)
  {
    float M = 0.5f*(imgErode(x,y) + imgDilate(x,y));
    imgOut(x,y)  = (imgIn(x,y)<=M ? imgErode(x,y) : imgDilate(x,y));
  }

  return imgOut;
}
```

4.3.2 Alternating sequential filters

Alternating sequential filters are widely used, e.g., to progressively filter out positive noise (narrow peaks) and negative noise (narrow valleys). They are built from sequences of morphological openings and closing operations of increasing size. In the digital case, such a filter applied to a function I is expressed as:

$$(\cdots(((I \circ B_1) \bullet B_1) \circ B_2) \bullet B_2)\cdots \circ B_n) \bullet B_n$$

| Original image | Filtered image, $n = 5$ | Filtered image, $n = 11$ |

Figure 4.9 – Kramer-Bruckner filter.

We thus obtain increasing and idempotent operations (thus morphological filters). The last structuring element (of size n) is determined according to the minimal size of the objects of the image that we want to keep after the filtering process (Code 4.4 and Fig. 4.10).

Code 4.4 – Alternating sequential filters.

```
/*
  Alternating sequential filters.

  imgIn : Input image
  n     : Maximum filter size
*/
CImg<> SAFiltering(CImg<>& imgIn, int n)
{
  CImg<> imgOut(imgIn);

  for (int k = 1; k<=n; ++k)
  {
    // Structuring element of size k x k.
    CImg<> mask = CImg<>(k,k).fill(1);

    // Opening.
    imgOut.erode(mask).dilate(mask);
```

```
    // Closing.
    imgOut.dilate(mask).erode(mask);
  }

  return imgOut;
}
```

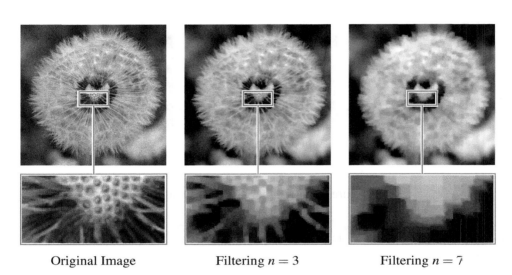

| Original Image | Filtering $n = 3$ | Filtering $n = 7$ |

Figure 4.10 – Some results of alternating sequential filters.

4.3.3 Morphological gradients

If B is a structuring element of small dimension, the operator $\nabla_E(A) = A - (A \ominus B)$, called erosion gradient, provides the inner contours of the image A. In the same way the dilation gradient $\nabla_D(A) = (A \oplus B) - A$ produces the outer contours of the image. It is then possible to combine these two new operators to extract the contours of A (code 4.5), by defining:

- Beucher's morphological gradient $\nabla_E(A) + \nabla_D(A) = (A \oplus B) - (A \ominus B)$
- White top-hat transform $(A - A \circ B)$ and black transform $(A \bullet B - A)$
- Edge detection operators $\min(\nabla_E(A), \nabla_D(A))$ and $\max(\nabla_E(A), \nabla_D(A))$
- The non-linear Laplacian $\nabla_D(A) - \nabla_E(A)$

Figure 4.11 shows some examples of morphological gradients in reversed colors.

Original Image   Beucher   Max contours

Figure 4.11 – Some morphological gradients (square structuring element of size 3).

Code 4.5 – Morphological gradient.

```
/*
  Morphological gradients.

  imgIn : Input image
  n     : size of the square structuring element
*/
void MorphologicalGradients(CImg<>& imgIn, int n)
{
  CImg<> B = CImg<>(n,n).fill(1),
        imgErode = imgIn.get_erode(B),
        imgDilate = imgIn.get_dilate(B),
        imgOpening = imgErode.get_dilate(B),
        imgClosing = imgDilate.get_erode(B),
        gradE = imgIn - imgErode,
        gradD = imgDilate - imgIn;
  // Beucher.
  CImg<> imgBeucher = imgDilate - imgErode;

  // Hop Hat.
  CImg<> whiteTopHat = imgIn - imgOpening,
        blackTopHat = imgClosing - imgIn;

  // Edge detector.
  CImg<> contourMin = gradE.min(gradD),
```

```
        contourMax = gradE.max(gradD);

    // Nonlinear laplacian.
    CImg<> Laplacien = gradD - gradE;
}
```

4.3.4 Skeletonization

Skeletonization (or thinning) is a classical technique in mathematical morphology whose objective is to reduce binary objects to a structure of a single pixel thick without breaking the topology and connectivity of the objects. This process is achieved by the iterative application of conditional erosions in a local neighborhood of each point, if a sufficient "thickness" remains in order not to modify the connectivity of the objects. This implies a local decision process which can make this skeletonization costly. Many skeletonization algorithms exist in the literature and we propose in the following to implement Zhang and Suen's algorithm [44].

Let I be a binary image containing a white object on a dark background. For each pixel in I, a 3×3 neighborhood N is analyzed, following Fig. 4.12.

N_3	N_2	N_1
N_4	(x,y)	N_0
N_5	N_6	N_7

Figure 4.12 – Neighborhood N of pixel (x,y). Neighbors are labeled from N_0 to N_7.

Two functions are then defined:

1. $B(N)$, giving the number of pixels of the binary object in N: $B(N) = \sum_{i=0}^{7} N_i$

2. $C(N)$, called connectivity number, expressing how many binary components are connected to the central pixel (x,y). It is therefore the number of $1 \rightarrow 0$ transitions in N, and thus $C(N) = \sum_{i=0}^{7} N_i(N_i - N_{(i+1) mod 8})$.

From B and N, one deduces two predicates:

$$\mathscr{R}_1(N) = \{(2 \le B(N) \le 6) \; AND \; (C(N) = 1) \; AND \; (N_6 N_0 N_2 = 0) \; AND \; (N_4 N_6 N_0 = 0)\}$$
$$\mathscr{R}_2(N) = \{(2 \le B(N) \le 6) \; AND \; (C(N) = 1) \; AND \; (N_0 N_2 N_4 = 0) \; AND \; (N_2 N_4 N_6 = 0)\}$$

Depending on the values of $\mathscr{R}_1(N)$ and $\mathscr{R}_2(N)$, the pixel (x,y) is eroded or marked as non-erodible in two passes.

Code 4.6 details the implementation of this skeletonization. Note the use of the neighborhood loops `cimg_for3x3()` of *CImg*, which allows an easy access to the neighborhoods of the current pixel.

Code 4.6 – Skeletonization step.

```cpp
int IterSkeleton(CImg<unsigned char>& imgIn)
{
  // Pixel tag image for removal.
  CImg<unsigned char> D(imgIn.width(),imgIn.height(),1,1,0);

  // Neighborhood.
  CImg_3x3(N,unsigned char);

  // Pass 1.
  int n1 = 0;
  cimg_for3x3(imgIn,x,y,0,0,N,unsigned char)
  {
    if (imgIn(x,y))
    {
      unsigned char
        B = Npp + Ncp + Nnp + Npc + Nnc + Npn + Ncn + Nnn,
        C = Nnc*(Nnc-Nnp) + Nnp*(Nnp-Ncp) +
            Ncp*(Ncp-Npp) + Npp*(Npp-Npc) +
            Npc*(Npc-Npn) + Npn*(Npn-Ncn) +
            Ncn*(Ncn-Nnn) + Nnn*(Nnn-Nnc);

      bool R1 = B>=2 && B<=6 && C==1 &&
                Ncn*Nnc*Ncp==0 &&
                Npc*Ncn*Nnc==0;
      if (R1)
      {
        // Tag (x,y).
        D(x,y) = 1;
        ++n1;
      }
    }
  }
  // Removing tagged pixels.
  cimg_forXY(imgIn,x,y)
    imgIn(x,y) -= (n1>0)*D(x,y);

  // Pass 2.
  int n2 = 0;
  D.fill(0);
```

```
cimg_for3x3(imgIn,x,y,0,0,N,unsigned char)
{
  if (imgIn(x,y))
  {
    unsigned char
        B = Npp + Ncp + Nnp + Npc + Nnc + Npn + Ncn + Nnn,
        C = Nnc*(Nnc-Nnp) + Nnp*(Nnp-Ncp) +
            Ncp*(Ncp-Npp) + Npp*(Npp-Npc) +
            Npc*(Npc-Npn) + Npn*(Npn-Ncn) +
            Ncn*(Ncn-Nnn) + Nnn*(Nnn-Nnc);

    bool R2 = B>=2 && B<=6 && C==1 &&
              Nnc*Ncp*Npc==0 &&
              Ncp*Npc*Ncn==0;
    if (R2)
    {
      // Tag (x,y)
      D(x,y) = 1;
      ++n2;
    }
  }
}
// Removing tagged pixels.
cimg_forXY(imgIn,x,y)
  imgIn(x,y) -= (n2>0)*D(x,y);

// Number of removed pixels.
return n1 + n2;
}
```

Code 4.7 uses the previous function in a loop, which ends after a maximum number of iterations or when no more pixels should be deleted.

Code 4.7 – Zhang and Suen's algorithm.

```
/*
  Thinning algorithm.

  imgIn    : Input image
  maxiter  : Maximum number of iterations
*/
int Skeletonization(CImg<unsigned char>& imgIn, int maxiter)
{
  int n, i = 0;
  do
  {
    ++i;
    n = IterSkeleton(imgIn);
```

```
    }
    while (n>0 && i<maxiter);
    return i;
}
```

Finally, Fig. 4.13 shows an example of results of this algorithm.

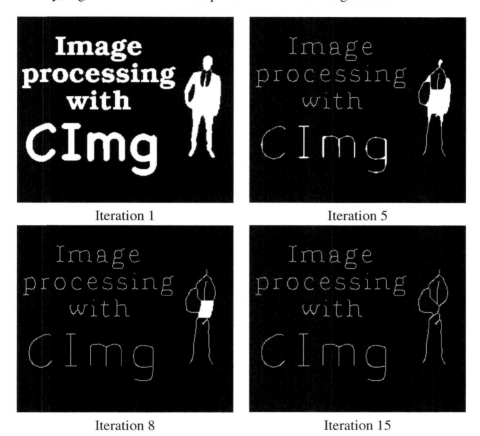

| Iteration 1 | Iteration 5 |
| Iteration 8 | Iteration 15 |

Figure 4.13 – Skeletonization using Zhang and Suen's algorithm.

5. Filtering

5.1 Spatial filtering

5.1.1 Introduction

The term "spatial" refers to the set of pixels of the image. Any spatial processing can be expressed as

$$J(x,y) = T[I(x,y)],$$

where I is the original image, J the processed one and T an operator acting on I, defined on a neighborhood of (x,y). If this neighborhood is of size 1, T acts pixel by pixel, and we related this filtering to point to point analysis (Chapter 3).

We consider in the following a neighborhood of size strictly greater than 1, centered in (x,y). We are then interested in *spatial filtering* (as opposed to frequency filtering, which we will discuss in the next section), and we detail here linear and non-linear filters.

Linear filters are based on the linearity assumption of the acquisition system. Low-pass filters attenuate or eliminate the high spatial frequencies in the image, leaving the low frequencies intact. On the contrary, high-pass filters leave the high frequencies intact, and lower the low frequencies. Finally, band-pass filters attenuate or eliminate a given frequency band.

Whatever the type of linear spatial filtering, the approach is identical. It consists in defining around a pixel (x,y) a mask W of odd size $M \times N$, centered in (x,y). W is described by a matrix of coefficients $w_{i,j}$ with $i \in [\![-\frac{M-1}{2}, \frac{M-1}{2}]\!]$ and $j \in [\![-\frac{N-1}{2}, \frac{N-1}{2}]\!]$. The filtering process consists then simply in scanning the image using W and in the assignment to the pixel (x,y) of the gray level resulting from the linear combination of the neighboring pixels weighted by the coefficients of the filter (Equation 5.1):

$$J(x,y) = \sum_{i=-\frac{M-1}{2}}^{\frac{M-1}{2}} \sum_{j=-\frac{N-1}{2}}^{\frac{N-1}{2}} w_{i,j} I(x+i, y+j) \tag{5.1}$$

This refers to discrete convolution and we note $J = W * I$. Very often $M = N$.

The `CImg<T>` class defines the method

```
CImg<> get_convolve(CImg<>& kernel,...)
```

which allows to perform the discrete convolution of the image instance by a mask `kernel` given in parameter. Code 5.1 presents an example of discrete convolution by a mask W, estimating the vertical gradient of an image.

Code 5.1 – Discrete convolution.

```
void MaskConv(CImg<>& imgIn)
{
   CImg<> W(3,3,1,1,0);
   W(0,1) = W(0,0) = W(0,2) = -1;
   W(2,1) = W(2,0) = W(2,2) = 1;
   CImg<> imgOut = imgIn.get_convolve(W);
   imgOut.display();
}
```

Non-linear filtering is also performed using centered neighborhoods, but it acts directly on the gray levels $I(x+i, y+j)$ by means of a non-linear transformation (e.g., with max, min, median operators, or non-linear functions of the gray levels).

A convolution mask cannot be applied entirely on the pixels located at the edges of the image: $\frac{M-1}{2}$ rows at the top and bottom of the image and $\frac{N-1}{2}$ columns on the left and right cannot be processed using Equation 5.1. Several strategies are then possible:
- do not calculate the convolution values for these rows and columns;
- assign a value (typically zero or the maximum gray-level) on the pixels that should be outside the definition domain of the image when computing the convolution (*padding*);
- assign to the outer pixels the values of their nearest neighbor;
- truncate the result image J into a smaller image, by suppressing the corresponding rows and columns in *I*.

5.1.2 Low-pass filters

Low-pass filters attenuate or remove high spatial frequencies in the image. Since these are characteristic of strong intensity variations in a small neighborhood, the noise will be attenuated, and the contours will also be impacted. Low-pass filtering therefore tends to smooth the image structures.

Linear filtering

A convolution mask for image smoothing has non-negative coefficients summing to 1 (ensuring the preservation of the mean value of the image). Generally speaking,

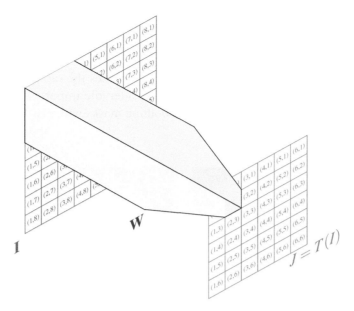

Figure 5.1 – Discrete convolution.

the coefficients can be manually given, or defined by a mathematical function (e.g., a Gaussian). Among the many smoothing masks that can be used, Fig. 5.2 presents two typical examples. Mask (a) simply operates an arithmetic mean in the 3×3 neighborhood of (x,y) in I and assigns this mean to $J(x,y)$. In mask (b), pixels close to the central pixel are given a larger contribution to the weighted average. Computing such filters is very easy with *CImg*. For example, the definition of a $n \times n$

1/9	1/9	1/9
1/9	1/9	1/9
1/9	1/9	1/9

a)

1/16	1/8	1/16
1/8	1/4	1/8
1/16	1/8	1/16

b)

Figure 5.2 – Two low-pass filter masks.

neighborhood averaging filter is done by defining a constant image W:

```
CImg<> W(n,n,1,1,1.0f/(n*n));
```

Smoothing the image generates a blurring effect. Since the coefficients of the mask sum up to 1, smoothing will preserve any area of the image where the gray level is almost constant. Therefore, this type of filtering does not modify the areas with small variations of gray levels and conversely, attenuates the rapid variations. The size of the convolution mask has of course a considerable importance in the result. Figure 5.3 shows filtering results for $n \times n$ smoothing masks with constant coefficients (all equal to $1/n^2$), for $n \in \{3, 7, 11\}$.

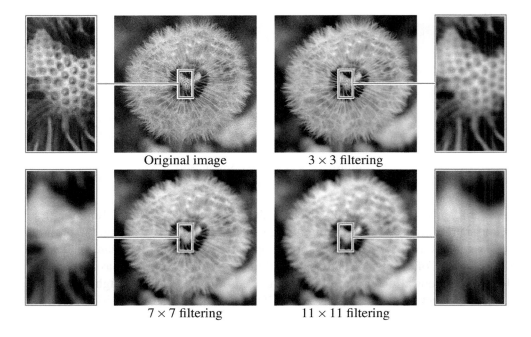

Figure 5.3 – Effect of mask size for neighborhood averaging.

In addition to removing small details, linear smoothing can be useful in certain circumstances, for example:

- to filter a noisy image;
- to create gradients in an image whose grayscales have been over-quantized;
- before an edge detection algorithm, to ease the analysis of the image geometry, and thus improve the detection results;
- To restore a halftone image (*half-toning*).

Figure 5.4 gives an example of noise reduction (image corrupted by Gaussian noise) using a neighborhood averaging filter.

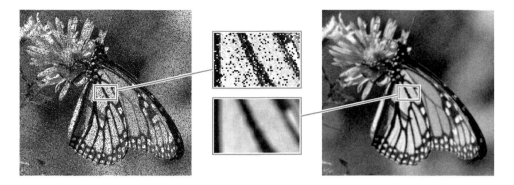

Figure 5.4 – Noise reduction.

Non-linear filtering

One of the main drawbacks of averaging filter smoothing methods is that the smoothing also applies to edge boundaries and high-frequency details, which introduces "blurring" into the image. If the objective of the processing is only noise reduction, one would like to preserve the natural contours in the image as much as possible.

Section 5.4 will introduce a technique based on partial differential equations to address this problem. Here we are interested in simpler methods, which can nevertheless be effective depending on the type of degradation (noise) encountered in the image.

Median filtering answers this problem for *impulse* noise. This filter also has the good property of leaving unchanged the monotonic transitions between neighboring regions of different intensities (Fig. 5.5). The principle is simple: replace the value of $I(x, y)$ by the median of the gray levels in a neighborhood of (x, y). If the computation is trivial, the method has some drawbacks. For noises with a low concentration distribution (Gaussian, uniform), its performance is poor compared to the optimal linear filter. In addition, it can still affect the geometry of the image regions: areas with an acute angle (corners of structures) tend to be rounded. Thus, geometric information is lost on angular points.

An immediate generalization of the median filter principle is the *order* filter. It consists in ordering in an increasing way the gray levels of the pixels contained in the neighborhood of (x, y), to obtain a vector $\mathbf{a}$, and to retain for $I(x, y)$ a function of the jth value a_j after sorting $\mathbf{a}$ (j^{th} order statistics). From these values, a L-filtering of the image is defined, which consists in applying a linear combination of the order

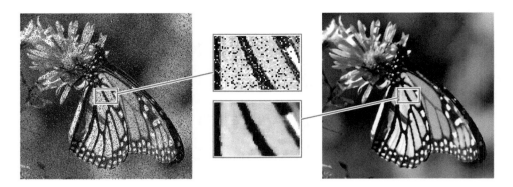

Figure 5.5 – Median filtering for impulse noise

statistics $\sum_{k=1}^{N} c_k a_k$ in replacement of $I(x,y)$.

In order not to modify the intensity of the homogeneous areas, coefficients are chosen to satisfy $\sum_{k=1}^{N} c_k = 1$. In the case where the image is homogeneous without transition and if the noise can locally be modeled by a white noise of density f and distribution function F, it is possible to optimize the choice of the c_k in the sense of a quadratic error criterion. It can be shown that the noise power at the output of an optimal L-filter is always less than or at worst equal to that of the best linear filter (mean filter). The values of the optimal coefficients depend on the shape of f.

- For a Gaussian noise of variance σ^2, $\forall k \quad c_k = \frac{1}{N}$ (mean filtering with variance $\frac{\sigma^2}{N}$);
- For a uniform noise, $c_k = \frac{1}{2}$ if $k = 1$ or $k = N$, 0 otherwise.

Moreover, if $c_k = \chi_{\{k=1\}}$ (χ_A indicator function of A), the filtering process is an erosion, and if $c_k = \chi_{\{k=N\}}$ it is a dilation. We thus find the two basic operations of mathematical morphology (cf. chapter 4), from which we can also perform non-linear filtering.

5.1.3 High-pass filters

Unlike low-pass filters, high-pass filters allow high spatial frequencies to pass and attenuate or suppress low frequencies. Since the large spatial variations in gray levels are characteristic of contours in the image, these filters therefore act as edge detectors.

Linear filtering

Sharpening consists in subtracting the smoothed image from the original one. We therefore calculate, for an image I and a smoothing mask W

$$I - (W * I) = (\delta - W) * I$$

where δ is the Kronecker delta (neutral element of the discrete convolution) defined by:

$$\delta[i,j] = \begin{cases} 1 & \text{if } i = j \\ 0 & \text{if } i \neq j \end{cases}$$

This is equivalent to applying to I the mask $W' = \delta - W$, which then has the following properties:

- the central value is $1 - w_{0,0}$;
- $-1 \leq w'_{ij} \leq 0$, for all $(i,j) \neq (0,0)$;
- $\sum\limits_{i=1}^{M} \sum\limits_{j=1}^{N} w'_{ij} = 0$.

Sharpening is related to the discrete version of the Laplacian (4- or 8-connexity approximation of partial derivatives by finite differences), which leads naturally to the notion of derivative filtering.

First order derivative filtering

Average filtering, modeled by the filter (a) in Fig. 5.2 tends to blur the image. This averaging is the approximation of an integration, and so we expect that differentiation will have the opposite effect, namely a strengthening of the image contours. The simplest differentiation operator to implement in image processing is the gradient. As a reminder, the gradient of a function $f : \mathbb{R} \times \mathbb{R} \rightarrow \mathbb{R}$ is the function:

$$\begin{aligned} \nabla : \mathbb{R} \times \mathbb{R} &\rightarrow \mathbb{R}^2 \\ (x,y) &\mapsto \begin{pmatrix} \frac{\partial f}{\partial x}(x,y) \\ \frac{\partial f}{\partial y}(x,y) \end{pmatrix} \end{aligned}$$

Since the image is discretized, the partial derivatives $\frac{\partial}{\partial x}$ and $\frac{\partial}{\partial y}$ must be approximated by left, right or centered finite differences, and for example (Fig. 5.6):

$$\frac{\partial I}{\partial x}(x,y) \approx I(x,y) - I(x+1,y) \quad \text{et} \quad \frac{\partial I}{\partial y}(x,y) \approx I(x,y) - I(x,y+1)$$

The `CImg<T>` class proposes the method

```
CImgList<> get_gradient(const char *axes=0, int scheme=0)
```

to compute the gradient of an image. Parameter `axes` specifies the set of axis along which the partial derivatives are to be computed (e.g., `"xy"`), and `scheme` specifies the desired discretization scheme (finite left, finite right, centered differences, etc.). The method returns a list of images CImgList<> where each element is an estimate of the partial derivative along each of the requested directions.

The gradient can also be decomposed at each point (Fig. 5.7) using:

- its norm $\|\nabla I(x,y)\|$, which defines the amplitude of the local variations ("contrast" of a contour);
- its phase $\phi(x,y) = \text{atan}\left(\frac{\partial I}{\partial y}(x,y) / \frac{\partial I}{\partial x}(x,y)\right)$, which defines the direction of the local variations (direction locally orthogonal to that of the contours).

Using CImg<T>::get_gradient(), it is then easy to compute derivative filters, and characteristics of these operators, as shown in Code 5.2 and Figs. 5.6 and 5.7.

Code 5.2 – Derivative filtering.

```
int Derivative(CImg<>& imageIn)
{
  // Gradient approximation using centered finite differences.
  CImgList<> grad = imageIn.get_gradient();

  // Norm and phase of the gradient.
  CImg<>
    norme = (grad[0].get_sqr() + grad[1].get_sqr()).sqrt(),
    phi = grad[1].get_atan2(grad[0]);

  // Display.
  (grad[0],grad[1],norme,phi).display();

  return 1;
}
```

It is also possible to approach the norm by cross-differences:

$$\sqrt{(I(x,y) - I(x+1,y+1))^2 + (I(x+1,y) - I(x,y+1))^2}$$

or

$$|I(x,y) - I(x+1,y+1)| + |I(x+1,y) - I(x,y+1)|$$

This leads to *Roberts's filters*. Finally, using a 3×3 neighborhood, it is possible to approximate the norm of the gradient by the *Prewitt* (Fig. 5.8a) or *Sobel* (Fig. 5.8b) operators in 4- or 8-connexity.

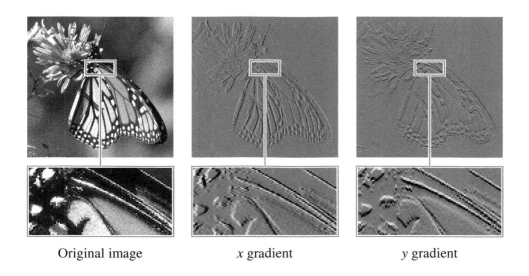

| Original image | x gradient | y gradient |

Figure 5.6 – Approximation of partial derivatives $\frac{\partial I}{\partial x}$ et $\frac{\partial I}{\partial y}$ using right finite differences.

Second order derivative filtering

By analyzing the intensity profiles of the images, contours can be seen as ramps between two areas having locally almost constant values. The first derivative on the ramp is constant, and depending on the "length" of this ramp, the contours will be more or less thick. The study of the second derivative, and more particularly of its zeros, thus makes it possible to detect edges, and in a sense to specify their orientation. Among all the second order derivative operators, the *Laplacian* is the most widely used. It is an isotropic operator, rotation invariant (the Laplacian of a rotated image is the rotated Laplacian of the original image) and can easily be approximated in a discrete way.

Formally the Laplacian, denoted ∇^2, is defined by

$$\begin{aligned} \nabla^2 : \mathbb{R} \times \mathbb{R} &\to \mathbb{R} \\ (x,y) &\mapsto \frac{\partial^2 f}{\partial x^2}(x,y) + \frac{\partial^2 f}{\partial y^2}(x,y) \end{aligned}$$

Approximating the second order derivatives using finite differences, for an image I:

$$\begin{aligned} \frac{\partial^2 I}{\partial x^2}(x,y) &\approx I(x+1,y) - 2I(x,y) + I(x-1,y) \\ \frac{\partial^2 I}{\partial y^2}(x,y) &\approx I(x,y+1) - 2I(x,y) + I(x,y-1) \end{aligned}$$

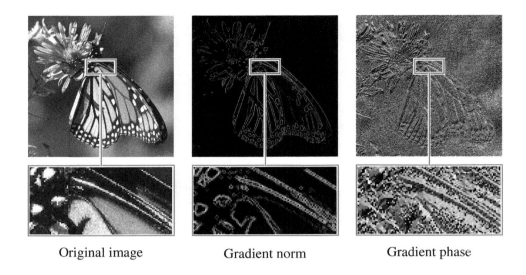

Original image   Gradient norm   Gradient phase

Figure 5.7 – Computing the norm and phase of the gradient.

and $\nabla^2 I(x,y) \approx I(x+1,y) + I(x-1,y) + I(x,y+1) + I(x,y-1) - 4I(x,y)$, which can be expressed using a convolution mask presented in Fig. 5.9a.

To compute the Laplacian, the `CImg<T>` class proposes the method

```
CImgList<> laplacian()
```

(R) From the Laplacian, it is possible to enhance edges in an image I by subtracting this operator to I: $I_E = I - \nabla^2(I)$ (Fig. 5.9b).

5.1.4 Adaptive filters

These filters are inspired by averaging filters, but each term in the sum is weighted by a coefficient that decreases with the similarity between the pixel considered and the pixel of the center of the window. Among these, the σ filter (Code 5.3) uses as weighting coefficient the inverse of the norm of the gradient, so that the points too different from the processed one do not contribute much to the smoothing. Another example is the Fairfield toboggan, which digs the histogram of the image by assigning to each pixel the gray level of the nearest minimum gradient point in a neighborhood. All points on the path connecting that pixel to the minimum gradient point are assigned this value and marked for further processing. The process is iterated until all points are marked.

-1	-1	-1
0	0	0
1	1	1

-1	0	1
-1	0	1
-1	0	1

Two of the 8 Prewitt filters   (up to a rotation)

-1	-2	-1
0	0	0
1	2	1

-1	0	1
-2	0	2
-1	0	1

Two of the 8 Sobel filters   (up to a rotation)

Figure 5.8 – Prewitt and Sobel masks.

0	1	0
1	-4	1
0	1	0

0	-1	0
-1	5	-1
0	-1	0

a) Laplacian mask   b) Edge enhancer

Figure 5.9 – Laplacian mask.

Code 5.3 – σ-filter.

```
CImg<> sigmaFilter(CImg<>& imgIn) {
  CImgList<> g = imgIn.get_gradient();
  CImg<> grad = (g[0].get_sqr() + g[1].get_sqr()).sqrt();

  // Sum of the  gradients on a 3x3 neiçghborhood
  CImg<> Sgrad = grad.get_convolve(CImg<>(3,3,1,1,1));

  float epsilon = 100;
  CImg_3x3(I,float);
  CImg<> rap = imgIn.get_div(grad + epsilon),
         imgOut(imgIn);

  cimg_for3x3(rap,x,y,0,0,I,float)
    imgOut(x,y) = (Ipp + Ipc + Ipn + Icp + Icc +
                   Icn + Inp + Inc + Inn)/(Sgrad(x,y) + epsilon);
  return imgOut;
}
```

5.1.5 Adaptive window filters

In the case of adaptive window filters, we search around each pixel for the most suitable window for filtering, either by selecting among a family of windows the most suitable one (e.g.,, Nagao, Kuwahara), or by growing a window and controlling its growth (e.g.,, Wu).

Nagao filter

We work on a neighborhood of fixed size (usually 5×5) surrounding the central pixel. We then define in this neighborhood 9 possible windows, all 9 pixel sizes, identified by an index k (Fig. 5.10). On each window we measure the mean μ_k and the variance σ_k of the gray levels, and we replace the gray level of the central pixel by the mean μ_k whose index minimizes the variance (Code 5.4).

Kuwahara filter

It is a variant of the Nagao filter, where only the definition of the neighborhoods changes (Fig. 5.11). Code 5.5 realizes this filter, and Fig. 5.12 proposes a comparison of these two filters on a noisy image.

Wu filter

This filter uses a homogeneity predicate on a region (often a measure of variance). It starts from a window of size 3×3, and extends it into a window of size $(2k + 1) \times (2k + 1)$ until the predicate is not verified anymore. In this case, the cause of heterogeneity is searched: if it is present only on one side of the window, the filter extends the window rectangularly by forbidding this side; if two adjacent sides are heterogeneous, the extension is done according to a triangle. When the window can no longer grow, the gray level of the central pixel is replaced by the average of the gray levels of the final window.

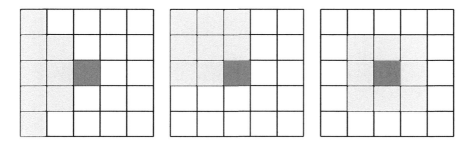

Figure 5.10 – Three of the nine Nagao windows. Three are deduced from the left window by iterated rotations of $\pi/2$, three from the center window using the same principle.

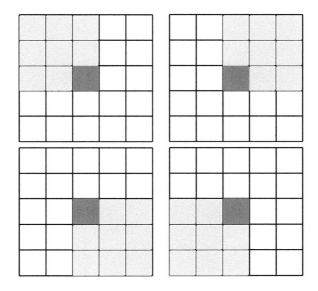

Figure 5.11 – Kuwahara neighborhoods.

Code 5.4 – Nagao filter.

```
CImg<> Nagao(CImg<>& imgIn)
{
  CImg<> imgOut(imgIn);

  //Nagao.
  CImgList<unsigned char> Nagao(9,5,5,1,1,0);
  Nagao(0,0,0) = Nagao(0,0,1) = Nagao(0,0,2) = Nagao(0,0,3) =
    Nagao(0,0,4) = Nagao(0,1,1) = Nagao(0,1,2) = Nagao(0,1,3) =
```

```
    Nagao(0,2,2) = 1;
  for (int i = 1; i<4; ++i) Nagao[i] = Nagao[0].get_rotate(i*90);


  Nagao(4,1,1) = Nagao(4,1,2) = Nagao(4,1,3) = Nagao(4,2,1) =
    Nagao(4,2,2) = Nagao(4,2,3) = Nagao(4,3,1) = Nagao(4,3,2) =
    Nagao(4,3,3) = 1;
  Nagao(5,0,0) = Nagao(5,0,1) = Nagao(5,0,2) = Nagao(5,1,0) =
    Nagao(5,1,1) = Nagao(5,1,2) = Nagao(5,2,0) = Nagao(5,2,1) =
    Nagao(5,2,2) = 1;
  for (int i = 1; i<4; ++i) Nagao[5 + i] = Nagao[5].get_rotate(i*90)
    ;


  // Neighborhood analysis.
  CImg<>
    mu(9,1,1,1,0),
    sigma(9,1,1,1,0),
    st,
    N(5,5);
  CImg<int> permutations;
  cimg_for5x5(imgIn,x,y,0,0,N,float)
  {
    CImgList<> res(9);
    for (int i = 0; i<9; ++i)
    {
      res[i] = N.get_mul(Nagao[i]);
      st = res[i].get_stats();
      mu[i] = st[2];
      sigma[i] = st[3];
    }
    // Searching minimal variance.
    sigma.sort(permutations);

    imgOut(x,y) = mu[permutations[0]];
  }
  return imgOut;
}
```

Code 5.5 – Kuwahara filter.

```
CImg<> Kuwahara(CImg<>& imgIn)
{
  CImg<> imgOut(imgIn);

  // Kuwahara.
  CImgList<unsigned char> Kuwahara(4,5,5,1,1,0);
  cimg_for_inXY(Kuwahara[0],0,0,2,2,i,j) Kuwahara(0,i,j) = 1;
  for (int i = 1; i<4; ++i)
    Kuwahara[i] = Kuwahara[0].get_rotate(i*90);
```

```
// Neighborhood analysis.
CImg<>
  mu(9,1,1,1,0),
  sigma(9,1,1,1,0),
  st,
  N(5,5);
CImg<int> permutations;

cimg_for5x5(imgIn,x,y,0,0,N,float)
{
  CImgList<> res(4);
  for (int i = 0; i<4; ++i)
  :
    res[i] = N.get_mul(Kuwahara[i]);
    st = res[i].get_stats();
    mu[i] = st[2];
    sigma[i] = st[3];
  :
  sigma.sort(permutations);
  imgOut(x,y) = mu[permutations[0]];
}
return imgOut;
}
```

Noisy image(Gaussian noise $\mathcal{N}(0,40)$)   Nagao filtering   Kuwahara filtering

Figure 5.12 – Comparison of Nagao and Kuwahara filters.

5.2   Recursive filtering

As seen before, the detection of contours in an image requires a signal derivation operation that can be implemented by a discrete convolution (Subsection 5.1.3, Equation 5.1). By this approach, this detection can be formalized as a filtering problem in the spatial domain. This numerical calculation is however not very efficient in the presence of noise, and several works therefore add a smoothing filter to the derivative calculations, allowing the signal to be regularized. The work of Prewitt and Sobel (Fig. 5.8), for example, proposed to use either an averaging or a Gaussian low-pass filter for this task.

The approach of coupling a smoothing filter to the estimation of the derivation is classical. A typical example of this approach can be found in [5] which developed an optimal finite impulse response (*FIR*) filter for edge detection, by maximizing different geometrical criteria. It leads to a complex solution, which is in practice approximated by a first derivative of a Gaussian. This operator, also known as *Canny's filter*, is implemented via a discrete convolution operation, which requires a number of operations proportional to the standard deviation of the Gaussian filter, in order to avoid the effects of filter truncations. In Deriche's work [10], the author takes up Canny's criteria and succeeds in developing a simpler analytical solution, in the form of an infinite impulse response (*IIR*) filter, which moreover has low algorithmic complexity via a clever recursive implementation with a constant number of operations whatever the width of the filter to be applied.

5.2.1   Optimal edge detection

In Canny's approach, we consider a continuous contour model (of the Heaviside distribution), noted $I(x)$, perturbed by an additive noise independent of the signal (Fig. 5.13). The objective of Canny's work is to find an optimal filter to detect this type of contours whose impulse response is noted $h_{opt}(x)$.

Canny's approach is based on three criteria that have to be met:

1. *Good detection*: a strong response of the detector even with weak contours which is equivalent to finding the best signal to noise ratio at the output of the filter $h_{opt}(x)$. This criterion is formalized by the maximization of:

$$\Sigma = \frac{\int_0^{+\infty} h_{opt}(x)\,dx}{\sqrt{\int_{-\infty}^{+\infty} h_{opt}^2(x)\,dx}};$$

2. *Good location*: the maximum of the detector response must be at a position closest to the actual position of the contour. Canny results in the maximization

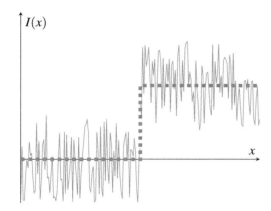

Figure 5.13 – Modeling a contour to study an optimal filter.

of:

$$\Lambda = \frac{\left| h'_{opt}(0) \right|}{\sqrt{\int_{-\infty}^{+\infty} h'^{2}_{opt}(x)\,dx}};$$

3. *No multiplicity of responses*: ensure that for a contour there will be only one detection. It can be shown that this is equivalent to optimizing the expression:

$$x_{max} = \sqrt{\frac{\int_{-\infty}^{+\infty} h'^{2}(x)\,dx}{\int_{-\infty}^{+\infty} h''^{2}(x)\,dx}}.$$

This criterion corresponds to the average distance between two local maxima detected in response to a contour.

The detection and localization criteria being antinomic, we combine them by maximizing the product $\Sigma\Lambda$, called Canny's criterion, under the constraint of the third one. This optimization leads to a differential equation which admits as a general solution:

$$h_{opt}(x) = c_0 + c_1 e^{\alpha x} \sin \omega x + c_2 e^{\alpha x} \cos \omega x + c_3 e^{-\alpha x} \sin \omega x + c_4 e^{-\alpha x} \cos \omega x \quad (5.2)$$

where the coefficients c_i and ω are determined from the filter size.

The scale parameter α is important since it indicates the maximum distance for two parallel contours to be merged into one through the detector.
Canny looks for a *FIR* filter of width L, i.e., defined on the interval $[\![-L; +L]\!]$, with slope s at the origin and with the following boundary conditions: $h(0) = 0$, $h(L) = 0$, $h'(0) = s$ and $h'(L) = 0$. Using numerical optimization, the optimal filter yields a Canny criterion of value 1.12. For implementation issues and ease of use, an

approximation by the derivative of a Gaussian function is proposed by the author (Equation 5.3). This filter allows to have a Canny criterion equal to $0,97$ and thus degrades the optimal result by 20%.

$$h_{opt}(x) \approx h_{canny}(x) = -x\exp\left(-\frac{(\alpha x)^2}{2\pi}\right) \tag{5.3}$$

The standard deviation of this function is proportional to the inverse of the scaling parameter of the optimal filter. It should be noted that a direct implementation of this operator, as proposed by Canny, requires a number of operations directly proportional to the standard deviation of the filter, which implies a high algorithmic complexity, especially in the case of very noisy images that require a large filter.

5.2.2 Deriche filter

In the work of Deriche [10], the author takes up Canny's criteria and succeeds in developing a simpler analytical solution in the form of an infinite impulse response (*IIR*) filter, whose recursive implementation ensures a constant number of operations whatever the width of the filter. By relaxing the choice of a FIR filter, the boundary conditions are chosen differently ($h(0) = 0$, $h(+\infty) = 0$, $h'(0) = s$ and $h'(+\infty) = 0$) and we obtain the following coefficient values: $c_0 = c_1 = c_2 = c_4 = 0$. Based on Equation 5.2, the optimal edge detection filter becomes:

$$h_{opt}(x) = c_3 e^{-\alpha|x|}\sin\omega x.$$

This operator has a Canny criterion $\Sigma\Lambda$ improved by 25% ($\Sigma\Lambda = \sqrt{3}$). The limit case $\omega \to 0$ presents the best compromise to respect the three performance criteria (Equation 5.4). This operator corresponds to the exact solution of the optimization problem of the Canny criterion. This optimal edge detection operator is known in the literature as *Deriche filter*.

$$h_{opt}(x) = h_{deriche}(x) = -cxe^{-\alpha|x|} \text{ with } c = \frac{(1-e^{-\alpha})^2}{e^{-\alpha}} \tag{5.4}$$

where c is a normalization coefficient of the function. In the literature, it is common to find different values of c, depending on the type of normalization desired. Figure 5.14 illustrates the Canny (Equation 5.3) and the Deriche (Equation 5.4) filters.

   This filter allows us to set up a contour detector based on a first order derivative approach. We can deduce a smoothing filter which is obtained by integrating the optimal filter $h_{deriche}(x)$. This smoothing filter, noted $f_{deriche}(x)$, is given by Equation 5.5. We can also deduce a second order derivative filter by derivation of the optimal filter.

$$f_{deriche}(x) = k(\alpha|x|+1)e^{-\alpha|x|} \text{ with } k = \frac{(1-e^{-\alpha})^2}{1+2\alpha e^{-\alpha} - e^{-2\alpha}} \tag{5.5}$$

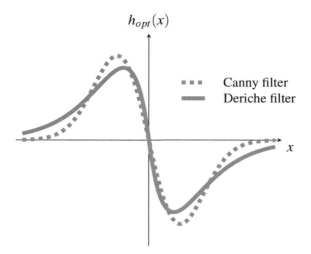

Figure 5.14 – The Canny filter and the Deriche filter in continuous form for the calculation of the first derivative.

IMPLEMENTATION OF THE DERICHE FILTER FAMILY

The Deriche contour filter not only corresponds to the exact solution of the optimization problem of the Canny criterion, it also has the remarkable property (shared also by its smoothing and derivative filter) to be implemented recursively with few operations, independently of the filter width.

Differences between finite and infinite impulse response filters

- *FIR* filters are filters whose finite size allows to implement their numerical convolution with a relation between the output, denoted $I_o[i]$, and the input, denoted $I_i[i]$, which is written as follows:

$$I_o[i] = \sum_{k=-L}^{L} H[k] \times I_i[i-k].$$

where $H[i]$ is the numerical impulse response of the filter. It is impossible to use this expression if the impulse response of the filter is infinite.

If a system is *BIBO* (*Bounded-Input / Bounded-Output*) stable, then for any bounded input, the output of the system is also stable. On discrete signals, a system is *BIBO* stable if and only if $\sum_{n=-\infty}^{\infty} |h(n)| = \|h\|_1 < \infty$. It is easy to show that if $L < \infty$, *FIR* filters are unconditionally stable, no matter what coefficients are used.

- *IIR* filters, which can be exactly recursively implemented, have a lower computational cost than the previous ones, but it is necessary to pay attention to their
stability. The relation between the output, denoted $I_o[i]$, and the input, denoted
$I_i[i]$, is written as follows:

$$I_o[i] = \sum_{k=0}^{N} b_k \times I_i[i-k] - \sum_{k=1}^{M} a_k \times I_o[i-k] \tag{5.6}$$

where the coefficients a_i and b_i are to be calculated from the impulse response
of the filter $H[i]$. This type of filter uses a recursive scheme and requires
$(N+M+1)$ operations, which is smaller and independent of the size of the
filter. It should also be noted that a convolution with the Deriche filter or its
derivatives and its smoothing filter can be implemented exactly in the form
of Equation 5.6. This remarkable property is not shared by all *IIR* filters (the
Gaussian filter and its derivatives, like the Canny filter cannot). A recursive
implementation by filters of order 2 to 4 approximating in a least squares sense
the convolution with the Gaussian and its derivatives has been developed by
Deriche [11] and by other authors [41, 43].

The convolution of a one-dimensional signal I_i composed of K samples with the
optimal Deriche contour detection filter is implemented in an exact way via the
following second-order recursive formula:

Derivation filter:

$$h_{deriche}(x) = -cxe^{-\alpha|x|}$$

$$\begin{cases} I^+[i] = aI_i[i] - b_1 I^+[i-1] - b_2 I^+[i-2] & \text{for } i \in [\![1,K]\!] \\ I^-[i] = -aI_i[i+1] - b_1 I^-[i+1] - b_2 I^-[i+2] & \text{for } i \in [\![K,1]\!] \\ I_o[i] = I^-[i] + I^+[i] & \text{for } i \in [\![1,K]\!] \end{cases}$$

with $a = ce^{-\alpha}$, $b_1 = -2e^{-\alpha}$ and $b_2 = e^{-2\alpha}$.

Smoothing filter:

$$f_{deriche}(x) = k(\alpha|x| + 1)e^{-\alpha|x|}$$

$$\begin{cases} I^+[i] = a_0 I_i[i] + a_1 I_i[i-1] - b_1 I^+[i-1] - b_2 I^+[i-2] & \text{for } i \in [\![1,K]\!] \\ I^-[i] = a_2 I_i[i+1] + a_3 I_i[i+2] - b_1 I^-[i+1] - b_2 I^-[i+2] & \text{for } i \in [\![K,1]\!] \\ I_0[i] = I^-[i] + I^+[i] & \text{for } i \in [\![1,K]\!] \end{cases}$$

with $a_0 = k$, $a_1 = k(\alpha - 1)e^{-\alpha}$, $a_2 = k(\alpha + 1)e^{-\alpha}$, $a_3 = -ke^{-2\alpha}$, $b_1 = -2e^{-\alpha}$ and $b_2 = e^{-2\alpha}$.

Code 5.6 allows to apply the Deriche filter along the X axis. The parameter `order` allows to select either the smoothing filter (order 0), the calculation of the first derivative (order 1) or the second derivative (order 2).

Code 5.6 – Deriche filter.

```
/*
  Deriche filter on a 1D signal (along the X axis).

  imgIn               : Input image
  alpha               : Scale parameter
  order               : Filter order
                        (0: smoothing, 1: first derivative,
                         2: second derivative)
  boundary_conditions : Boundary conditions
*/
void deriche(CImg<>& imgIn, float alpha, unsigned int order=0,
             bool boundary_conditions=true)
{
  // Filter coefficients.
  float
    ema = std::exp(-alpha),
    ema2 = std::exp(-2*alpha),
    b1 = -2*ema,
    b2 = ema2,
    a0 = 0, a1 = 0, a2 = 0, a3 = 0,
    coefp = 0, coefn = 0;

  switch (order)
  {
  case 0 : { // Order 0 (smoothing)
    float k = (1 - ema)*(1 - ema)/(1 + 2*alpha*ema - ema2);
    a0 = k;
    a1 = k*(alpha - 1)*ema;
    a2 = k*(alpha + 1)*ema;
```

```
      a3 = -k*ema2;
  } break;
  case 1 : { // Order 1 (first derivative)
      float k = -(1 - ema)*(1 - ema)*(1 - ema)/(2*(ema + 1)*ema);
      a0 = a3 = 0;
      a1 = k*ema;
      a2 = -a1;
  } break;
  case 2 : { // Order 2 (second derivative)
      float
        ea = std::exp(-alpha),
        k = -(ema2 - 1)/(2*alpha*ema),
        kn = -2*(-1 + 3*ea - 3*ea*ea + ea*ea*ea)/
              (3*ea + 1 + 3*ea*ea + ea*ea*ea);
      a0 = kn;
      a1 = -kn*(1 + k*alpha)*ema;
      a2 = kn*(1 - k*alpha)*ema;
      a3 = -kn*ema2;
  } break;
  }
  coefp = (a0 + a1)/(1 + b1 + b2);
  coefn = (a2 + a3)/(1 + b1 + b2);

  // Application of the recursive filter (row by row).
  CImg<> Y(imgIn.width());

  cimg_forYC(imgIn,y,c)
  {
      float *X = imgIn.data(0,y,0,c);

      // Computation from left to right.
      float yb = 0, yp = 0, xp = 0;
      if (boundary_conditions) {
        xp = X[0];
        yb = yp = coefp*xp;
      }
      cimg_forX(imgIn,m)
      {
        float
          xc = X[m],
          yc = Y[m] = a0*xc + a1*xp - b1*yp - b2*yb;
        xp = xc;
        yb = yp;
        yp = yc;
      }

      // Computation from right to left.
      float xn = 0, xa = 0, yn = 0, ya = 0;
      if (boundary_conditions) {
```

```
    xn = xa = X[imgIn.width() - 1];
    yn = ya = coefn*xn;
  }

  for (int n = imgIn.width() - 1; n>=0; --n)
  {
    float
      xc = X[n],
      yc = a2*xn + a3*xa - b1*yn - b2*ya;
    xa = xn;
    xn = xc;
    ya = yn;
    yn = yc;
    X[n] = Y[n] + yc;
  }
}
}
```

RESULTS OF THE DERICHE FILTERS

Several interesting and fast processings can be performed using the Deriche filter.

Smoothing of an image (order 0 filter)

Due to its recursive implementation, the Deriche smoothing filter has a constant computational complexity regardless of the width of the filter specified by the scale parameter α. Using the separability property of the filter, we can smooth a 2D image I first by filtering I along the X axis, then by transposing the image (equivalent to a 90° rotation), reapplying the filter and transposing the image again (Code 5.7).

Code 5.7 – Smoothing of a 2D image by the Deriche filter.

```
CImg<> imgIn("test.bmp");  // Loading the image
deriche(imgIn,alpha,0);    // X filtering
imgIn.transpose();
deriche(imgIn,alpha,0);    // Y filtering <=>
imgIn.transpose();         // X filtering of transposed image
```

Figure 5.15 presents the result of the smoothing filter for several values of α. The larger this scale parameter is, the less the image is smoothed.

| Input image | $\alpha = 0.25$ | $\alpha = 0.5$ | $\alpha = 1.0$ |

Figure 5.15 – Results of the order 0 Deriche filter (smoothing filter) for several values of the scale parameter α.

Computation of the gradient norm (first order filter):

To compute the norm of the gradient, we can compute the first derivative along X and the first derivative along Y (by transposing the image), then compute the norm of the gradient from the two filtered images. For each derivative, it is convenient to pre-smooth the image along the opposite axis, with an order 0 Deriche filter, in order to obtain derivatives computed on a spatially smoothed image in an isotropic way (Code 5.8).

$$\begin{cases} \dfrac{\partial I}{\partial x}(x,y) = (I * f_{deriche}(y)) * h_{deriche}(x) \\[2mm] \dfrac{\partial I}{\partial y}(x,y) = (I * f_{deriche}(x)) * h_{deriche}(y) \\[2mm] |\nabla I|(x,y) = \sqrt{\left(\dfrac{\partial I}{\partial x}(x,y)\right)^2 + \left(\dfrac{\partial I}{\partial y}(x,y)\right)^2} \end{cases}$$

Code 5.8 – Computation of the gradient norm by the Deriche filter.

```
CImg<>{}
  imgIn("image.bmp"), // Loading the image
  imgX = imgIn.get_transpose(),
  imgY = imgIn;

deriche(imgX,alpha,0);   // Pre-smooth along 'Y' for 'd/dX'
deriche(imgY,alpha,0);   // Pre-smooth along 'X' for 'd/dY'
```

```
imgX.transpose();imgY.transpose();
deriche(imgX,alpha,1);    // First derivative along 'X'
deriche(imgY,alpha,1);    // First derivative along 'Y'
imgY.transpose();

CImg<> Norme = (imgX.sqr() + imgY.sqr()).get_sqrt();
```

Figure 5.16 illustrates the result of the Deriche filter for the computation of the gradient norm, for several values of the parameter α. Extracting the local maxima of the norm of the gradient of the image allows us to detect the contours.

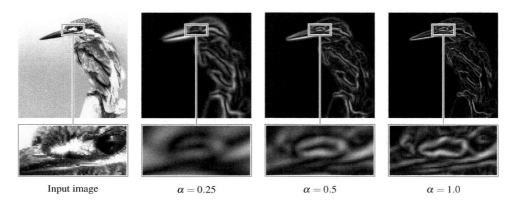

| Input image | $\alpha = 0.25$ | $\alpha = 0.5$ | $\alpha = 1.0$ |

Figure 5.16 – Results for order 1 Deriche filtering (gradient norm calculation) for several values of the scaling parameter α.

Computation of the Laplacian (second order filter):

The Laplacian is equal to the sum of the second derivatives of the image along the X and Y axes. It can be easily and quickly computed with the order 2 Deriche filters (Code 5.9).

Code 5.9 – Computation of the Laplacian by the Deriche filter.

```
CImg<>
  imgIn("test.bmp"), // Loading the image
  img2X = imgIn,
  img2Y = imgIn.get_transpose();
deriche(img2X,alpha,2);    // Second derivative along 'X'
deriche(img2Y,alpha,2);    // Second derivative along 'Y'
img2Y.transpose();

CImg<> laplacian = img2X + img2Y;
```

Figure 5.17 shows the result of Code 5.9 for several values of α. The zero crossings of the Laplacian allow us to detect the contours.

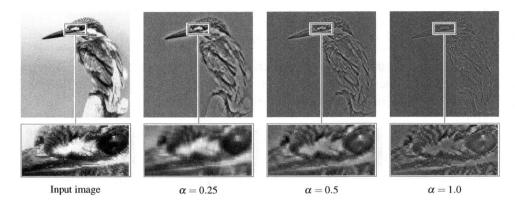

| Input image | $\alpha = 0.25$ | $\alpha = 0.5$ | $\alpha = 1.0$ |

Figure 5.17 – Results for order 2 Deriche filtering (Laplacian computation) for several values of the scaling parameter α.

5.3   Frequency filtering

We are now interested in the frequency content of an image and the definition of a linear filtering in the frequency domain rather than the spatial domain.

5.3.1   Introduction

Linear filters are defined as linear time-invariant systems. It can be shown that the relation between the input signal, denoted $I_e(x,y)$, and the output signal, denoted $I_s(x,y)$, of such a filter can be written as a convolution product. The quantity characterizing the filter, denoted $H(x,y)$, is called the impulse response. This convolution approach has been described in Section 5.1.

This processing can also be seen in the frequency domain by using the Fourier transform of the images (Fig. 5.18). The Fourier transform of the output image, denoted $\widehat{I_s}(f_x, f_y)$, is equal to the multiplication between the Fourier transform of the input image, denoted $\widehat{I_e}(f_x, f_y)$, and the frequency response, denoted $\widehat{H}(f_x, f_y)$, defined as the Fourier transform of the impulse response $H(x,y)$.

In the same way as for spatial filtering, notions of smoothing filters and edge enhancers are defined. However, in the frequency domain, these notions are more easily understood. Indeed, the frequency content (obtained by the Fourier transform)

Spatial domain

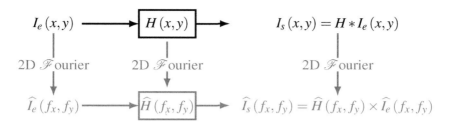

Figure 5.18 – Equivalence of linear filtering in the spatial and frequency domain.

can be decomposed into low frequency and high spatial frequency domains (Fig. 5.19). The first refers to the domain of low spatial gray levels variations (the rather homogeneous areas of the image), while the second refers to the high spatial variations (the contours).

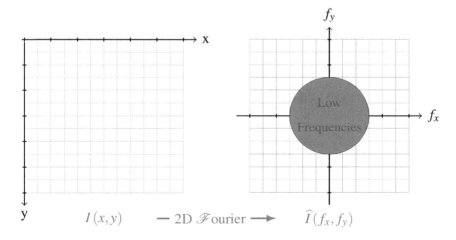

Figure 5.19 – From spatial to frequency domain.

We will thus find the filters known as "low-pass" which attenuate or eliminate high frequencies in the Fourier domain without modifying the low frequencies. The high frequency components characterize the contours and other abrupt details in the image, the overall effect of the filter is a smoothing. Similarly, a "high-pass" filter attenuates or eliminates low-frequency components. Because these frequencies are responsible for slow variations in the image such as overall contrast or average intensity, the effect of this filter is to reduce these characteristics and thus provide an apparent edge enhancement. The third type of filter is called a "bandpass" filter, which retains only the intermediate frequency components.

5.3.2 The Fourier transform

THE CONTINUOUS FOURIER TRANSFORM

The Fourier transform projects an image into a frequency space characterized by spatial frequencies f_x and f_y. It allows to analyze image properties in this new space.

> **Definition 5.3.1** The Fourier transform of a continuous image $I(x, y)$, assumed to have infinite support is given by
>
> $$TF : \mathbb{R} \times \mathbb{R} \mapsto \mathbb{C}$$
> $$f_x, f_y \rightarrow \widehat{I}(f_x, f_y) = \iint I(x, y) e^{-j(2\pi f_x x + 2\pi f_y y)} \mathrm{d}x \mathrm{d}y$$

This is a bidimensional complex transform in the frequency domain and can be represented:

- either by its modulus (spectrum) and its argument (phase);
- or by its real and imaginary parts.

From this, the original image can be recovered:

$$I(x, y) = \iint \widehat{I}(f_x, f_y) e^{j(2\pi f_x x + 2\pi f_y y)} \mathrm{d}f_x \mathrm{d}f_y$$

Figure 5.20 shows the modulus of the Fourier transform of a two-dimensional rectangular function. One can easily recognize the sinc function. It is also possible to identify the orientation of the shape. Indeed, in the second set of figures, this same function is rotated by 45° and this change in spatial variations is reflected in the frequency content in terms of orientation.

In Fig. 5.21, we notice the presence of energy in particular directions; this phenomenon is characteristic of the presence of oblique lines or contours, whose frequency decomposition is wide spectrum (f large in the direction perpendicular to the line).

Working in the frequency domain has many applications in image processing: filtering, texture analysis (Section 6.3), image registration (Section 8.2.2), compression (Section 11.1).

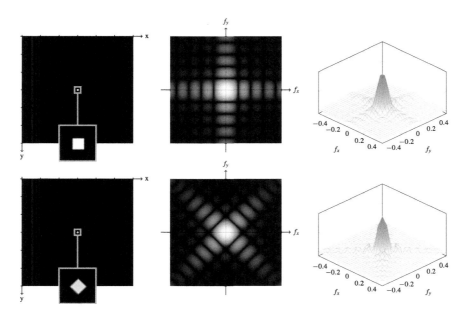

Figure 5.20 – Example of amplitude spectrum of the rectangular function, with two different orientations.

DISCRETE FOURIER TRANSFORM

FFT algorithm - Fast Fourier Transform

To compute the Fourier transform on digital images, the *Fast Fourier Transform* (*FFT*) is classicaly used and computed in *CImg* using CImg<T>::get_FFT():

```
CImgList<> get_FFT(const char *axis, bool is_inverse=false)
```

Parameter axis is a string specifying the axes along which the Fourier transform must be computed (for example "xy" for a 2D image) and the argument is_inverse allows to specify if one wishes to calculate a direct or an inverse transform. Computing the Fourier transform in this way returns an object of type CImgList<T> containing two images, because this transformation returns a complex function. This list of images allows to store the real part (first image [0] of the list) and the imaginary part (second image [1]) of the transform.

Code 5.10 presents an example, where we create a synthetic image by mixing the modulus of the Fourier transform of a first image with the argument of the Fourier transform of a second image. The result is given in Fig. 5.22.

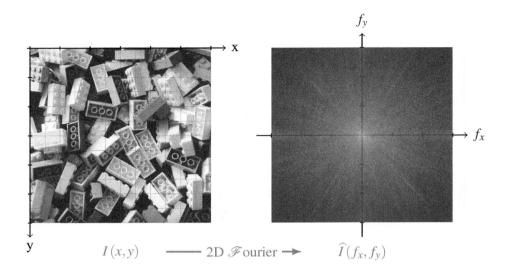

Figure 5.21 – Amplitude spectrum (in db) of a real image.

Code 5.10 – Using CImg<T>::get_FFT().

```
CImg<> Mix(CImg<>& imgIn1, CImg<>& imgIn2)
{
  // Fourier transform of two images.
  CImgList<>
    F_Img1 = imgIn1.get_FFT(),
    F_Img2 = imgIn2.get_FFT();

  // Modulus of the first Fourier transform.
  CImg<> Img1_Mag = (F_Img1[0].get_pow(2) + F_Img1[1].get_pow(2)).
                     sqrt();

  // Argument of the second Fourier transform.
  CImg<> Img2_Arg(imgIn2.width(),imgIn2.height());
  cimg_forXY(Img2_Arg,x,y)
    Img2_Arg(x,y) = std::atan2(F_Img2(1,x,y),F_Img2(0,x,y));

  // Real and imaginary parts of the combination
  CImg<>
    R_img3(imgIn1.width(),imgIn1.height()),
    I_img3(R_img3);

  cimg_forXY(R_img3,x,y) {
```

```
    R_img3(x,y) = Img1_Mag(x,y)*std::cos(Img2_Arg(x,y));
    I_img3(x,y) = Img1_Mag(x,y)*std::sin(Img2_Arg(x,y));
  }

  // Inverse Fourier transform and return the real part.
  return (R_img3,I_img3).get_FFT(true)[0].normalize(0,255);
}
```

Input image 1   Input image 2   Output image

Figure 5.22 – Mixing modulus and argument of two images.

Visualization of an image spectrum

The Fourier transform of a discrete signal is periodic with period $F_e = \frac{1}{T_e}$ on all axes. In practice, only one period is computed. Graphically and theoretically, it is classical to represent the frequency domain in the range $\left[-\frac{F_e}{2}, \frac{F_e}{2}\right]$ for a 2D image. One can also choose normalized frequencies $\tilde{f} = f/F_e$ and so the range $\left[-\frac{1}{2}, \frac{1}{2}\right]$.

The *FFT* algorithm outputs data in the range $[0, F_{e_x}] \times [0, F_{e_y}]$ or in $[0,1] \times [0,1]$ when using normalized frequencies (Fig. 5.23). It is necessary to take this data arrangement into account when calculating or visualizing.

Code 5.11 allows to visualize the spectrum (in decibels) of an image from the raw data of the *FFT* and the spectrum by rearranging the data of the *FFT* to center the zero frequency in the middle of the interval.

Code 5.11 – Visualizing an image spectrum.

```
CImg<> img("image.bmp");

// Fast Fourier Transform.
CImgList<> imgFFT = img.get_FFT();
```

```
// Computing the spectrum.
CImg<> imgS = (imgFFT[0].pow(2) +
              imgFFT[1].pow(2)).get_sqrt() + 0.01f;
imgS.log10();

// Rearrange the data (place the zero in the middle).
CImg<> imgSR = imgS.get_shift(imgS.width()/2,imgS.height()/2,0,0,2);

// Image display
(img,imgS,imgSR).display("Input image - "
                         "Spectrum (Raw FFT data) - "
                         "Spectrum (Rearranged FFT data)");
```

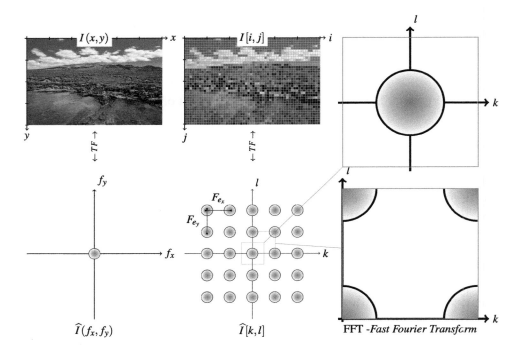

Figure 5.23 – Interpreting *FFT* output. A digital image has a periodic Fourier transform. We represent the spectrum on a period with the zero frequency in the middle. The *FFT* algorithm focuses on another period and the zero is found in the corners.

Figure 5.24 shows an image spectrum with raw and rearranged *FFT* data.

In the remainder of this section, the natural arrangement of the data from the *FFT* algorithm will be taken into account.

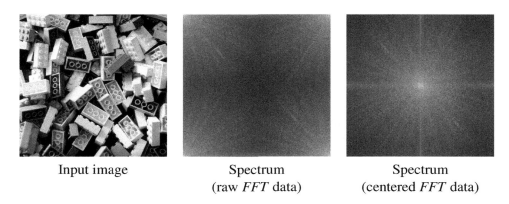

| Input image | Spectrum (raw *FFT* data) | Spectrum (centered *FFT* data) |

Figure 5.24 – Visualizing an image spectrum from *FFT*: raw and centered data.

5.3.3 Frequency filtering

Smoothing by reducing the high frequency content or enhancing contours by increasing the high frequency components with respect to the low frequencies come from concepts directly related to the Fourier transform. In fact, the idea of linear filtering is more intuitive in the frequency domain. In practice, spatial masks (see Section 5.1) are much more used than the Fourier transform because of their simplicity of implementation and their speed. But the understanding of the phenomena in the frequency domain is essential to solve problems that are difficult to grasp with purely spatial techniques. Linear filtering can thus be calculated, either in the spatial domain by a discrete convolution in the case of digital images (Equation 5.1), or by a complex multiplication in the frequency domain. The principle of frequency filtering is simple: take the Fourier transform of the image to be filtered, multiply the spectrum obtained by the frequency response of the filter, then take the inverse Fourier transform to produce the filtered image (Algorithm 2).

IDEAL LOW-PASS FILTER

The ideal low-pass filter is described by the frequency response:

$$\widehat{H_I}(f_x, f_y) = \begin{cases} 1 \text{ if } \rho(f_x, f_y) \leq f_c \\ 0 \text{ if } \rho(f_x, f_y) > f_c \end{cases}$$

Algorithm 2: Linear filtering in the frequency domain.

Input: Input image: $I_e(x,y)$
Data: Frequency response: $\widehat{H}(f_x, f_y)$
Result: Output (filtered) image: $I_s(x,y)$
begin

  Fourier transform of the input image: $I_e(x,y) \overset{2D-\mathscr{F}\text{ourier}}{\longleftrightarrow} \widehat{I_e}(f_x, f_y)$;
  Filtering in the frequency domain: $\widehat{I_s}(f_x, f_y) = \widehat{H}(f_x, f_y) \times \widehat{I_e}(f_x, f_y)$;
  Output image: $\widehat{I_s}(f_x, f_y) \overset{2D \text{ inverse } \mathscr{F}\text{ourier}}{\longleftrightarrow} I_s(x,y)$;

---

where f_c is the cutoff frequency and $\rho(f_x, f_y)$ is the distance from (f_x, f_y) to the origin of the frequency plane:

$$\rho(f_x, f_y) = \sqrt{f_x^2 + f_y^2}$$

Figure 5.25 shows a representation of $\widehat{H_I}(f_x, f_y)$.

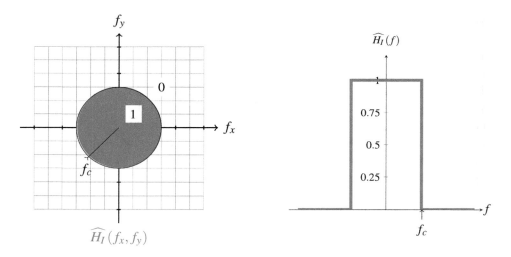

Figure 5.25 – Frequency response of the ideal low-pass filter.

It is an ideal filter because all frequencies inside a circle of radius f_c are restored without attenuation, while all others are cancelled. Low-pass filters considered in this chapter have radial symmetry, so it is sufficient to know the profile of the filter on one of its radii. The disadvantage of the ideal low-pass filter is that it introduces ripples in the spatial domain: its impulse response is none but the Bessel function of order 1 (inverse Fourier transform of the frequency response). This phenomenon is called the Gibbs effect. To reduce these ripples, it is necessary to avoid having too abrupt variations of the filter in the frequency domain, and in this context, Butterworth filters are a possible solution.

BUTTERWORTH FILTERS

The nth-order Butterworth filter is defined by:

$$\widehat{H_B}(f_x, f_y) = \frac{1}{1 + [\rho(f_x, f_y)/f_0]^{2n}}$$

where f_0 is related to the cutoff frequency. Figure 5.26 shows the frequency response of Butterworth filters for $n = 1$ and $n = 10$, for a given value of f_0. In contrast to the

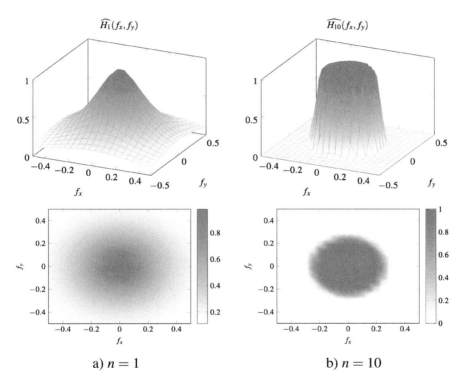

a) $n = 1$ b) $n = 10$

Figure 5.26 – Frequency response of the Butterworth filter, with $f_0 = 0,25$.

theoretical low-pass filter, the Butterworth filter does not have a sharp cutoff between low and high frequencies. This variation of the passband at the cutoff band is set by the value of n (Fig. 5.27a). In general, the cutoff frequency is defined at the point where the transfer function goes below $1/\sqrt{2}$ of the maximum (equivalent to -3dB in logarithmic scale). We can modify the previous equation so that it is expressed as a function of the cutoff frequency f_c:

$$\widehat{H_B}(f_x, f_y) = \frac{1}{1 + [\sqrt{2} - 1][\rho(f_x, f_y)/f_c]^{2n}}$$

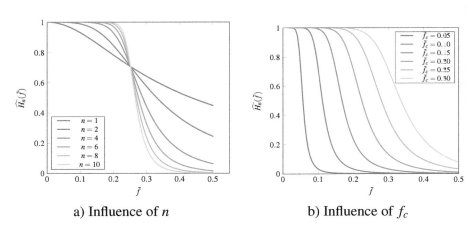

a) Influence of n b) Influence of f_c

Figure 5.27 – Frequency response of Butterworth filters - Influence of n and f_c.

Filtered images show less ripples than in the ideal filter case. Moreover, the smoothing rate varies more slowly as f_c decreases (Fig. 5.27b).

GAUSSIAN FILTER

In the isotropic case, the Gaussian filter as for impulse response:

$$H(x, y) = \frac{1}{\sqrt{2\pi\sigma_s^2}} e^{-\frac{x^2 + y^2}{2\sigma_s^2}}$$

The frequency response is also a Gaussian function (Fig. 5.28), with the standard deviation proportional to the inverse of the spatial standard deviation:

$$\widehat{H}(f_x, f_y) = e^{-2\pi^2\sigma_s^2(f_x^2 + f_y^2)} = e^{-\frac{f_x^2 + f_y^2}{2\sigma_f^2}} \quad \text{where } \sigma_f = \frac{1}{2\pi\sigma_s}$$

This is the optimal filter for removing additive Gaussian noise. Code 5.12 implements Gaussian filtering in the frequency domain. The frequency response of this filter is illustrated in Fig. 5.28.

Code 5.12 – Gaussian filtering in the frequency domain.

```
CImg<> GaussianFilter(CImg<>& imgIn,float sigma)
{
  // FFT
  CImgList<> fImg = imgIn.get_FFT();

  // Frequency response of the filter.
  CImg<> gaussMask(imgIn.width(),imgIn.height());
  float sigma2 = cimg::sqr(sigma);
  cimg_forXY(gaussMask,x,y)
  {
    float fx = x/(float)imgIn.width()  - 0.5f,
          fx2 = cimg::sqr(fx),
          fy = y/(float)imgIn.height() - 0.5f,
          fy2 = cimg::sqr(fy);
    gaussMask(x,y) = 2*cimg::PI*sigma2*
      std::exp(-2*cimg::sqr(cimg::PI)*sigma2*(fx2 + fy2));
  }
  // Zero shift.
  gaussMask.shift(-imgIn.width()/2,-imgIn.height()/2,0,0,2);

  // Filtering
  cimglist_for(fImg,k)
    fImg[k].mul(gaussMask);

  // Inverse FFT and real part.
  return fImg.get_FFT(true)[0].normalize(0,255);
}
```

The result of this processing is represented in Fig. 5.29 where the image is corrupted with a Gaussian noise.

5.3.4 Processing a Moiré image

The objective here is to propose a method restoring a Moiré image, i.e., having a very specific raster noise (Moiré) that we want to remove. First, we propose a model of this noise and calculate the Fourier transform of the image using this model. We then observe how noise acts in the frequency domain, and we deduce a frequency-based filtering method to restore the image.

MODELING A MOIRÉ IMAGE

The input image I_t can be modeled as the product of a pattern T and the image to restore I (Equation 5.7 and Fig. 5.30).

$$\forall (x,y) \in \Omega \subset \mathbb{R}^2 \quad I_t(x,y) = T(x,y) \times I(x,y) \tag{5.7}$$

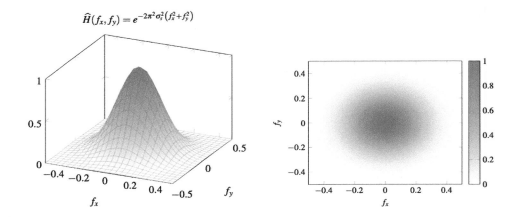

Figure 5.28 – Frequency response of the Gaussian filter with a spatial standard deviation $\sigma_s = 1$, corresponding to a frequency standard deviation of $\sigma_f = \frac{1}{2\pi\sigma_s}$.

T can be written as the convolution product of a Dirac comb following the y axis and of period P with the rectangular function of width $P/2$ in the y direction:

$$T(x,y) = \text{III}_P * \mathbb{1}_{[-\infty,+\infty] \times \left[-\frac{P}{4}, \frac{P}{4}\right]}(x,y)$$

with

$$
\begin{aligned}
\mathbb{1}_E : F &\longrightarrow \{0,1\} \\
m &\longmapsto \begin{cases} 1 \text{ if } m \in E \\ 0 \text{ if } m \notin E \end{cases}
\end{aligned}
\quad \text{and} \quad
\begin{aligned}
\text{III}_{(\infty,P)} : \mathbb{R}^2 &\longrightarrow \mathbb{R} \\
(x,y) &\longmapsto \sum_{j=-\infty}^{+\infty} \delta(x, y - jP)
\end{aligned}
$$

FREQUENCY REPRESENTATION OF THE MOIRÉ IMAGE

If spatial techniques exist (such as *inpainting*) to restore this type of images, we wish here to work in the frequency domain by using filtering. First, we compute the two-dimensional Fourier transform of Equation 5.7:

$$\widehat{I_t}(f_x, f_y) = \widehat{T} * \widehat{I}(f_x, f_y). \tag{5.8}$$

To carry out this calculation, it is initially necessary to calculate the Fourier transform of $\widehat{T}$. Let's recall that:

$$
\begin{cases}
\text{III}_P(x,y) & \overset{TF}{\leftrightarrow} & f_p \text{III}_{f_p}(f_x, f_y) \\
\mathbb{1}_{[-\infty,+\infty] \times \left[-\frac{P}{4}, \frac{P}{4}\right]}(x,y) & \overset{TF}{\leftrightarrow} & \frac{P}{2}\text{sinc}\left(\pi f_y \frac{P}{2}\right)
\end{cases}
\quad \text{with } f_p = \frac{1}{P}.
$$

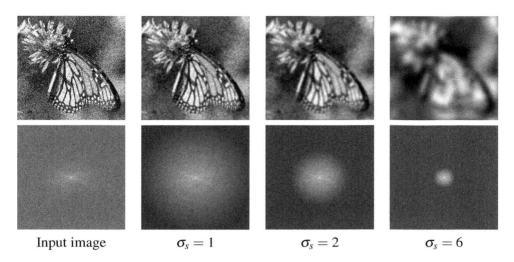

Figure 5.29 – Result of the Gaussian filtering for different standard deviations. The first row visualizes the images, the second row their spectrum in the frequency domain.

Knowing that $F * G(x,y) \overset{TF}{\leftrightarrow} \widehat{F}(f_x, f_y) \times \widehat{G}(f_x, f_y)$, the Fourier transform of T is expressed as:

$$
\begin{aligned}
\widehat{T}(f_x, f_y) &= \frac{1}{2} \mathrm{III}_{f_p}(f_x, f_y) \times \mathrm{sinc}\left(\pi f_y \frac{P}{2}\right) \\
&= \frac{1}{2} \sum_{i=-\infty}^{+\infty} \mathrm{sinc}\left(\frac{\pi}{2} f_y P\right) \delta\left(f_x, f_y - i f_p\right)
\end{aligned}
$$

$G(f_x, f_y) \delta(f_x - f_{x_0}, f_y - f_{y_0}) = G(f_{x_0}, f_{y_0}) \delta(f_x - f_{x_0}, f_y - f_{y_0})$ corresponds to a "selection" operation and thus:

$$
\widehat{T}(f_x, f_y) = \frac{1}{2} \sum_{i=-\infty}^{+\infty} \mathrm{sinc}\left(i\frac{\pi}{2}\right) \delta\left(f_x, f_y - i f_p\right) \tag{5.9}
$$

With Equations 5.8 and 5.9, the Fourier transform of $\widehat{I}$ is given by

$$
\widehat{I_t}(f_x, f_y) = \frac{1}{2} \sum_{i=-\infty}^{+\infty} \mathrm{sinc}\left(i\frac{\pi}{2}\right) \widehat{I_r} * \delta\left(f_x, f_y - i f_p\right). \tag{5.10}
$$

$G * \delta(f_x - f_{x_0}, f_y - f_{y_0}) = G(f_x - f_{x_0}, f_y - f_{y_0})$ is a shift operation, and thus:

$$
\widehat{I_t}(f_x, f_y) = \frac{1}{2} \sum_{i=-\infty}^{+\infty} \mathrm{sinc}\left(i\frac{\pi}{2}\right) \widehat{I}(f_x, f_y - i f_p) \tag{5.11}
$$

The graphical representation of the modulus of the Fourier transform of the Moiré image, considering that the image we wish to restore is band-limited in $[-f_0, f_0] \times [-f_0, f_0]$, is given in Fig. 5.11. The shape of $\widehat{I}$ in this figure is arbitrary.

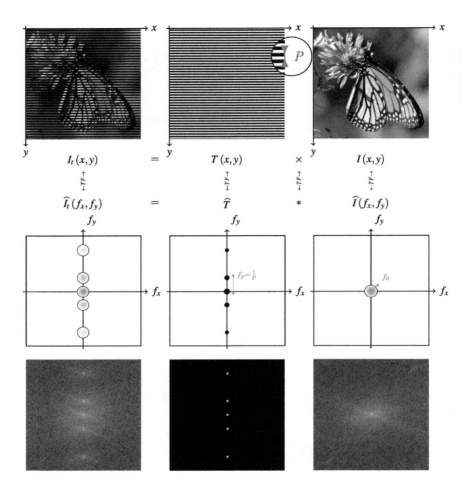

Figure 5.30 – Spatial and frequency models of a Moiré image. First row: spatial modeling as the multiplication by a pattern. Second row: frequency modeling as convolution with set of Dirac distributions. Third row: Image spectrum. Here, $P = 8$.

RESTORING THE IMAGE USING FREQUENCY FILTERING

The Fourier transform of the Moiré image consists of a repetition of the Fourier transform of the image to be restored (Equation 5.11 and Fig. 5.30).

1. In the case where the image to be restored is band-limited in $[-f_0, f_0]$ with $2f_0 < f_p$ (Fig. 5.30), it is possible to restore "ideally" the corrupted image by a vertical low-pass filtering with a cutoff frequency $f_c = \frac{f_p}{2}$.
2. In the case where the image to be restored is band-limited with $2f_0 > f_p$ or is not band-limited, it is impossible to "ideally" restore the image. With the method described above, the restored image will have frequency aliasing.

Images are of size $N \times N$ and we set the sampling period $T_e = 1$ (equivalent to work with normalized frequencies). We use the discrete Fourier transform.

Working with digital signals, the Fourier transform lives on a $\left[-\frac{F_e}{2}, \frac{F_e}{2}\right]$ support sampled in N points in each direction, the frequency resolution (distance between 2 pixels) is thus $\frac{1}{N}$. In practice, setting up a low-pass filter with a cut-off frequency of $f_c = \frac{f_p}{2}$ is equivalent to keeping the "pixels" in the interval $[\![-\frac{N}{2P}, \frac{N}{2P}]\!]$.

The full implementation is given in Code 5.13.

Code 5.13 – Removing Moiré pattern.

```
/*
  Moiré removal.

  imgIn   : Input image
  period  : Period of the pattern to remove
  imgOut  : Output image
*/
CImg<> Detramage(CImg<>& imgIn, int period)
{
  // FFT.
  CImgList<> F_Img = imgIn.get_FFT();

  // Cutoff frequency.
  int Freq_c = imgIn.height()/(2*period);

  // Frequency filtering.
  cimg_forXYC(F_Img[0],x,y,c)
  {
    if (y>Freq_c && y<F_Img[0].height() - Freq_c)
      F_Img[0](x,y,c) = F_Img[1](x,y,c) = 0;
  }
  // Inverse FFT and real part.
  return F_Img.get_FFT(true)[0].normalize(0,255);
}
```

Figure 5.31 shows an example on a synthetic result. In the original image, half of the lines are cancelled with a pattern of 6 pixels period. The result shows that there is a significant difference with the original image. This can be explained by the fact that the image is not band-limited (the frequency filtering has therefore removed a significant amount of information).

Figure 5.32 presents the results on a real image extracted from a video sequence where the lines are interlaced. After separating the odd and even lines, a frequency filter is applied taking into account that the pattern has a period of 2 pixels.

Input image   Restored image

Figure 5.31 – Removing Moiré. A simulated example.

5.4 Diffusion filtering

5.4.1 Introduction

In Sections 5.1 and 5.3 we studied linear filters, i.e.,, linear and translation invariant systems. We have seen that the relation between the output and the input is written using a convolution product where the impulse response is introduced. Geometrically, this can be seen as a process of diffusion of the amount of gray levels of the pixel on its neighborhood. The calculation of the numerical convolution realizes this process. However, linear filtering acts in a *homogeneous* way on the image, i.e., the processing is applied in an identical way to all the pixels (property of invariance by translation), leading to possible defaults in the resulting image. For example, the Gaussian filter is widely used to reduce noise, but it alters and delocalizes the contours. But this filter can also be seen as a diffusion process, where the gray level of the image diffuses homogeneously and *isotropically*. By "isotropic" we mean that the diffusion takes place in all spatial directions without preferential orientation.

The idea of diffusion filtering consists in applying a physical diffusion process of pixel values to an image. Several approaches exist. They are based on the

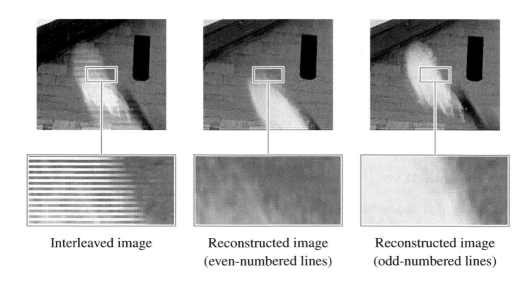

| Interleaved image | Reconstructed image (even-numbered lines) | Reconstructed image (odd-numbered lines) |

Figure 5.32 – Correction of interleaving in a video. (Source of the original video: [42].)

non-linear character of the diffusion process, thus allowing to obtain locally differentiated *anisotropic* smoothing according to the type of structures encountered. Diffusion filtering is a process allowing in particular to attenuate the noise of an image, while preserving the important information, in particular the contours of the objects.

5.4.2 Physical basis of diffusion

This method is based on the physical principles of diffusion between fluids: the diffusion equation is similar to that of local concentrations of a fluid that equilibrate under the condition of conservation of matter. The transfer to reach the equilibrium of concentrations is expressed with the first Fick's empirical law:

$$\mathbf{j} = -\mathbf{D}\,\nabla U,$$

where
- $\mathbf{D}$ is the diffusion tensor, a symmetric and positive definite matrix;
- $U(\mathbf{x}, t)$ is the concentration of matter in $\mathbf{x}$ at time t, $U : \mathbb{R}^d \times [0; +\infty[\to \mathbb{R}$;
- ∇U is the spatial gradient of the concentration of matter;
- $\mathbf{j}$ is the diffusion flux.

Note that, in a simplified version of this equation, $\mathbf{D}$ can be replaced by a scalar d, named *diffusivity*. This is equivalent to choose a diffusion tensor equal to either

$\mathbf{D} = d\,\mathrm{I}_d$ (I_d is the identity matrix), or $\mathbf{D} = d\,\frac{\nabla U \nabla U^T}{\|\nabla U\|^2}$.

The property of matter transport under the conservation condition is expressed with the continuity equation:

$$\frac{\partial U}{\partial t} = -div\,(\mathbf{j})\,.$$

Combining these two equations lead to the diffusion equation (second Fick's empirical law):

$$\frac{\partial U}{\partial t} = div\,(\mathbf{D}.\nabla U) \tag{5.12}$$

This equation is encountered in many fields. For example, it is the heat equation (or Fourier's law) when considering the study of heat transfer in homogeneous or inhomogeneous medium.

In image processing, we can imagine that the concentration $U(x,y)$ at a given point is given by the gray level $I(x,y)$ of the image at this point, and the initial conditions of the evolution of the diffusion equation, by the input image that we want to filter. In this case, the diffusion tensor (or diffusivity) defines how the diffusion should be done and is not necessarily constant. In practice, there is an advantage in choosing this tensor as a function of the local characteristics of the image. Two cases can be considered (Fig. 5.33):

- the *linear isotropic diffusion filter*, using a constant diffusivity;
- the *non-linear anisotropic diffusion filter* using a diffusion tensor or a diffusivity adapted to the local characteristics of the image.

5.4.3 Linear diffusion filter

In the case of homogeneous linear diffusion, Equation (5.12) is written in 2D:

$$\frac{\partial}{\partial t}I(x,y,t) = \nabla^2 I(x,y,t) \tag{5.13}$$

where $I(x,y,t=0)$ corresponds to the input image (initial condition) and the output image, solution of the equation, corresponds to the image after diffusion for a time $t = t_0 > 0$. The analytical solution of Equation 5.13 is:

$$I(x,y,t=t_0) = H_{\sqrt{2t_0}} * I(x,y)\,,$$

where H_σ is the impulse response which is a Gaussian function of standard deviation σ. It is thus a Gaussian filtering of the image.

In this case, it is not necessary to use Equation 5.12, since one can directly carry out a Gaussian filtering by using the `CImg<T>::get_blur()` method:

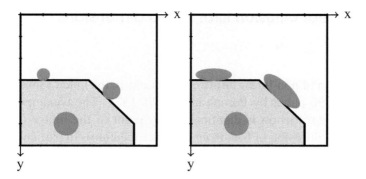

Figure 5.33 – Illustration of the different diffusion filters. Left: in the homogeneous linear case, we have a constant diffusion. Right: in the anisotropic case, the diffusion is done parallel to the contours, by exploiting for example the orientation of the spatial gradient.

```
CImg<> filtered_img = input_img.get_blur(sigma);
```

Historically, this is the first multi-scale filtering that has been studied. However, if this filtering reduces noise, it also blurs the image and attenuates the contours. In Fig. 5.34 is illustrated the application of a Gaussian filter with increasing diffusion times (i.e., increasing standard deviation values of σ).

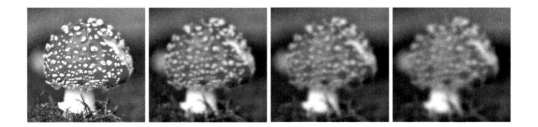

Figure 5.34 – Linear diffusion filtering, equivalent to Gaussian filtering.

The idea is then to adapt the diffusivity to a local "measure" of the contours (for example, based on the spatial gradient of the image), leading to non-linear diffusion filtering techniques.

5.4.4 Non-linear diffusion filter in two dimensions

PERONA AND MALIK'S ALGORITHM

The introduction of non-linear diffusion equations in the field of image processing dates back to a 1990 paper by Perona and Malik [32]. The weakness of the heat equation is that the diffusion is identical at any point of the image (this equation initially models the diffusion of heat in an isotropic medium). In particular, as we saw in the previous paragraph, the image is smoothed both in the homogeneous areas and along the contours.

The idea of Perona and Malik is to smooth the image in the homogeneous areas, and not to make the image evolve along the contours, or even to enhance them, as we will see more precisely. The corresponding equation is written:

$$\frac{\partial}{\partial t} I(x,y,t) = div\left(g\left(\|\nabla I\|(x,y,t)\right)\nabla I(x,y,t)\right)$$

where g is a decreasing function, with $g(0) = 1$ and $\lim_{x\to\infty} g(x) = 0$. The equation is therefore close to the heat equation at the points where $\|\nabla I\|$ is close to 0. As an example, we will consider the following function, originally proposed in [32].

$$g_1(s) = \frac{1}{1+(\lambda s)^2} \qquad\qquad (5.14)$$

This metric imposes a lower diffusion for higher gradient values (in norm). So the contours are preserved. The parameter λ allows to set a more or less important diffusion compared to the value of the norm of the gradient. Indeed, a high λ value will preserve contours with gradients which are lower in norm.

DISCRETIZATION SCHEME

The explicit discretization scheme of Perona-Malik's method for all points $[i,j]$ and at time $t + \Delta t$ is the following:

$$I_{i,j}^{t+\Delta t} = I_{i,j}^t + \Delta t\left(c_{E_{i,j}}^t \nabla_E I_{i,j}^t + c_{W_{i,j}}^t \nabla_W I_{i,j}^t + c_{N_{i,j}}^t \nabla_N I_{i,j}^t + c_{S_{i,j}}^t \nabla_S I_{i,j}^t\right)$$

where N, S, E and W represent the north, south, east and west spatial directions, the symbol ∇ denotes the spatial gradient in the direction indicated by the subscript, and coefficients c are defined by:

$$c^t_{N_{i,j}} = g\left(\left|\nabla_N I^t_{i,j}\right|\right) \quad c^t_{S_{i,j}} = g\left(\left|\nabla_S I^t_{i,j}\right|\right)$$
$$c^t_{E_{i,j}} = g\left(\left|\nabla_E I^t_{i,j}\right|\right) \quad c^t_{W_{i,j}} = g\left(\left|\nabla_W I^t_{i,j}\right|\right)$$

The directions to the cardinal points are shown in Fig. 5.35.

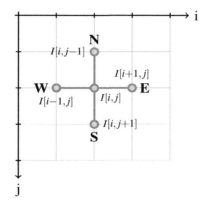

Figure 5.35 – Relationship between discrete positions (i,j) and spatial directions North, South, East, and West.

In order to compute the spatial gradients in these directions, we use numerical partial derivative computation by left and right finite difference techniques by using the CImg<T>::get_gradient() method:

```
// Gradient calculated by finite left differences.
CImgList<> gradient_g = img.get_gradient("xy",-1);
// Gradient calculated by finite right differences.
CImgList<> gradient_d = img.get_gradient("xy",1);
```

The relationships between the spatial gradients in the north, south, east and west directions and the finite differences are then:

$$\begin{cases} \nabla_N I[i,j] = I[i,j-1] - I[i,j] = (-1) \times \text{ finite left difference following } y \\ \nabla_S I[i,j] = I[i,j+1] - I[i,j] = \text{ finite right difference following } y \\ \nabla_W I[i,j] = I[i-1,j] - I[i,j] = (-1) \times \text{ finite left difference following } x \\ \nabla_E I[i,j] = I[i+1,j] - I[i,j] = \text{ finite right difference following } x \end{cases}$$

Code 5.14 implements Perona and Malik's algorithm in two dimensions.

Code 5.14 – Diffusion filter (Perona and Malik) in two dimensions.

```
/*
  2D diffusion filtering (Perona and Malik method).

  imgIn    : Input image
  nbiter   : Maximum diffusion time
  dt       : Time step in the discretization scheme
  lambda   : Diffusivity parameter to be set in relation
             to the gradient norm to be "kept".
*/
CImg<> PeronaMalik2D(CImg<>& imgIn, int nbiter, float dt, float
    lambda)
{
  CImg<> imgOut= imgIn;

  for (int iter = 0; iter<nbiter; ++iter)
  {
    // Computation of spatial derivatives by finite differences.
    CImgList<>
      NW = imgOut.get_gradient("xy",-1),
      SE = imgOut.get_gradient("xy",+1);

    cimg_forXY(imgOut,x,y)
    {
      float
        cN = 1/(1 + cimg::sqr(lambda*NW(1,x,y))),
        cS = 1/(1 + cimg::sqr(lambda*SE(1,x,y))),
        cE = 1/(1 + cimg::sqr(lambda*SE(0,x,y))),
        cW = 1/(1 + cimg::sqr(lambda*NW(0,x,y)));

      imgOut(x,y)  += dt*(-cN*NW(1,x,y) + cS*SE(1,x,y) +
                          cE*SE(0,x,y) - cW*NW(0,x,y));
    }
  }
  return imgOut;
}
```

RESULTS

Figure 5.36 presents the result of such a filtering for increasing diffusion times ($t_0 < t_1 < t_2 < t_3$) and for decreasing parameters of the diffusivity function ($\lambda_0 > \lambda_1 > \lambda_2 > \lambda_3$). The expression of this diffusivity is not the only one, and for example, Perona and Malik proposed $g_2(s) = e^{-(\lambda s)^2}$. The parameter λ allows to define the level of contrast (through the norm of the gradient of the image) which reduces the diffusion phenomenon. This is the non-linear character of this processing. It allows to set the type of contour preserved during filtering (Fig. 5.36).

	t_0	$t_1 > t_0$	$t_2 > t_1$	$t_3 > t_2$
λ_0				
λ_1				
λ_2				
λ_3				

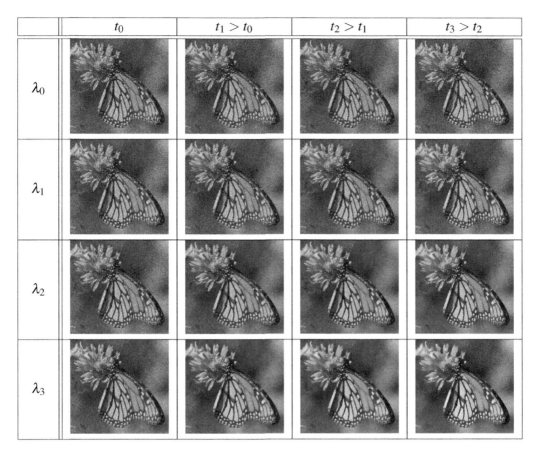

Figure 5.36 – Results of non-linear diffusion filtering by the Perona-Malik method.

5.4.5 Non-linear diffusion filter on a video sequence

Note that it is very easy to generalize Perona and Malik's method for images with a higher number of dimensions (e.g., 3D volumetric images or 2D+t video sequences). The example Code 5.15 illustrates a modification of Algorithm 5.14 for processing several consecutive images from a video sequence. Here, we take into account the temporal variation of light intensities.

We can notice that algorithmically, this adds terms which are linked to the gradients in the directions along the z axis, which is used to store the different timesteps of the sequence.

Figure 5.37 compares results of the linear and non-linear isotropic diffusion filtering in the case of a video sequence.

Code 5.15 – Diffusion filter (Perona and Malik) on a video sequence.

```
/*
  2D+T diffusion filtering (Perona and Malik method).

  seqIn    : Input images (the images of the sequence are
             arranged in the "z" axis of the CImg object)
  nbiter   : Maximum diffusion time
  dt       : Time step in the discretization scheme
  lambda   : Diffusivity parameter to be set in relation to
             the norm of the gradient to be "kept".
*/
CImg<> PeronaMalik2D(CImg<>& seqIn, int nbiter, float dt, float
    lambda)
{
  CImg<> seqOut = seqIn;

  for (int iter = 0; iter<nbiter; ++iter)
  {
    // Computation of spatial and temporal derivatives by finite
       differences.
    CImgList<>
      NWP = seqIn.get_gradient("xyz",-1),
      SEF = seqIn.get_gradient("xyz",+1);

    cimg_forXYZ(seqOut,x,y,t)
    {
      float
        cW = 1/(1 + cimg::sqr(lambda*NWP(0,x,y,t))),
        cE = 1/(1 + cimg::sqr(lambda*SEF(0,x,y,t))),
        cN = 1/(1 + cimg::sqr(lambda*NWP(1,x,y,t))),
        cS = 1/(1 + cimg::sqr(lambda*SEF(1,x,y,t))),
        cP = 1/(1 + cimg::sqr(lambda*NWP(2,x,y,t))),
        cF = 1/(1 + cimg::sqr(lambda*SEF(2,x,y,t)));

      seqOut(x,y,t)  += dt*(-cW*NWP(0,x,y,t) + cE*SEF(0,x,y,t)
                           -cN*NWP(1,x,y,t) + cS*SEF(1,x,y,t)
                           -cP*NWP(2,x,y,t) + cF*SEF(2,x,y,t));
    }
  }
  return seqOut;
}
```

Figure 5.37 – Results of the diffusion filtering. Top left: the noisy input image. Top right: linear isotropic diffusion filtering with a diffusion time of $t = 12.5$ s, equivalent to a Gaussian filtering of standard deviation $\sigma = 5$. Bottom left: non linear isotropic filtering in two dimensions by the Perona-Malik method. Bottom right: non-linear isotropic filtering in two dimensions + time by the Perona-Malik method. (Source of the video sequence: *SBI Database* [27].)

6. Feature Extraction

Features play a central role in image processing. These numerical values, derived from direct calculations on the image, allow:

- to represent each pixel i by a vector $\mathbf{x_i} \in \mathbb{R}^d$, each of the components reflecting a feature relevant to the problem at hand;
- to detect points of interest in the image, for further processing (registration, matching, ...).

We illustrate the first aspect in Sections 7.2 and 6.3. We focus on the second aspect in the two other sections of this chapter, and we more particularly search for particular geometric objects (points, shapes) in the image. First, we detail a method dedicated to the detection of points of interest and more particularly corners. Then we focus on a method for the detection of parametric shapes in images, allowing to locate for example lines, circles or ellipses.

6.1 Points of interest

Points of interest, especially corners, represent key information for many applications such as object tracking, stereo image matching, geometric feature measurement or camera calibration.

6.1.1 Introduction

A corner in an image can be seen as a point for which there are two dominant and different contour directions in a local neighborhood. Even if this definition seems simple, and even if our visual system is very good at detecting these features, automatic corner detection is not an easy task for a computer. A good detector must meet many criteria, including low false positive detection, robust detection to illumination changes, noise, partial occlusions, accurate precision constraint, or an implementation allowing real time detection.

Numerous corner detection methods have been proposed in the literature and most of them are based on the following principle: while a contour is classically defined by a strong gradient in one direction of space and weak in the others (see Section 5.1 of Chapter 5), a corner is defined by the location of high gradient points along several directions simultaneously. Many algorithms exploit the first and second derivatives of the image to perform this detection. We present in the following two of these methods.

6.1.2 Harris and Stephens detector

The Harris and Stephens corner detector [16] and its derivatives are among the most used methods. This detector is invariant to scaling, rotations, noise and illumination variations [35]. The principle is based on the analysis of a local weighted sum of quadratic differences measuring local changes of the signal with pixel neighborhoods shifted by a small amount in different directions.

For a 2D image I and $\mathbf{x} = (x,y)^\top$, this sum is computed for a shift $\delta = (\delta x, \delta y)^\top$ by

$$S(\mathbf{x}) = \sum_{(x_i,y_i)\in W} G_\mathbf{x}(x_i,y_i)\left(I(x_i,y_i) - I(x_i+\delta x, y_i+\delta y)\right)^2$$

where W is a window of points (x_i,y_i) centered on $\mathbf{x}$ and $G_\mathbf{x}$ is a kernel centered on $\mathbf{x}$. Choosing a Gaussian kernel gives an isotropic response of the detector. If δ is small, a first order approximation gives

$$I(x_i+\delta x, y_i+\delta y) \approx I(x_i,y_i) + \nabla I(x_i,y_i)^\top \delta$$

and then $S(\mathbf{x}) \approx \displaystyle\sum_{(x_i,y_i)\in W} G_\mathbf{x}(x_i,y_i)\left(\nabla I(x_i,y_i)^\top \delta\right)^2 = \delta^\top \mathbf{M}(\mathbf{x})\delta.$

$\mathbf{M}(\mathbf{x})$, called *structure tensor*, is a semi-definite positive matrix capturing the intensity structure of the gray levels in the neighborhood W. It is defined by:

$$\mathbf{M}(\mathbf{x}) = \begin{pmatrix} A(\mathbf{x}) & B(\mathbf{x}) \\ B(\mathbf{x}) & C(\mathbf{x}) \end{pmatrix}$$

with

$$A(\mathbf{x}) = \sum_{(x_i,y_i)\in W} G_\mathbf{x}(x_i,y_i)\left(\frac{\partial I}{\partial x}(x_i,y_i)\right)^2$$

$$B(\mathbf{x}) = \sum_{(x_i,y_i)\in W} G_\mathbf{x}(x_i,y_i)\left(\frac{\partial I}{\partial x}(x_i,y_i)\right)\left(\frac{\partial I}{\partial y}(x_i,y_i)\right)$$

$$C(\mathbf{x}) = \sum_{(x_i,y_i)\in W} G_\mathbf{x}(x_i,y_i)\left(\frac{\partial I}{\partial y}(x_i,y_i)\right)^2$$

A corner (or more generally a point of interest) is expected to have a large variation of S in all spatial directions. The matrix $\mathbf{M}(\mathbf{x})$ being real symmetric, its spectral factorization is $\mathbf{Q}(\mathbf{x})\Lambda(\mathbf{x})\mathbf{Q}^\mathbf{T}(\mathbf{x})$, with:

- $\Lambda(\mathbf{x}) = \mathrm{diag}\,(\lambda_1(\mathbf{x}), \lambda_2(\mathbf{x}))$ the diagonal matrix of eigenvalues, assuming $\lambda_1(\mathbf{x}) \geq \lambda_2(\mathbf{x}) \geq 0$;
- $\mathbf{Q}(\mathbf{x}) = (\mathbf{q}_1(\mathbf{x})\ \mathbf{q}_2(\mathbf{x}))$ the orthogonal matrix of the eigenvectors.

In the eigenvectors' basis, with coordinates (X,Y), the first order approximation of S is then $S(X,Y) \approx \lambda_1(\mathbf{x})X^2 + \lambda_2(\mathbf{x})Y^2$. Depending on the respective value of these eigenvalues, three cases have to be considered in the neighborhood W (Fig. 6.1):

1. If $\lambda_1(\mathbf{x})$ and $\lambda_2(\mathbf{x})$ are small, $S(\mathbf{x})$ is small in all directions and the image on W can be considered as constant in terms of intensity;
2. If $\lambda_1(\mathbf{x}) \gg \lambda_2(\mathbf{x})$, a small shift in the direction of $\mathbf{q}_2(\mathbf{x})$ slightly changes $S(\mathbf{x})$, whereas a small shift in the direction of $\mathbf{q}_1(\mathbf{x})$ makes $S(\mathbf{x})$ change significantly. An edge therefore passes through the point $\mathbf{x}$;
3. If $\lambda_1(\mathbf{x})$ and $\lambda_2(\mathbf{x})$ are large, a small variation of position makes $S(\mathbf{x})$ vary significantly. The point $\mathbf{x}$ is then a point of interest (a corner).

The exact computation of $\lambda_1(\mathbf{x}), \lambda_2(\mathbf{x}), \mathbf{x} \in I$ can be expensive, and it has been suggested in [16] to use

$$R(\mathbf{x}) = det\,(\mathbf{M}(\mathbf{x})) - k.Tr\,(\mathbf{M}(\mathbf{x}))^2 = \lambda_1(\mathbf{x})\lambda_2(\mathbf{x}) - k(\lambda_1(\mathbf{x}) + \lambda_2(\mathbf{x}))^2$$

where k allows to tune the detector sensitivity ($k \in [0.04, 0.15]$ empirically gives good results). Then,

1. on an homogeneous area, $R(\mathbf{x}) \approx 0$;
2. on an edge, $R(\mathbf{x}) < 0$ and $|R(\mathbf{x})|$ is high;
3. on a point of interest, $R(\mathbf{x}) > s$ where s is a (high) threshold value.

It is also possible to detect a pre-defined number n of points of interest, to avoid giving an arbitrary value to s.

To compute such a detector with *CImg*, we start by writing a windowing function W, which we will suppose to be Gaussian of standard deviation sigma.

Code 6.1 – Gaussian window.

```
CImg<> W(int size, float sigma) {
  CImg<> res(size,size);

  int center = size / 2 + 1;
  float sigma2 = cimg::sqr(sigma);

  cimg_forXY(res,i,j)
    res(i,j) = std::exp(-(cimg::sqr(center - i) +
                          cimg::sqr(center - j))/(2*sigma2)));
  return res;
}
```

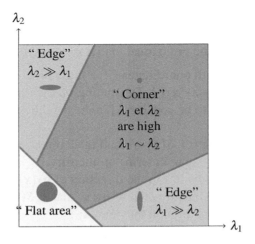

Figure 6.1 – Interpreting the eigenvalues of M.

It is possible of course to define alternative kernels.

We then write Code 6.2, which implements the detection algorithm itself. We give as parameters the k value, the number of points of interest to detect and the variance of the Gaussian kernel. Figure 6.2 presents two outputs of this algorithm.

Code 6.2 – Harris and Stephens detector.

```
/*
  Corner detector using Harris and Stephens algorithm.

  imgIn : Input image
  k     : Sensitivity parameter
  n     : Number of points to detect
  sigma : Variance of the Gaussian window
*/
CImg<> HarrisDetector(CImg<>& imgIn, float k, int n, float sigma) {
  CImg<> harris(imgIn);
  CImgList<> gradXY = imgIn.get_gradient();
  const float eps = 1e-5f;

  // Windowing.
  CImg<> G = W(7,sigma);

  // Structure tensor.
  CImg<>
    Ixx = gradXY[0].get_mul(gradXY[0]).get_convolve(G),
    Iyy = gradXY[1].get_mul(gradXY[1]).get_convolve(G),
```

```
    Ixy = gradXY[0].get_mul(gradXY[1]).get_convolve(G);

  // R function.
  CImg<>
    det = Ixx.get_mul(Iyy) - Ixy.get_sqr(),
    trace = Ixx + Iyy,
    R = det - k*trace.get_sqr();

  // Local maxima of R.
  CImgList<> imgGradR = R.get_gradient();
  CImg_3x3(I,float);
  CImg<> harrisValues(imgIn.width()*imgIn.height(),1,1,1,0);
  CImg<int>
    harrisXY(imgIn.width()*imgIn.height(),2,1,1,0),
    perm(imgIn.width()*imgIn.height(),1,1,1,0);

  int nbHarris = 0;
  cimg_for3x3(R,x,y,0,0,I,float) {
    if (imgGradR[0](x,y)<eps && imgGradR[1](x,y)<eps) {
      float
        befx = Ipc - Icc,
        befy = Icp - Icc,
        afty = Icn - Icc,
        aftx = Inc - Icc;
      if (befx<0 && befy<0 && aftx<0 && afty<0) {
        harrisValues(nbHarris) = R(x,y);
        harrisXY(nbHarris,0) = x;
        harrisXY(nbHarris++,1) = y;
      }
    }
  }
  // Sorting.
  harrisValues.sort(perm,false);

  // Display of the points of interest.
  unsigned char red[3] = { 255,0,0 };
  for (int i = 0; i<n; ++i)
  {
    int
      pos = perm(i),
      posx = harrisXY(pos,0),
      posy = harrisXY(pos,1);
    harris.draw_line(posx-1,posy,posx,posy,red);
    harris.draw_line(posx,posy,posx+1,posy,red);
    harris.draw_line(posx,posy-1,posx,posy,red);
    harris.draw_line(posx,posy,posx,posy+1,red);
  }
  return harris;
}
```

Checkboard (n=200, $k = 0.4$, $\sigma = 5$)   Building ($n = 100$, $k = 0.1$, $\sigma = 10$)

Figure 6.2 – Harris and Stephens detector.

In the previous algorithm, *CImg* allows to directly compute M using

```
CImg<> get_structure_tensors(unsigned int scheme=1)
```

6.1.3   Shi and Tomasi algorithm

An eigenvalue analysis can also be performed for each point **x**. Shi and Tomasi [39] proposed to classify a point **x** as a point of interest if $\min(\lambda_1(\mathbf{x}), \lambda_2(\mathbf{x})) > \lambda$, where λ is a pre-defined threshold. For 2D matrices, an elegant method to determine the eigenvalues, without solving $x^2 - Tr(M)x + det(M) = 0$, nor calling the function

```
CImg<T>& eigen(CImg<>& val, CImg<>& vec)
```

is to use:
$$(\lambda_1(\mathbf{x}) + \lambda_2(\mathbf{x}))^2 - (\lambda_1(\mathbf{x}) - \lambda_2(\mathbf{x}))^2 = 4\lambda_1(\mathbf{x})\lambda_2(\mathbf{x})$$
and then $(\lambda_1(\mathbf{x}) - \lambda_2(\mathbf{x}))^2 = (\lambda_1(\mathbf{x}) + \lambda_2(\mathbf{x}))^2 - 4\lambda_1(\mathbf{x})\lambda_2(\mathbf{x})$ or

$$(\lambda_1(\mathbf{x}) - \lambda_2(\mathbf{x})) = \sqrt{Tr^2(\mathbf{M}(\mathbf{x})) - 4det(\mathbf{M}(\mathbf{x}))}$$

Knowing the sum and the difference of the eigenvalues, we can then determine the latter easily for all the pixels of the image:

```
CImg<>
  diff = (trace.get_sqr() - 4*det).sqrt(),
  lambda1 = (trace + diff)/2,
  lambda2 = (trace - diff)/2,
  R = lambda1.min(lambda2);
```

6.1.4 **Points of interest with sub-pixel accuracy**

Of course, the smallest accessible part of an image is the pixel and no information "between these pixels" is accessible. However, it may be necessary to improve the accuracy provided by this sampling, for example for 3D reconstruction problems. We propose in the following a simple method to improve the accuracy of points of interest detection, and more particularly the corners.

Suppose that $\mathbf{x}$ is a corner, detected in the image I, e.g., using one of the former detectors, and let $\mathscr{V}_{\mathbf{x}}$ denote a neighborhood of size n of this point. Since $\mathbf{x}$ is a corner, any point $\mathbf{y} \in \mathscr{V}_{\mathbf{x}}$ can be of two types: either a point on a homogeneous region, or an edge point:

- if $\mathbf{y}$ is in a homogeneous region, then $\nabla I(\mathbf{y}) = 0$ and also $\nabla I(\mathbf{y})^{\top}(\mathbf{x} - \mathbf{y}) = 0$
- if $\mathbf{y}$ is on an edge, then $\mathbf{x} - \mathbf{y}$ follows this edge, and since the gradient is orthogonal to the edge in $\mathbf{y}$ we also have $\nabla I(\mathbf{y})^{\top}(\mathbf{x} - \mathbf{y}) = 0$

The idea is then to form and solve for any $\mathbf{y_i} \in \mathscr{V}_{\mathbf{x}}$ a linear system

$$\nabla I(\mathbf{y_i})^{\top}\mathbf{x} = \nabla I(\mathbf{y_i})^{\top}\mathbf{y_i}$$

in order to improve the location of points of interest.

If $\mathbf{A}$ is the matrix whose rows are the $\nabla I(\mathbf{y_i})^{\top}$ and $\mathbf{b}$ is the vector of components $\nabla I(\mathbf{y_i})^{\top}$, the overdetermined system is $\mathbf{Ax} = \mathbf{b}$ and $\mathbf{x}$ is the solution of the system with normal equations $\mathbf{A}^{\top}\mathbf{Ax} = \mathbf{A}^{\top}\mathbf{b}$. Since $n \gg 2$, $\mathbf{A}$ (and thus $\mathbf{A}^{\top}\mathbf{A}$) is most likely of rank 2 and $\mathbf{x} = (\mathbf{A}^{\top}\mathbf{A})^{-1}\mathbf{A}^{\top}\mathbf{b}$. Code 6.3 implements such a sub-pixel corner detection algorithm.

Code 6.3 – Sub-pixel detection of the points of interest.

```
/*
   Improvement of the position of the points of interest.

   imgIn : Input image
   p     : Point of interest
   n     : Size of the window around p
*/
CImg<> SubpixelCornerDetection(CImg<>& imgIn, CImg<int>& p, int n)
{
   int n2 = n/2, i = 0;

   // Image gradients.
   CImgList<> grad = imgIn.get_gradient();

   // Looking inside the neighborhood.
   CImg<>
```

```
    gx = grad(0).crop(p(0) - n2,p(1) - n2,
                      p(0) + n2,p(1) + n2),
    gy = grad(1).crop(p(0) - n2,p(1) - n2,
                      p(0) + n2,p(1) + n2),
    A,
    b(1,n*n);
  cimg_forXY(gx,x,y)
  {
    // yi coordinates in the original image.
    CImg<int> yi(1,2);
    yi[0] = p(0) - n2 + x;
    yi[1] = p(1) - n2 + y;
    CImg<> gradi(2,1);
    gradi[0] = gx(x,y);
    gradi[1] = gy(x,y);
    A.append(gradi,'y');
    b(i) = gradi.dot(yi);
    ++i;
  }


  // Solving the linear system.
  return (A.get_transpose()*A).get_invert()*A.transpose()*b;
}
```

6.2 Hough transform

6.2.1 Introduction

The Hough transform [31] is a general method for feature extraction in an image I, allowing to localize certain classes of shapes. The transformation is particularly well suited for parametric shapes $f(\theta)$, which can be described by a vector of parameters $\theta \in \mathbb{R}^d$. For each position $\mathbf{x}$ in I, the transform associates a description of this parametrization. A discretization of the parameter space Θ is then generated, the values of θ being accumulated at each point θ_i of this space, measuring at which point a shape $f(\theta_i)$ corresponds to a shape present in I. The cells of Θ with high accumulation values are finally located to back-project the corresponding detected shapes in the image space.

6.2.2 Line detection

ALGORITHM

The first and simplest shape that can be detected by the Hough transform is the *line*. A line can be parameterized in several ways, with only two parameters ($d = 2$).
The most intuitive method is to consider a Cartesian equation $y = ax + b$ and thus $\theta = (a\ b)^{\top}$. A naive method to search for lines in an image I would be to find the

values of a and b such that "as many" of the possible $\mathbf{x} = (x,y)^\top$ contour points in I satisfy the equation. This approach in practice is unfeasible, since it is impossible from a combinatorial point of view to determine the number of points belonging to a given line.

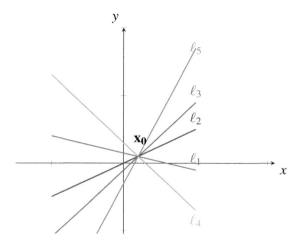

Figure 6.3 – A set of lines passing through $\mathbf{x_0}$ For each of these lines, the equation $y_0 = a_j x_0 + b_j$ is verified, for a certain pair (a_j, b_j).

Hough adopts another strategy: the algorithm examines all the lines that pass through a given point $\mathbf{x_0} = (x_0, y_0)^\top$ of I. Each line $\ell_j : y = a_j x + b_j$ that passes through $\mathbf{x_0}$ verifies $y_0 = a_j x_0 + b_j$. This equation is underdetermined and the set of solutions (a_j, b_j) is infinite (Fig. 6.3). Note that for a fixed a_j, $b_j = y_0 - a_j x_0$ and a_j, b_j are now variables, (x_0, y_0) being fixed parameters. The set of solutions of this last equation then describes the set of parameters of all lines ℓ_j which pass through $\mathbf{x_0}$.

However, this parametrization poses a problem, since it does not allow to represent the vertical lines ($a = \infty$). Moreover, a priori $a, b \in \mathbb{R}$ and the parameter space Θ is therefore $\mathbb{R}^2$. For this reason, the Hough transform uses more specifically the Hessian normal form, or polar representation of a line (Fig. 6.4):

$$r = x.\cos\alpha + y.\sin\alpha$$

or

$$y = -\frac{\cos\theta}{\sin\alpha}x + \frac{r}{\sin\alpha}$$

A line ℓ_j is then described by $\theta = (r_j, \alpha_j)^\top$.

As previously described, the fundamental concept of the Hough transform is the matching of points between the image space I and the parameter space Θ, here equal

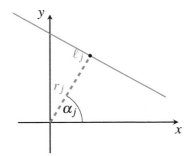

Figure 6.4 – Polar representation of a line. $r \in \mathbb{R}$ is the distance of the line from the origin and $\alpha \in [0, \pi[$ is the angle that the line makes with the x-axis.

to $\Theta = \mathbb{R} \times [0, \pi[$, a point $\mathbf{x_0}$ of I being matched to all the lines that can pass through this point. In the case of the polar parametrization, since these lines can be written as

$$r(\alpha) = x_0 cos\alpha + y_0 sin\alpha$$

the projection of $\mathbf{x_0}$ is represented in Θ by a sinusoidal curve (Figs. 6.5a and 6.5b). When more than one point of I is considered, the result is a set of sinusoidal curves (Fig. 6.5c) in Θ.

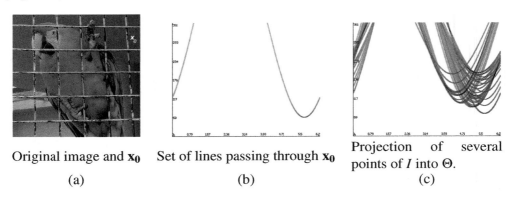

Original image and $\mathbf{x_0}$ Set of lines passing through $\mathbf{x_0}$ Projection of several points of I into Θ.

(a)   (b)   (c)

Figure 6.5 – Projection of several points of I into Hough space Θ.

Once this matching is done, the Hough algorithm proceeds according to the following steps:
1. Detect edge points in I: set of points $\mathscr{B}$;
2. Discretize the Hough space Θ into a grid of accumulators;
3. Project points of $\mathscr{B}$ into Θ. For each projection, increment the accumulators of all the lines that pass through this point. The accuracy with which the lines can be detected is determined by the resolution of the grid in Θ;
4. Threshold the grid: the accumulators with higher values represent the lines most likely to be present in I. A simple thresholding is often not sufficient

(detection of close but distinct lines possible, since close accumulators can have approximately the same value). A local analysis of the accumulators must therefore be defined. For example, for each accumulator, we search if there is a larger value in its neighborhood. If this is not the case, we leave this value; if not, we set the accumulator to 0;

5. Convert infinite lines into segments: since $\Theta = \mathbb{R} \times [0, \pi[$ no information on the length of the lines is available in the Hough space. If the objective is to detect segments, rather than lines, it is necessary to use algorithms in Θ to limit the length of the detected lines: for example, scan the lines in the edge image of I to detect segment boundaries, or directly integrate the length constraint in the Hough transform [13].

IMPLEMENTATION

Code 6.4 details the function to threshold the accumulator grid. Each accumulator is compared to the values of its neighborhood in a window of size $2*wsize+1$ after a thresholding of value th. The number $accnb$, as well as the list of positions $accXY$ are returned by the function. This function is then used in the line detection algorithm itself (Code 6.5). Figure 6.6 shows the result of the line detection by the Hough transform.

Code 6.4 – Thresholding the accumulator grid.

```
/*
  Accumulator thresholding

  acc   : accumulator grid
  th    : threshold
  wsize : half size of the neighborhood
  accXY : positions of the thresholded accumulators
  accnb : number of thresholded accumulators
*/
void AccThreshold(CImg<>& acc, float th, int wsize,
                  CImg<int>& accXY, int& accnb)
{
  cimg_for_insideXY(acc,x,y,wsize)
  {
    float value = acc(x,y);
    if (value<th) continue;

    bool ismax = true;
    for (int ny = y - wsize; ny<=y + wsize; ++ny)
      for (int nx = x - wsize; nx<=x + wsize; ++nx)
        ismax = ismax && (acc(nx,ny)<=value);
    if (!ismax) continue;
```

```
      accXY(accnb,0) = x;
      accXY(accnb++,1) = y;
  }
}
```

Code 6.5 – Hough transform for line detection.

```
/*
  Line detection using the Hough transform

  imgIn : Input image
  thr   : accumulator threshold
*/
CImg<> Hough(CImg<>& imgIn, float thr)
{
  CImg<>
    acc(500,400,1,1,0),
    imgOut(imgIn);
  int
    wx = imgIn.width(),
    wy = imgIn.height();

  // Bounds of the parameters.
  float
    rhomax = std::sqrt((float)(wx*wx + wy*wy))/2,
    thetamax = 2*cimg::PI;

  // Gradient and smoothing.
  CImgList<> grad = imgIn.get_gradient();
  cimglist_for(grad,l)
    grad[l].blur(1.5f);

  // Hough space.
  cimg_forXY(imgIn,x,y)
  {
    float
      X = (float)x - wx/2,
      Y = (float)y - wy/2,
      gx = grad(0,x,y),
      gy = grad(1,x,y),
      theta = std::atan2(gy,gx),
      rho = std::sqrt(X*X + Y*Y)*std::cos(std::atan2(Y,X) - theta);
    if (rho<0)
    {
      rho *= -1;
      theta += cimg::PI;
    }
    theta = cimg::mod(theta,thetamax);
```

```
        acc((int)(theta*acc.width()/thetamax),
            (int)(rho*acc.height()/rhomax)) += (float)std::sqrt(gx*gx
                + gy*gy);
    }

    // Smoothing the accumulators.
    acc.blur(0.5f);
    CImg<> acc2(acc);
    cimg_forXY(acc2,x,y)
      acc2(x,y) = (float)std::log(1 + acc(x,y));

    // Thresholding and filtering the accumulators.
    int taille_max = acc2.get_threshold(thr*acc2.max()).get_label().
        max();
    CImg<int> coordinates(taille_max,2,1,1,0);
    int accNumber = 0;
    AccThreshold(acc2,thr*acc2.max(),4,coordinates,accNumber);

    // Line display.
    unsigned char col1[3] = { 255,255,0 };
    for (unsigned i = 0; i<accNumber; ++i)
    {
      float
        rho = coordinates(i,1)*rhomax/acc.height(),
        theta = coordinates(i,0)*thetamax/acc.width(),
        x = wx/2 + rho*std::cos(theta),
        y = wy/2 + rho*std::sin(theta);
      int
        x0 = (int)(x + 1000*std::sin(theta)),
        y0 = (int)(y - 1000*std::cos(theta)),
        x1 = (int)(x - 1000*std::sin(theta)),
        y1 = (int)(y + 1000*std::cos(theta));

      imgOut.
        draw_line(x0,y0,x1,y1,col1,1.0f).
        draw_line(x0+1,y0,x1+1,y1,col1,1.0f).
        draw_line(x0,y0+1,x1,y1+1,col1,1.0f);
    }
    return imgOut;
}
```

In some applications (e.g., detecting corners of a polygonal shape), the Hough transform can be used to detect line intersection: to compute the point of intersection $\mathbf{x_i} = (x_i, y_i)^\top$ of two lines $\ell_1 = (r_1, \alpha_1)$ and $\ell_2 = (r_2, \alpha_2)$, it is necessary to solve the linear system

$$\begin{cases} x_i\cos(\alpha_1) & + & y_i\sin(\alpha_1) & = r_1 \\ x_i\cos(\alpha_2) & + & y_i\sin(\alpha_2) & = r_2 \end{cases}$$

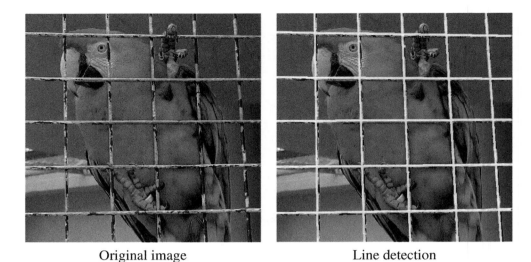

Original image   Line detection

Figure 6.6 – Line detection using the Hough transform.

The solution, defined if $\alpha_1 \neq \alpha_2$ (i.e., if the two lines are not parallel, which makes sense) is given by

$$\mathbf{x_i} = \frac{1}{sin(\alpha_2 - \alpha_1)} \begin{pmatrix} r_1 sin(\alpha_2) - r_2 sin(\alpha_2) \\ r_2 cos(\alpha_1) - r_1 cos(\alpha_1) \end{pmatrix}$$

6.2.3 Circle and ellipse detection

CIRCLE DETECTION

The principle of the Hough transform can be applied to the detection of circles in images. A circle can be parameterized in a three-dimensional Θ space by (Fig. 6.8a):

$$(x - x_0)^2 + (y - y_0)^2 = r^2$$

where $\mathbf{O} = (x_0, y_0)^\top$ if the circle center and r its radius.

If the phase ϕ of the gradient of the contours in I is available, it provides a constraint that reduces the number of degrees of freedom of the shape (since it determines the direction of the vector connecting $\mathbf{O}$ to each point of the contours), and r is the only parameter left in Θ. Using a polar parametrization, a circle can be written as

$$x = x_0 + r.cos\alpha \quad \text{and} \quad y = y_0 + r.sin\alpha$$

and then

$$x_0 = x - r.cos\alpha \quad \text{and} \quad y_0 = y - r.sin\alpha$$

Given ϕ at point $\mathbf{x} = (x,y)^\top$, the parameter r can be eliminated to lead to

$$y_0 = x_0.tan\phi - x.tan\phi + y$$

The Hough transform for circle detection then consists in:
1. Detect edges in I;
2. Compute the phase ϕ of the gradient;
3. Project the edge points $\Theta = (x_0, y_0)\top$ and increment the points in the accumulator grid along $y_0 = x_0.tan\phi - x.tan\phi + y$;
4. Threshold the accumulator grid.

The computation of the accumulator grid is given in Code 6.6. Of course, it is then necessary to calculate the maximum in the accumulator and then draw the circles in the image for example. Figure 6.7 shows a result on an image of globules.

Code 6.6 – Computing the accumulator for circle detection.

```
/*
  Accumulator for circle detection.

  ImgIn : Input image
  Acc   : Accumulator (output)
  a     : Gradient regularization
  s     : Threshold
  Rmin  : Minimum radius
*/
void Hough_Circle(CImg<>& ImgIn, CImg<>& Acc, float a, float s, int
    Rmin)
{
  // Initialization.
  Acc.fill(0);

  // Gradient
  CImgList<> imgGrad = ImgIn.get_gradient();
  imgGrad[0].blur(a);
  imgGrad[1].blur(a);

  cimg_forXY(ImgIn,x,y)
  {
    float
      gx = imgGrad(0,x,y),
      gy = imgGrad(1,x,y),
      norm = std::sqrt(gx*gx + gy*gy);
```

```
if (norm>s)
{
   cimg_forZ(Acc,r)
   {
      // Center in the direction of the gradient
      int
         xc = (int)(x + (r + Rmin)*gx/norm),
         yc = (int)(y + (r + Rmin)*gy/norm);

      // Voting scheme
      if (xc>=0 && xc<Acc.width() && yc>=0 && yc<Acc.height())
         Acc(xc, yc,r) += norm;

      // Center in the opposite direction of the gradient.
      xc = (int)(x - (r + Rmin)*gx/norm);
      yc = (int)(y - (r + Rmin)*gy/norm);

      if (xc>=0 && xc<Acc.width() && yc>=0 && yc<Acc.height())
         Acc(xc,yc,r) += norm;
   }
}
}
}
```

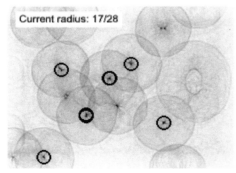

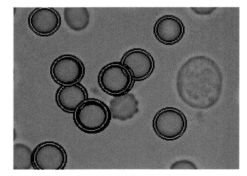

(a) Hough space   (b) Circle detection in the image space

Figure 6.7 – Detection of circles by Hough transform. (a) shows the result for $r = 17$.

ELLIPSES

In the case of ellipse detection, five parameters are *a priori* needed (Fig. 6.8b): the center **O**, the half-lengths of the axis r_a, r_b and the orientation α of the major axis with respect to the X axis. The Θ space is therefore a 5D space and it must be discretized in a sufficiently fine way to be able to detect ellipses in I. A quick calculation gives an idea of the memory occupation of such an algorithm: with a grid of resolution 128 along each dimension, Θ has to be discretized into 2^{35} accumulators which, if coded on long integers, require no less than 128 GB of memory for their storage.

As soon as the number of parameters of the shape to be detected increases, it is therefore necessary to turn to alternatives to the initial Hough algorithm. The generalized Hough transform [20] allows for example to detect any 2D shape. In this method, the shape of the desired contour is first encoded point by point in a table, and the associated parameter space is related to the position, scale and orientation of the shape. The method thus requires only four parameters, one less in the case of the ellipse, than the classical Hough transform.

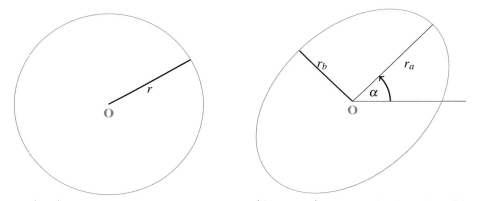

(a) - $(\mathbf{O}, r)$ parameterization of a circle   (b) - $(\mathbf{O}, r_a, t_b, \alpha)$ parameterization of an ellipse

Figure 6.8 – Circle and ellipse parameterization.

6.3 Texture features

Texture is a feature implicitly used by the human perception system to recognize and characterize surfaces. A texture refers mostly to the repetition of one or more patterns at different relative spatial positions, the repetition involving variations in scale, orientation or other geometric and optical properties. A texture can be described in three ways:
- a visual aspect, which describes its "geometry" (smooth, rough, coarse, fine, ...);
- a constitutive aspect, which describes if/how the texture is generated from simple patterns (primitives or texels);
- an informational aspect, which quantifies the statistical characteristics of the texture.

In the literature, many works try to describe textures by their frequency and/or spatial aspects (e.g., Gabor filters or wavelets) or statistical aspects (Markov field models). We propose here to describe simple methods that compute, for each pixel of an image, quantities allowing to characterize the underlying texture. These quantities are then used locally to segment textures (by a region segmentation method using these quantities as features, see Section 7.2), or computed on the whole image to allow *Content Based Image Retrieval* (CBIR).

Texture means elementary spatial pattern, and these methods are therefore based on indices computed in spatial neighborhoods of each pixel.

6.3.1 Texture spectrum

The approach proposed by [17] is a feature extraction method and texture classification. Each pixel $\mathbf{x}$ of I is compared to its neighbors $\mathbf{x}_i$ in a mask of a given size (and usually odd, here of size 3×3 pixels), using a threshold τ. For $i \in [\![1,8]\!]$, the quantity E_i is then defined:

$$E_i = \begin{cases} 0 & \text{if } I(\mathbf{x_i}) < I(\mathbf{x}) - \tau \\ 1 & \text{if } |I(\mathbf{x}) - I(\mathbf{x}_i)| < \tau \\ 2 & \text{otherwise} \end{cases}$$

The vector $(E_1 \cdots E_8)^\top$ gives a *texture unit*. Each E_i can take 3 values, so there are $3^8 = 6561$ possible texture units. We choose to identify a given unit by its representation in base 3: $N(\mathbf{x}) = \sum_{i=1}^{8} E_i 3^{i-1}$, and we assign this value to the central pixel (Code 6.7). The distribution S of the $N(\mathbf{x})$'s is called the *texture spectrum* of I. The parameter τ allows to encode the notion of homogeneity in an area, in a different way than the equality $I(\mathbf{x}) = I(\mathbf{x}_i)$ (Fig. 6.9).

Code 6.7 – Texture unit and spectrum.

```
unsigned char valE(float val1, float val2, float tau)
{
  return val1<val2 - tau ? 0 : cimg::abs(val1 - val2)<=tau ? 1 : 2;
}


CImg<> TextureUnit(CImg<>& imgIn)
{
  CImg<unsigned char> E(8);
  CImg<> N(imgIn);
  CImg_3x3(I,float);
  float tau = 5;
  cimg_for3x3(imgIn,x,y,0,0,I,float)
  {
```

```
if (x>0 && y>0)
{
  // The neighborhood is labeled counterclockwise
  E(0) = valE(Ipp,Icc,tau);
  E(1) = valE(Ipc,Icc,tau);
  E(2) = valE(Ipn,Icc,tau);
  E(3) = valE(Icn,Icc,tau);
  E(4) = valE(Inn,Icc,tau);
  E(5) = valE(Inc,Icc,tau);
  E(7) = valE(Icp,Icc,tau);
  E(6) = valE(Inp,Icc,tau);

  N(x,y) = E(0);
  for (int j = 1; j<8; ++j)
    N(x,y) += E(j)*pow(3,j);
}
}
return N;
}
```

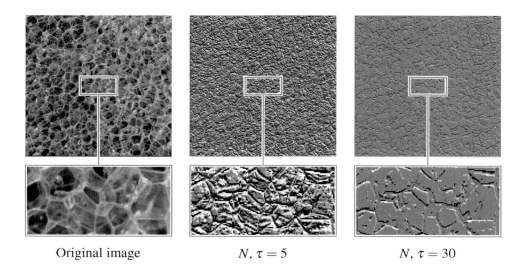

| Original image | $N, \tau = 5$ | $N, \tau = 30$ |

Figure 6.9 – Coding of the texture spectrum for different values of τ.

From this distribution, [17] defines a set of features, including:

1. geometric symmetry: let's assume that the neighbors are clockwise oriented, starting ($j=1$) from the top left neighbor.

$$GS = 100 \left[1 - \frac{1}{4} \sum_{j=1}^{4} \frac{\sum_{i=0}^{6560} |S_j(i) - S_{j+4}(i)|}{2 \sum_{i=0}^{6560} S_j(i)} \right]$$

2. direction degree: using the same convention

$$DD = 100 \left[1 - \frac{1}{6} \sum_{m=1}^{3} \sum_{n=m+1}^{4} \frac{\sum_{i=0}^{6560} |S_m(i) - S_n(i)|}{2 \sum_{i=0}^{6560} S_m(i)} \right]$$

6.3.2 Tamura coefficients

Tamura et al. [40] elaborated six indices, based on results of psychological experiments, allowing to characterize textures in images. Among these six indices, three are commonly used, the other three (regularity, line likeness and roughness) are correlated to the first three, which we present below.

CONTRAST

The *contrast* measures the distribution of gray levels in the image. It is equal to the ratio between the standard deviation and a power n (parameter, whose usual values are around 0.25) of the kurtosis of the empirical distribution (histogram, see Chapter 3) of the gray levels (Code 6.8).

Code 6.8 – Tamura's contrast.

```
/*
    Tamura's contrast.

    imgIn : Input image
    n     : integer, power of the kurtosis
    nbins : number of bins of the histogram
*/
float Contrast(CImg<>& imgIn, float n, int nbins)
```

```
{
  CImg<> h = imgIn.get_histogram(nbins);
  float
    mean = h.mean(),
    variance = h.variance(),
    kurtosis = 0;

  cimg_forX(h,x)
    kurtosis += cimg::sqr(cimg::sqr((h(x) - mean)));
  kurtosis /= (nbins*cimg::sqr(variance));

  return std::sqrt(variance)/std::pow(kurtosis,n);
}
```

COARSENESS

Coarseness (granularity) is related to the mean distance of noticeable variations of gray levels (and thus related to the characteristic size of the texels). For each pixel $\mathbf{x} = (x, y)^\top$:

1. We compute the average of the gray levels in five neighborhoods of size $2^k \times 2^k$, $k \in [1, 5]$:

$$A_k(\mathbf{x}) = \frac{1}{2^{2k}} \sum_{i=x-2^{k-1}}^{x+2^{k-1}} \sum_{j=y-2^{k-1}}^{y+2^{k-1}} I(i, j)$$

For an efficient implementation, we use the integral image (image of the same size as the original image, each pixel containing the sum of the pixels located above and to the left of this point). Code 6.9 allows to compute the mean at the point (x, y) for a neighborhood of size 2^k.

Code 6.9 – Local mean using the integral image.

```
/*
  Integral image of a point.

  imgInt : integral image
  x,y    : pixel
  k      : size of the window
*/
float IntegralMean(CImg<>& imgInt, int x, int y, int k)
{
  int
    k2 = k/2,
    startx = std::max(0,x - k2),
    starty = std::max(0,y - k2),
    stopx = std::min(imgInt.width() - 1,x + k2 - 1),
    stopy = std::min(imgInt.height() - 1,y + k2 - 1);

  float
    l1 = startx - 1<0 ? 0 : imgInt(startx - 1,stopy,0),
    l2 = starty - 1<0 ? 0 : imgInt(stopx,starty - 1,0),
    l3 = starty - 1<0 || startx - 1<0 ? 0 :
      imgInt(startx - 1,starty - 1,0),
    l4 = imgInt(stopx,stopy,0);

  return (l4 - l1 - l2 + l3)/
         ((stopy - starty + 1)*(stopx - startx + 1));
}
```

Code 6.10 allows a fast computation of the $A_k(\mathbf{x})$.

Code 6.10 – Local mean computation.

```
CImg<> ComputeAk(CImg<>& imgIn)
{
  CImg<>
    integralImage(imgIn.width(),imgIn.height(),1,1,0),
    Ak(imgIn.width(),imgIn.height(),5,1,0);

  // Initialization using integral images
  cimg_forXY(integralImage,x,y)
  {
    float
      l1 = x==0 ? 0 : integralImage(x - 1,y),
      l2 = y==0 ? 0 : integralImage(x,y - 1),
      l3 = x==0 || y==0 ? 0: integralImage(x - 1,y - 1);
    integralImage(x,y) = imgIn(x,y) + l1 + l2 - l3;
  }
```

```
// Computing the Ak.
int kp = 1;
cimg_forZ(Ak,k)
{
  kp *= 2;
  cimg_forXY(Ak,x,y)
    Ak(x,y,k) = IntegralMean(integralImage,x,y,kp);
}
return Ak;
}
```

2. For each $k \in [\![1,5]\!]$ absolute differences $E_k(\mathbf{x})$ between pairs of non-overlapping neighborhood means in the horizontal and vertical directions are then computed (Code 6.11):

$$
\begin{array}{rcl}
E_k^h(\mathbf{x}) & = & |A_k(x+2^{k-1},y) - A_k(x-2^{k-1},y)| \\
E_k^v(\mathbf{x}) & = & |A_k(x,y+2^{k-1}) - A_k(x,y-2^{k-1})|
\end{array}
$$

Code 6.11 – Absolute differences computation.

```
/*
  Absolute difference computation
  Ak      : Image of local means
  Ekh,Ekv : Images of horizontal and vertical differences
            the k scale is encoded in z
*/
void ComputeE(CImg<>& Ak, CImg<>& Ekh, CImg<>& Ekv)
{
  int kp = 1;
  cimg_forZ(Ekh,k)
  {
    int k2 = kp;
    kp *= 2;
    cimg_forXY(Ekh,x,y)
    {
      int
        posx1 = x + k2,
        posx2 = x - k2,
        posy1 = y + k2,
        posy2 = y - k2;
      if (posx1<Ak.width() && posx2>=0)
        Ekh(x,y,k) = cimg::abs(Ak(posx1,y,k) - Ak(posx2,y,k));

      if (posy1<Ak.height() && posy2>=0)
```

```
            Ekv(x,y,k) = cimg::abs(Ak(x,posy1,k) - Ak(x,posy2,k));
      }
   }
}
```

3. We look for the value of k maximizing these absolute differences in one or the other direction. We then note $S(\mathbf{x}) = 2^k$ and we deduce the *coarseness* of I by averaging S over the whole image (Code 6.12, only one property for the texture present in the image) or by studying the histogram of S (several possible *coarseness* for the texture).

Code 6.12 – Tamura's *Coarseness*.

```
/*
  Tamura's coarseness.

  Ekh,Ekv : Images of horizontal and vertical differences
            the k scale is encoded in z
*/
float ComputeS(CImg<>& Ekh, CImg<>& Ekv)
{
  float sum = 0;

  cimg_forXY(Ekh,x,y)
    {
      float maxE = 0;
      int maxk = 0;
      cimg_forZ(Ekh,k)
        if (std::max(Ekh(x,y,k),Ekv(x,y,k))>maxE)
        {
          maxE = std::max(Ekh(x,y,k),Ekv(x,y,k));
          maxk = k + 1;
        }
      sum += pow(2,maxk);
    }
  return sum/(Ekh.width()*Ekh.height());
}
```

DIRECTIONALITY

Directionality is measured by computing the frequency distribution of the orientations of the contours. A histogram h of the phases $\phi(\mathbf{x})$ of the gradients is computed whose norm $\|\nabla I(\mathbf{x})\|$ is greater than a threshold τ. A texture with no preferred orientation has a relatively uniform histogram and an oriented texture has one or more marked peaks. We then deduce the directionality of the texture:

$$D = 1 - r.n \sum_{p=1}^{n} \sum_{\phi \in w_p} (\phi - \phi_p)^2 h(\phi)$$

where n is the number of peaks, ϕ_p is the pth peak position, w_p is the phase spreading of the peak, r is a normalizing factor related to the angle discretization of the phase space. Code 6.13 implements this feature when w_p covers the whole phase space.

Code 6.13 – Tamura's directionality computation.

```
float Directionality(CImg<>& imgIn)
{
  CImgList<> g = imgIn.get_gradient();
  CImg<>
    phi = g(1).get_atan2(g(0)),
    norm = (g[0].get_sqr() + g[1].get_sqr()).sqrt();

  float tau = 0.01f;
  cimg_forXY(phi,x,y)
    phi(x,y) = norm(x,y)>tau ? phi(x,y) : 0;

  CImg<> h = phi.get_histogram(100);
  h /= (imgIn.width()*imgIn.height());

  // Searching the maxima
  h.threshold(0.7*h.max());
  int nb_pics = h.sum();

  // Location of the maxima
  CImg<int> perm;
  h.get_sort(perm,false);

  float D = 0;
  for (int p = 0; p<nb_pics; ++p)
    cimg_forX(h,x) D -= h(x)*(cimg::sqr(x - perm(p)));

  float r = 1;
  D *= r*nb_pics;

  return D + 1;
}
```

6.3.3 Local binary pattern

Ojala et al. [28] described a texture T as the joint distribution of $p+1$ gray levels of $(I(\mathbf{x}), I(\mathbf{x}_0) \cdots I(\mathbf{x}_{p-1}))$, where $\mathbf{x}$ is the location of the central pixel and $\mathbf{x}_0 \cdots \mathbf{x}_{p-1}$ are

p equally spaced neighbors on a circle of radius R centered on $\mathbf{x}$ (if $\mathbf{x}_i$ is not on the pixel grid, the gray level is interpolated). A simple texture operator is then defined, the *Local Binary Pattern* (*LBP*). We present and implement the rotation and gray level invariant version of LBP, proposed in [28]:

$$LBP_{p,R} = \begin{cases} \sum_{i=0}^{p-1} \sigma(I(\mathbf{x}_i) - I(\mathbf{x})) & \text{if } U(LBP_{p,R}) \leq 2 \\ p+1 & \text{otherwise} \end{cases}$$

where

$$\begin{aligned} U(LBP_{p,R}) &= |\sigma(I(\mathbf{x}_{p-1}) - I(\mathbf{x})) - \sigma(I(\mathbf{x}_0) - I(\mathbf{x}))| \\ &+ \sum_{i=1}^{p-1} |\sigma(I(\mathbf{x}_i) - I(\mathbf{x})) - \sigma(I(\mathbf{x}_{i-1}) - I(\mathbf{x}))| \end{aligned}$$

and $\sigma(.)$ is the sign function. The uniformity function $U(LBP_{p,R})$ corresponds to the number of spatial transitions in the neighborhood of $\mathbf{x}$: the larger it is, the more chances there are that a spatial transition occurs. If $LBP_{p,R}$ captures the spatial structure of the texture, the contrast of the texture is not expressed. We therefore add an additional feature

$$C_{p,R} = \frac{1}{p}\sum_{i=0}^{p-1}(I(\mathbf{x}_i) - \bar{I})^2 \quad \text{where} \quad \bar{I} = \frac{1}{p}\sum_{i=0}^{p-1} I(\mathbf{x})$$

A texture can then be characterized by the joint distribution of $LBP_{p,R}$ and $C_{p,R}$. Code 6.14 implements this version of *LBP* and Fig. 6.10 shows a result on a grass-like texture.

Code 6.14 – *LBP* and contrast.

```
/*
   LBP and contrast - rotation invariant version

   imgIn : input image
   R     : neighborhood radius
   P     : number of neighbors
   lbp,C : output images
*/
void LBP(CImg<>& imgIn, float R, int p, CImg<>& lbp, CImg<>& C)
{
   float PI2 = 2*cimg::PI;

   cimg_for_insideXY(imgIn,x,y,(int)(R + 1))
   {
```

```
float
  Ibar = 0,
  Vc = imgIn(x,y);

// Sampling p points on the circle of radius R
CImg<> xi(p,2,1,1,0), V(p);
cimg_forX(V,n)
{
  xi(n,0) = x - R*std::sin(PI2*n/p);
  xi(n,1) = y + R*std::cos(PI2*n/p);
  V(n) = imgIn.linear_atXY(xi(n,0),xi(n,1));
  Ibar += V(n);
}
// Mean of the grey-levels
Ibar /= p;

// Computing U.
float U = 0;
for (int n = 1; n<p; ++n)
{
  float Vj = imgIn.linear_atXY(xi(n - 1,0),xi(n - 1,1));
  U += cimg::abs(V(n) - Vc>0 ? 1 : 0) -
       cimg::abs(Vj - Vc>0 ? 1 : 0);
}
float
  Vi = imgIn.linear_atXY(xi(p - 1,0),xi(p - 1,1)),
  Vj = imgIn.linear_atXY(xi(0,0),xi(0,1));
U += cimg::abs((Vi - Vc>0 ? 1 : 0) -
               (Vj - Vc>0 ? 1 : 0));

if (U>2) lbp(x,y) = p + 1;
else
  cimg_forX(V,n)
    lbp(x,y) += (V(n) - Vc>0 ? 1 : 0);

cimg_forX(V,n)
  C(x,y) += cimg::sqr(V(n) - Ibar);
C(x,y) /= p;
}
}
```

Note that the *LBP* are used:

- to segment textures in images: in this case, $LBP_{p,R}$ and $C_{p,R}$ are components of the pixel features;
- to search for similar textures: in this case, we use the distribution of these parameters, and we define a metric between distributions to judge the similarity between two images (see the example below).

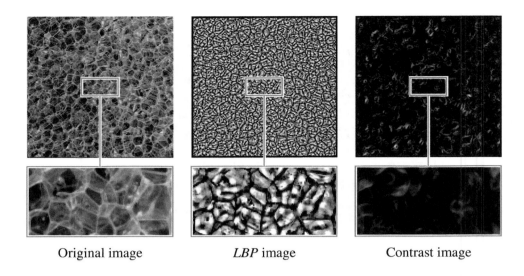

| Original image | *LBP* image | Contrast image |

Figure 6.10 – *LBP* and contrast image for *R*=2 and *p*=20.

6.3.4 Application

Section 7.2 will focus on the creation of local features for the segmentation of an image into regions. We propose here the use of these texture features for image search in large databases. To be more precise, we propose to search in an image database the "closest" image to a given target image. Many methods exist, and we implement in the following a method based on [2]. The idea is simple and is specified in Algorithm 3: the image I is cut into *patches* (i.e., small rectangular thumbnails of the same size), on which the *LBP* are computed, from which we then draw the distributions. The set of distributions (histograms) is then concatenated to form a global feature of I.

The interest of representing the image by the concatenated histogram is that it offers three levels of representation:

- at the pixel level, the *LBP* coefficients carry this information;
- at the regional level, by the representation of the histograms of the *patches*;
- at the global level, by concatenation.

The algorithm depends on a metric between histograms, and we choose in the following the simplest one, the L_1 norm of the difference:

$$d(h_I, h_J) = \sum_{k=1}^{nbins} |h_I(k) - h_J(k)|$$

Code 6.15 implements the first part of the algorithm (and uses Code 6.14).

Algorithm 3: Searching similar images to a query using *LBP*.

Input: A database $\mathscr{B}$ of images, a query image I, a metric d

Output: $\hat{I} \subset \mathscr{B}$ closest to I

for *All J in $\mathscr{B}$* **do**

    Cut J in rectangular patches

    for *each patch* **do**

        Compute the *LBP* histogram

    Concatenate the histograms to define a representation h_j of J

Compute the concatenated histogram h_I of I;

$\hat{I} = Arg\min_{J\in\mathscr{B}} d(h_I, h_J)$

> **Code 6.15 – *LBP* concatenated histogram.**

```
CImg<> LBPHistogram(CImg<>& imgIn) {
  int dx = imgIn.width(), dy = imgIn.height();

  // Number of patches in x and y.
  int nbX = 5, nbY = 5;

  // LBP and histogram parameters
  float R = 2;
  int p = 20, nbins = 20;

  // Concatenated histogram.
  CImg<> hglobal(nbins*nbX*nbY);
  for (int i = 0; i<nbX; ++i)
  {
    for (int j = 0; j<nbY; ++j)
    {
      CImg<>
        patch = imgIn.get_crop(i*dx/nbX,j*dy/nbY,0,0,
                               (i + 1)*dx/nbX,(j + 1)*dy/nbY,0,0),
        lbp(patch.width(),patch.height(),1,1,0),
        C(lbp);

      LBP(patch,R,p,lbp,C);
      CImg<> hlbp = lbp.get_histogram(nbins);
      cimg_forX(hlbp,x) hglobal((j + i*nbY)*nbins + x) = hlbp(x);
    }
  }
  return hglobal;
}
```

Computing d is simple

```
double dist = (hI - hJ).get_abs().sum();
```

Results (Fig. 6.11) are presented using UTK[1] dataset. This database contains 20,000 images of people, from 0 to 116 years old, covering a wide range of poses, expressions and lighting conditions. All ethnicities and genders are represented.

Query   Result   Query   Result

Query   Result   Query   Result

Query   Result   Query   Result

Figure 6.11 – Results of the CBIR algorithm using *LBP* histograms. On the first and third columns are the query images, on the second and fourth are the closest images in the database.

---

[1] https://www.kaggle.com/abhikjha/utk-face-cropped

7. Segmentation

Segmentation consists in identifying and defining objects in the image: it is no longer a collection of pixels, but a set of disjointed regions forming a scene. Ideally, regions have a meaning (object, structure, signal, ... or background) apart from their own characteristics (gray levels, shape).

Segmentation algorithms can be divided into two groups:
- region-based segmentation: pixels with common characteristics (called attributes or features), derived from the intensity of the pixels or from characteristics calculated on these intensities, are gathered together; the grouping criterion is evaluated in absolute (amplitudes) or in relative terms; decision rules (thresholds or metrics on the feature space) are then used to define which pixels belong to the same region, whether it is connected or not;
- edge-based segmentation: boundaries are set up [6] at positions that locally maximize the variation of a criterion; a contour is a closed curve or surface (in the case of 3D images) 1 pixel thick, which is generally closed.

These are two dual conceptions: a region has a closed contour, and a closed contour defines an inner and an outer region.

7.1 Edge-based approaches

There are several ways to perform an image segmentation by an "edge" approach. We introduce here a popular method called *active contours*.

7.1.1 Introduction to implicit active contours

Active contours are a method of image analysis which allows the extraction of primitives under constraints. They are objects of mathematical nature (contours noted γ) which are given a realistic mechanical behavior by the minimization of a total energy:

$$E_{\text{total}} = E_{\text{potential}} + E_{\text{kinetic}}$$

The potential energy is calculated from the image. As in physics, this minimization will result in the conversion of the potential energy into kinetic energy which causes the contour to move. γ is thus a function of time $\gamma(t)$. The objective is to make the contour converge toward the structures of interest that we wish to extract. This method has the advantage, among others, to control the shape of the solution curve, which can be forced to be closed using an adapted contour representation. The principle of active contours is represented in Fig. 7.1. The method is initialized by defining an initial contour $\gamma(t=0)$, to which we associate an energy that we minimize. The convergence of the motion of the curve allows to obtain a segmentation of the image. The rest of this study focuses on the so-called *implicit* representation of active contours.

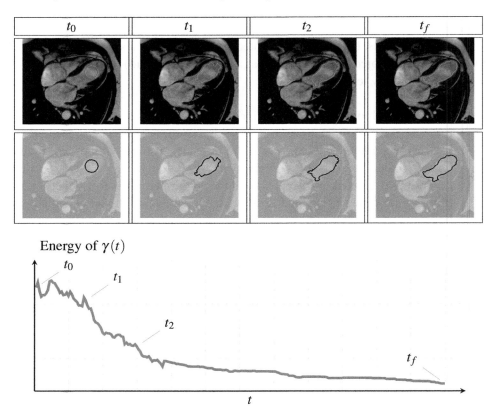

Figure 7.1 – Presentation of the active contour method. The iterative minimization of the energy associated to a contour γ will allow γ to move.

As opposed to explicit representations (polygonal approximation, parametric curves, decomposition on a basis of functions), the implicit representation, also called level curve representation or *level set* representation, presents less constraints as for the geometry of the objects which can be irregular (presence of strong curvatures) or whose topology can even vary during the convergence (by separation or fusion of curves).

From a chronological point of view, the original active contours model was proposed by Kass et al. [22] and consists of an intrinsically closed deformable model that evolves to the boundaries of the desired region. The deformation is based on a Lagrangian formulation of energy minimization, expressed as the sum of an image data related term and a regularization term. This method does not allow for simple topological changes, and the value of the energy depends strongly on the parametrization of the curve.

Caselles et al. [7] introduced a geometric model of active contours formulated by partial differential equations of curve evolution. Each point of the curve moves in the direction of its normal vector at a speed proportional to the curvature. This approach is an alternative to energy minimization which can be seen as a search for the solution of a Hamilton-Jacobi equation, and thus be solved efficiently by using the Osher and Sethian level curve method [29]. The use of this implicit representation explains the success of this approach.

Caselles et al. [6] subsequently proposed an equivalent energy minimization problem, based on the search for a minimal geodesic path in a Riemann space. This problem, which can also be solved numerically by *level set*, allows in theory to solve the initialization problem of active contours. Theoretical results have shown the existence, uniqueness and stability of the solution.

Many other models deriving from geometric and geodesic approaches have been proposed. Rather than presenting a catalog of the different variants described in the literature, the following paragraph unifies them in a single energy minimization formalism. The link between energy decay and velocity field generating a displacement is also presented, in order to have both an energetic and a geometrical approach.
The use of an implicit representation has as a main disadvantage a higher computation time. In this section, we will not discuss the fast algorithms for solving the implicit active contour methods, which exist but are more complex to implement.

GENERAL PRINCIPLE

Let us denote $\gamma(\mathbf{p})$ a closed curve defined on $\Omega \subset \mathbb{N}^2$ and parametrized by a vector $\mathbf{p}$. The inner region bounded by this contour is denoted R_γ. The active contours method in two dimensions is based on a deformable model considering that the curve $\gamma(\mathbf{p})$ is dynamic, i.e., $\gamma(\mathbf{p}) = \gamma(\mathbf{p},t)$. The model must evolve toward the boundaries of the object to be segmented R_i. The problem is therefore to find the vector **p** which verifies $R_\gamma = R_i$. In order to constrain the progression of the model, an energy E is associated to it. It is composed of the sum of a data attachment term and a regularization term. The system minimizes E by converting it into kinetic energy until a stopping criterion is verified. This energy problem can be formulated by a force balance, corresponding to a numerical gradient descent problem:

$$\frac{\partial \gamma(\mathbf{p},t)}{\partial t} = \mathbf{F} \quad \text{with} \quad \begin{cases} \gamma(\mathbf{p}, t = 0) = \gamma_0(\mathbf{p}) \\ \mathbf{F} = \dfrac{\delta E}{\delta \gamma} \end{cases}$$

In this model, three degrees of freedom are left to the user:
- the representation of the curve (**p**), which can be explicit, parametric or implicit;
- the definition of the energy function (E or $\mathbf{F}$ by calculation), which is based on geometrical constraints and/or data extracted from the image (gradient, texture parameters, temporal information ...) ;
- the initialization of the method ($\gamma(\mathbf{p}, t = 0)$) which influences the solution found because of the possible non-convexity of the energy function.

In most cases, the energy attached to the model can be described as a combination of integral, curvilinear and/or surface functions. The partial differential equation for the evolution of the γ contour can be deduced mathematically by calculus of variations.

ENERGY FORMULATION

Curvilinear integral energy

This contour energy can be expressed as a simple integral along the contour of a function f depending on the characteristics of the image (boundaries for example):

$$E_b = \int_{\gamma(\mathbf{p})} f(\mathbf{m}) \, \mathrm{da}(\mathbf{m})$$

In [6] authors have shown that this form of energy leads to the velocity field:

$$\mathbf{F}_b = [\nabla . (f(\mathbf{m})\mathbf{n})] \mathbf{n} = [f(\mathbf{m})\kappa - \nabla f(\mathbf{m}).\mathbf{n}] \mathbf{n} \tag{7.1}$$

where **n** is the unit normal vector, κ the Euclidean curvature and ∇ the gradient operator.

Integral surface energy

A regional energy can be expressed as a double integral over a subdomain of Ω of a function g of the image characteristics:

$$E_r = \iint\limits_{R_\gamma} g\left(\mathbf{m}, R_\gamma\right) d\mathbf{m}$$

In the literature, the special case of independence with respect to the region considered, i.e., $g\left(\mathbf{m}, R_\gamma\right) = g\left(\mathbf{m}\right)$, is widely used:

$$\mathbf{F}_r = g\left(\mathbf{m}\right)\mathbf{n}$$

ENERGY FORMULATION IN IMAGE PROCESSING

A wide variety of energy terms can be implemented from the curvilinear or surface integral function formulation. They can be classified into two categories: internal energy terms, favoring coherence and regularization of the contour, and data attachment energy terms, allowing the contour to be attracted to the structures of interest.

Regularization energies

- When $f\left(\mathbf{m}\right) = 1$, the energy is equivalent to the Euclidean length of the curve γ. This case is widely used for its regularization properties and leads to the field:

$$\mathbf{F}_b = \kappa\mathbf{n}$$

  This term tends to make γ more regular, by attenuating the discontinuities of the curve.
- When $g\left(\mathbf{m}\right) = \mu$, the energy is proportional to the domain surface. This energy corresponds to a widely used velocity corresponding to a surface force homogeneous to a pressure called balloon force [8], which constrains the model to a global contraction or dilation motion. In this case:

$$\mathbf{F}_r = \mu\mathbf{n}$$

  Each point on the contour experiences a constant force in the normal direction of the contour, which is equivalent to applying a homothetic motion to the shape. This energy is commonly used to push the curve toward the valleys of potential.

Data driven energies

The information from the image can be derived from data extracted along the γ contour (curvilinear integral) or within R_γ (surface integral). The associated energies are called "boundary" energy or "region" energy, respectively.

For the boundary term, the function f usually defined in the curvilinear integral is called the stopping function. It depends on a derivative operator, for example the norm of the gradient, which has a maximum response on the amplitude jumps in the image; it decreases when the operator increases and theoretically tends toward zero when it tends to infinity. In practice, the following form is commonly used:

$$f(\mathbf{m}) = \frac{1}{1 + \|\nabla \hat{I}(\mathbf{m})\|^p}$$

where $\hat{I}$ is a regularized version of I (for example, a Gaussian smoothing version of the image) and the power p is generally chosen equal to 1 or 2. The corresponding model is called geodesic active contour [6].

7.1.2 Implicit representation of a contour

The mathematical representations of a contour can be divided into three classes:
- explicit representation (polygonal approximation ...) ;
- parametric representation (Fourier descriptors, B-splines ...) ;
- implicit representation (*level set*).

The *level set* method is an analytical framework for the geometric evolution of objects. Instead of using a classical Lagrangian representation to describe the geometries, the *level set* method describes them through a scalar function ψ defined on a fixed grid. The evolution equation, formalized as a partial differential equation, is constrained by a velocity field imposed in the normal direction of the contour. This field is constructed in such a way as to attract the model to the objects to be extracted in the image under geometric regularization constraints. The normal and curvature of the contour at each point are easily defined from the geometric differential properties of this representation.

One of the main advantages of the implicit contour description is that it intrinsically handles topological changes during convergence. For example, if a segmentation process is initialized by multiple seeds, collisions and merges of related components are automatically managed without modification of the algorithm, which is not the case for example with active contours with explicit representation. The counterpart of this flexibility is an additional cost in computation time, which requires in practice the use of optimized algorithms [37].

In the *level set* formalism, the γ curve is not parametrized, but implicitly defined through a higher dimensional function:

$$\psi: \begin{array}{ccc} \mathbb{R}^2 \times \mathbb{R} & \rightarrow & \mathbb{R} \\ \mathbf{m} \times t & \mapsto & \psi(\mathbf{m}, t) \end{array}$$

The 2D front at a time t is then defined by the zero isolevel of the function ψ at this time:

$$\gamma(t) = \left[\psi^{-1}(0) \right](t)$$

Code 7.1 allows to extract the contour γ from an implicit function ψ, by looking for the zero crossings of ψ.

Code 7.1 – Extraction of the contour from the 0 level of ψ.

```
/*
  ExtractContour : Calculation of the approximate position of the
  contour from the levelset map (psi): Isocontour with value 0.

  LevelSet : Level set (psi function)
  Return   : Binary image (1 <=> contour)
*/
CImg<> ExtractContour(CImg<>& LevelSet)
{
 CImg<> Contour(LevelSet.width(),LevelSet.height(),1,1,0);
 CImg_3x3(I,float);
 cimg_for3x3(LevelSet,x,y,0,0,I,float)
 {
   // Search for the set of pixels with a neighbor of opposite sign.
   if (Icc*Icp<=0 || Icc*Icn<=0 || Icc*Ipc<=0 || Icc*Inc<=0)
     Contour(x,y) = 1;
 }

 return Contour;
}
```

The principle of contour evolution under this representation was introduced by Osher and Sethian [29]. Generally, the initial *level set* function ψ_0 is obtained by using the signed distance to an initial curve γ_0 [14]:

$$\psi_0(\mathbf{m}) = \psi(\mathbf{m}, 0) = \begin{cases} +d(\mathbf{m}, \gamma_0) & \text{if } \mathbf{m} \in R_\gamma \\ -d(\mathbf{m}, \gamma_0) & \text{if } \mathbf{m} \notin R_\gamma \end{cases}$$

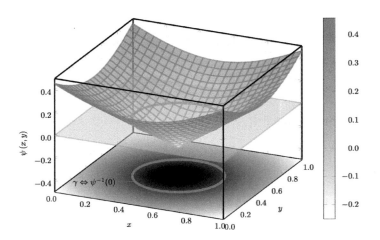

Figure 7.2 – Implicit representation of a curve γ in the form of a *level set*: $\gamma = \psi^{-1}(0)$. In this example, the contour is a circle so the function ψ is a cone.

where $d\,(\bullet)$ is the Euclidean distance, and $\mathbf{m}$ is a point of $\Omega \subset \mathbb{R}^2$.

What makes this formalism interesting is that the normal $\mathbf{n}$ at each point of the contour γ, as well as its curvature κ, are easily computable using differential operators applied to the implicit map ψ:

$$\mathbf{n} = \frac{\nabla \psi}{\|\nabla \psi\|} \text{ and } \kappa = \nabla \cdot \frac{\nabla \psi}{\|\nabla \psi\|},$$

where ∇ is the spatial gradient, i.e., relative to $\mathbf{m}$.

To initialize the ψ function, we generally use a signed distance computation algorithm (*Fast Marching* algorithm of [37] for example). In the case where the initial curve γ_0 has a simple form, one can even have an analytical form of ψ. This is what we do in Code 7.2, where the initial curve is a circle, and the values of ψ thus correspond to the distance to this circle.

Code 7.2 – Initialization of the function ψ in the particular case of a circle.

```
/*
  InitLevelSet: Initialization of the LevelSet (psi) using the
  signed euclidean distance. The initial contour is a circle of
  center (x0,y0) and radius r.

  imgIn : Level-set function to be initialized
  x0,y0,r : Circle parameters to initialize
*/
void InitLevelSet(CImg<>& imgIn, int x0, int y0, int r)
{
  cimg_forXY(imgIn,x,y)
    imgIn(x,y) = std::sqrt(cimg::sqr(x - x0) + cimg::sqr(y - y0)) -
      r;
}
```

7.1.3 Evolution equation

It has been shown in [37] that if $\gamma(t)$ evolves according to the evolution equation $\frac{\partial \gamma}{\partial t} = F.\mathbf{n}$ then its implicit representation (i.e., the ψ function) evolves according to the equation:

$$\frac{\partial \psi(\mathbf{m},t)}{\partial t} = F\|\nabla \psi(\mathbf{m},t)\| \tag{7.2}$$

where F is the normal component of the velocity field $\mathbf{F} : F = \mathbf{F}.\mathbf{n}$. This is true only if the property $\|\nabla \psi(\mathbf{m},t)\| = 1$ is preserved over time (*Eikonal* equation). The evolution problem is then solved for the function ψ, since it is possible to deduce the evolution of $\gamma(t)$ from that of $\psi(t)$. With this implicit representation of γ by ψ, note that only the component normal to the contour is used in the propagation of the model. In the following, we will refer to the velocity field or the velocity value at a point.

In order to extract the desired region R_i from the image, it is necessary to construct a velocity field F adapted from various sources. As an example, in the *level set* formulation, the geodesic model of Caselles *et al.* proposes the equation:

$$\frac{\partial \psi(\mathbf{m},t)}{\partial t} = f(\mathbf{m})\|\nabla \psi(\mathbf{m},t)\|\kappa + \nabla f(\mathbf{m}) \cdot \nabla \psi(\mathbf{m},t).$$

Note that whatever the rate of evolution $\mathbf{F}$, it is important that the implicit representation ψ keeps its property $\|\nabla \psi(\mathbf{m})\| = 1$ during its evolution, so that the equivalence (Equation 7.2) between the evolution of ψ and the γ curve it represents remains valid. In practice, a normalization of the ψ gradients is performed at regular time intervals. This normalization is not algorithmically simple to achieve, and we will not go into the theoretical details of its implementation.

7.1.4   Discretization of the evolution equation

The core of the method is an iterative scheme guided by the velocity function F, for which a stopping criterion must be defined. The front propagation problem is solved numerically by discretizing the domains in space $\mathbf{m} \to (i,j)$ and in time $t \to n$. The values of the function ψ and of the velocity F at the point $\mathbf{m}$ and at time t are respectively noted ψ_{ij}^n and F_{ij}^n. The function ψ is initialized by the signed distance. Using the finite difference method, the evolution equation becomes:

$$\psi_{ij}^{n+1} = \psi_{ij}^n + \Delta t F_{ij}^n \|\nabla \psi_{ij}^n\|$$

A complete first-order convex numerical scheme can be found in [37] for estimating the spatial derivatives of the previous equation when the velocity function can be written as:

$$F = F_{prop} + F_{curv} + F_{adv} = F_0 - \varepsilon\kappa + \mathbf{U}(\mathbf{m},t) \cdot \mathbf{n}$$

where $F_{prop} = F_0$ is a propagation velocity, $F_{curv} = -\varepsilon\kappa$ is a curvature-dependent velocity term and $F_{adv} = \mathbf{U}(\mathbf{m},t) \cdot \mathbf{n}$ is an advection term where $\mathbf{U}(\mathbf{m},t) = (u(\mathbf{m},t),v(\mathbf{m},t))^\top$. The numerical calculation of the boundary and region velocity terms uses this scheme because it is possible to approximate the two terms of the geodesic velocity to F_{curv} and F_{adv} and the region velocity field is analogous to F_{prop}:

$$\psi_{ij}^{n+1} = \psi_{ij}^n + \Delta t \left[\begin{array}{c} -\left[\max\left(F_{0ij},0\right)\nabla^+\left(\psi_{ij}^n\right) + \min\left(F_{0ij},0\right)\nabla^-\left(\psi_{ij}^n\right)\right] \\[4pt] +\left[\varepsilon\kappa_{ij}^n \sqrt{D^{0x}\left(\psi_{ij}^n\right)^2 + D^{0y}\left(\psi_{ij}^n\right)^2}\right] \\[4pt] -\left\{ \begin{array}{l} \max\left(u_{ij}^n,0\right)D^{-x}\left(\psi_{ij}^n\right) + \min\left(u_{ij}^n,0\right)D^{+x}\left(\psi_{ij}^n\right) + \\ \max\left(v_{ij}^n,0\right)D^{-y}\left(\psi_{ij}^n\right) + \min\left(v_{ij}^n,0\right)D^{+y}\left(\psi_{ij}^n\right) \end{array}\right\} \end{array} \right],$$

where $\min(\bullet,\bullet)$ and $\max(\bullet,\bullet)$ correspond to the minimum and maximum operators, $D^{+\beta}(\bullet)$, $D^{-\beta}(\bullet)$ and $D^{0\beta}(\bullet)$ are respectively the finite difference derivatives on the right, on the left and centered with respect to the variable β. Finally, $\nabla^+(\bullet)$ and $\nabla^-(\bullet)$ are the following derivative operators:

$$\nabla^+(\bullet) = \sqrt{\begin{array}{c} \max\left(D^{-x}(\bullet),0\right)^2 + \min\left(D^{+x}(\bullet),0\right)^2 \\ + \max\left(D^{-y}(\bullet),0\right)^2 + \min\left(D^{+y}(\bullet),0\right)^2 \end{array}} \, ,$$

$$\nabla^-(\bullet) = \sqrt{\begin{array}{c} \max\left(D^{+x}(\bullet),0\right)^2 + \min\left(D^{-x}(\bullet),0\right)^2 \\ + \max\left(D^{+y}(\bullet),0\right)^2 + \min\left(D^{-y}(\bullet),0\right)^2 \end{array}} \, .$$

There are also higher order schemes that apply to convex or non-convex functionals to iteratively solve the problem. However, since the application of image segmentation does not require a high accuracy in the resolution of the contour propagation, these schemes are not necessary in practice.

7.1.5 Geodesic model propagation algorithm

The geodesic model is based on Equation 7.1. In terms of discretization, we can identify an advection term $\nabla f(\mathbf{m}).\mathbf{n}$ and a curvature term $f(\mathbf{m})\kappa$. In order to simplify the code, we consider that the curvature term is a propagation term $f(\mathbf{m})\kappa \to f(\mathbf{m})$. In practice, this change will reduce the regularization of the contour during its propagation and obtain a result with larger curvatures. In this part we will not discuss the stopping criterion of the evolution algorithm, we will define more simply a maximal number of iterations.

The sign of the data-driven function will cause the contour to expand or contract. Algorithmically, we can force the contour to move by fixing the sign of this function. Code 7.3 allows to set up the iterative scheme calculating the propagation of the contour with a propagation speed term and an advection speed term.

Note that the unit normalization step of the ψ gradient norms is performed every 20 iterations, by the call to `CImg<T>::distance_eikonal()`:

```
CImg<T>& distance_eikonal(unsigned int nb_iterations, float
    band_size=0, float time_step=0.5f)
```

Code 7.3 – Propagation algorithm of the simplified geodesic model.

```
/*
  Propagate : Propagation algorithm of an implicit contour
  (geodesic model)

  imgIn :     Image to be segmented
  LevelSet : Level-set function (initialized)
*/
void Propagate(CImg<>& imgIn, CImg<>& LevelSet)
{
  float
    delta_t = 2.0f,     // Temporal step
    alpha = 0.05f,      // Weighting of the propagation term
    beta = 0.8f,        // Weighting of the advection term
    ballon = 0;         // Balloon force (>0)
  int
    nbiter = 50000,     // Number of iterations
    exp_cont = 1;       // Expansion (1) or contraction (-1) of F0

  // Computation of regularized gradients.
  CImgList<> GradImg = imgIn.get_gradient("xy",4);
```

```cpp
// Function of the geodesic model.
CImg<> f(imgIn.width(),imgIn.height());
cimg_forXY(f,x,y)
{
  float gx = GradImg(0,x,y), gy = GradImg(1,x,y);
  f(x,y) = exp_cont*(1./(1 + std::sqrt(gx*gx + gy*gy)) + ballon);
}


// Computation of the gradient of f.
CImgList<> Grad_f = f.get_gradient();

// Iterative scheme of the propagation algorithm.
for (int iter = 0; iter<nbiter; ++iter)
{
// Spatial gradient of psi.
  CImgList<>
    GradLS_moins = LevelSet.get_gradient("xy",-1),
    GradLS_plus = LevelSet.get_gradient("xy",1);

  cimg_forXY(LevelSet,x,y)
  {
    float
      Dxm = GradLS_moins(0,x,y),  Dxp = GradLS_plus(0,x,y),
      Dym = GradLS_moins(1,x,y),  Dyp = GradLS_plus(1,x,y);

    // Propagation speed term: F0.
    float
      Nabla_plus = std::sqrt(cimg::sqr(std::max(Dxm,0)) +
                             cimg::sqr(std::min(Dxp,0)) +
                             cimg::sqr(std::max(Dym,0)) +
                             cimg::sqr(std::min(Dyp,0))),
      Nabla_moins = std::sqrt(cimg::sqr(std::max(Dxp,0)) +
                              cimg::sqr(std::min(Dxm,0)) +
                              cimg::sqr(std::max(Dyp,0)) +
                              cimg::sqr(std::min(Dym,0))),

      Fprop = -(std::max(f(x,y),0)*Nabla_plus + std::min(f(x,y),0)
          *Nabla_moins);

    // Advection speed term: Fadv.
    float
      u = Grad_f(0,x,y),
      v = Grad_f(1,x,y),
      Fadv = -(std::max(u,0)*Dxm + std::min(u,0)*Dxp +
              std::max(v,0)*Dym + std::min(v,0)*Dyp);

    // Update of the level-set function.
    LevelSet(x,y) += delta_t*(alpha*Fprop + beta*Fadv);
```

```
    }
    if (!(iter%20)) LevelSet.distance_eikonal(10,3);
  }
}
```

Figure 7.1 shows a result of this algorithm.

7.2 Region-based approaches

7.2.1 Introduction

In region-based approaches, pixels with homogeneous features are assigned to the same region or more generally to the same class. In the example of Fig. 7.3, the original image (Fig. 7.3a) is composed of two textures. By using the gradient norm as a feature for a pixel (Fig. 7.3b) we obtain information that is impossible to use to segment the image correctly (i.e., to separate the two textures). Conversely, by using the local variance of the image, segmentation becomes possible (Fig. 7.3c).

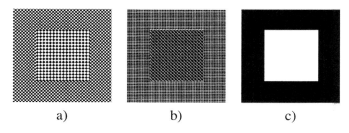

a)   b)   c)

Figure 7.3 – Region-based approach (synthetic case). (a) original image, (b) using gradient, (c) using local variance.

The feature is a concept (most often a vector $\mathbf{x_i} \in \mathbb{R}^d$) that we attach to each pixel i of the image. The computation of features consists in characterizing the pixel by values relative to its intensity (Chapter 3), its gradient (Section 5.1), attributes of geometric type (Section 6.1), texture (Section 6.3) or any other value depending on the application. In the vector, several types of features can coexist.

7.2.2 Histogram-based methods

These methods, although simple to implement, are often of reduced performance because they do not take into account the spatial information underlying the image data. Nevertheless, they can be useful when the images are very well contrasted or when the segmentation is done from a set of images representing the same scene measured with several channels (e.g., radar) or various modalities (e.g., medical imaging). The main idea is to find the different modes of the histogram, representative of as many classes of objects in the image.

If some knowledge about the classes we are looking for is available (in particular the probability of occurrence of a gray level for each class, and a priori probabilities of the classes), then it is possible to use Bayesian decision theory, and choose thresholds which minimize the cost of false errors (Bayesian thresholding, Neyman-Pearson for example). If not, we look for the threshold(s) in the case of several regions or classes from an analysis of the histogram:

- Direct thresholding: thresholds are automatically derived from statistical calculations on the gray levels histogram (modes, zero crossings, maximum entropy, maximum variance, conservation of moments, etc.) and a priori constraints on the number of classes;
- Adaptive thresholding, which uses the previous computation techniques, but with a focus on the local study of the criteria, i.e., on sub-regions (managing the size of the regions, overlaps);
- Hysteresis thresholding, where four threshold values are interactively or automatically defined, determining three classes of pixels: rejected pixels (range s_1-s_2), accepted pixels (range s_3-s_4), and candidate pixels (range s_2-s_3). A connectivity test of the sets (s_2-s_3) and (s_3-s_4) allows to validate or invalidate the candidate pixels: (s_3-s_4) is used as a marker for the reconstruction of (s_2-s_3). It is also possible to control the extension of the reconstruction of (s_2-s_3) by geodesic reconstruction.

OTSU ALGORITHM

Otsu Algorithm [30] supposes that image I of size $nx \times ny$ is composed of only two distinct classes, whose gray level distribution is unknown. The objective is then to find a threshold s such that the distributions of the two classes are separated at best, i.e.,:

1. their means are farthest apart;
2. the distributions are as compact as possible (minimal variances).

Let M be the maximum gray level in I. Given s, the image is partitioned into two classes R_0 and R_1 of cardinalities:

$$n_0(s) = \sum_{g=0}^{s} h(g) \ \text{ and } \ n_1(s) = \sum_{g=s+1}^{M-1} h(g)$$

where h is the histogram of I. Means and variances of both classes are then:

$$\mu_0(s) = \frac{1}{n_0(s)} \sum_{g=0}^{s} gh(g) \ ; \ \mu_1(s) = \frac{1}{n_1(s)} \sum_{g=s+1}^{M-1} gh(g)$$

and $\sigma_0^2(s) = \frac{1}{n_0(s)} \sum_{g=0}^{s} (g - \mu_0(s))^2 h(g)$; $\sigma_1^2(s) = \frac{1}{n_1(s)} \sum_{g=s+1}^{M-1} (g - \mu_1(s))^2 h(g)$.

The sum of intra-class variances is then:

$$\sigma_w^2(s) = \mathbf{P}_0(s)\sigma_0^2(s) + \mathbf{P}_1(s)\sigma_1^2(s) = \frac{\left(n_0(s)\sigma_0^2(s) + n_1(s)\sigma_1^2(s)\right)}{nx \times ny}$$

with: $\mathbf{P}_0(s) = \frac{1}{nx \times ny} \sum_{g=0}^{s} h(g)$ and $\mathbf{P}_1(s) = \frac{1}{nx \times ny} \sum_{g=s+1}^{M-1} h(g)$.

Similarly, the inter-class variance is calculated by:

$$\sigma_b^2(s) = \mathbf{P}_0(s)(\mu_0(s) - \mu_I)^2 + \mathbf{P}_1(s)(\mu_1(s) - \mu_I)^2$$

where $\mu_I = \frac{1}{nx \times ny}(n_0(s)\mu_0(s) + n_1(s)\mu_1(s))$ is the mean of gray levels of I.

The total variance of I is the sum of $\sigma_b^2(s)$ and $\sigma_w^2(s)$. Since it is constant for a given I, the threshold s can be found either by minimizing $\sigma_w^2(s)$, or by maximizing $\sigma_b^2(s)$. This latter choice is used since it depends only on order 1 statistics. Rewriting $\sigma_b^2(s)$ using the expression of μ_I:

$$\sigma_b^2(s) = \frac{n_0(s)n_1(s)(\mu_0(s) - \mu_1(s))^2}{(nx \times ny)^2}$$

that has to be maximized.

Code 7.4 implements the Otsu algorithm and Fig. 7.4 shows some results of the algorithm.

Code 7.4 – Thresholding using Otsu algorithm.

```
/*
  Otsu algorithm

  imgIn      : input image
  nb_levels  : number of bins
*/
float Otsu(CImg<>& imgIn, int nb_levels)
{
  float sigmaBmax = 0;
  long n0 = 0, n1;
  int th = -1;

  CImg<> hist = imgIn.get_histogram(nb_levels);
  cimg_forX(hist,i)
```

```
{
  if (i<nb_levels - 1)
    // If i==nb_levels - 1, all the pixels belong to class 0.
    {
      n0 += hist[i];
      n1 = imgIn.size() - n0;

      float mu0 = 0, mu1 = 0;
      for (int j = 0; j<=i; ++j) mu0 += j*hist[j];
      for (int j = i + 1; j<nb_levels; ++j) mu1 += j*hist[j];
      mu0 /= n0;
      mu1 /= n1;

      if (n0*n1>0)
      {
        float sigmaB = n0*n1*cimg::sqr(mu0 - mu1)/
                            cimg::sqr(imgIn.size());
        if (sigmaB>sigmaBmax)
        {
          sigmaBmax = sigmaB;
          th = i;
        }
      }
    }
}
return (float)th;
}
```

Original image   Thresholded image

Figure 7.4 – Example of use of Otsu algorithm.

BERNSEN ADAPTIVE THRESHOLDING

Bernsen algorithm [4] computes for each pixel (x,y) a threshold based on the minimum and maximum intensities in a neighborhood $\mathcal{V}(x,y)$. If:

$$I_{min}(x,y) = \min_{(i,j)\in\mathcal{V}(x,y)} I(i,j)$$

$$I_{max}(x,y) = \max_{(i,j)\in\mathcal{V}(x,y)} I(i,j)$$

the threshold is simply defined as the mean $s(x,y) = (I_{max}(x,y) + I_{min}(x,y))/2$, as long as the local contrast $c(x,y) = I_{max}(x,y) - I_{min}(x,y)$ is greater than a limit c_{min}. Otherwise, pixels of $\mathcal{V}(x,y)$ all belong to the same region. Code 7.5 implements this algorithm in a very efficient way, thanks to the structure of neighborhoods of *CImg*.

Code 7.5 – Thresholding using Bernsen algorithm.

```
/*
  Bernsen algorithm.

  imgIn : input image
  cmin  : lower bound for the contrast
*/
CImg<> Bernsen(CImg<>& imgIn, float cmin)
{
  CImg<> imgOut(imgIn.width(),imgIn.height(),1,1,0);
  float valClass = 0;

  CImg<> N(5,5);
  cimg_for5x5(imgIn,x,y,0,0,N,float)
  {
    float min, max = N.max_min(min);
    imgOut(x,y) = max - min>cmin ? (max + min)/2 : valClass;
  }
  return imgOut;
}
```

Figure 7.5 presents an example of result.

7.2.3 Thresholding by clustering

Considering features as points of $\mathbb{R}^d$, it is possible to use an unsupervised classification algorithm (also known as clustering algorithm) in this space to find the regions of I: vectors belonging to the same class in $\mathbb{R}^d$ define the pixels belonging to the same region in I. Among all the unsupervised classification algorithms (see for example [3]), we propose to use function minimization methods.

| Original image | Threshold map (c_{min}=20) | Thresholded image |

Figure 7.5 – Bernsen adaptive thresholding.

Formally, the objective is to compute a partition from a set of features of the n pixels of the image $X = \{\mathbf{x}_i, i \in [\![1, n]\!], \mathbf{x}_i \in \mathbb{R}^d\}$, i.e.,, a set of g non-empty parts $P = (P_1, P_2, \cdots P_g)$ of X such that:

1. $(\forall k \neq l) P_k \cap P_l = \emptyset$
2. $\cup_{i=1}^{g} P_i = X$

Clustering methods using function minimization define a cost on the parameterized set of all partitions, and optimize this cost to find the "best" possible partition. Very often, the objective function requires to know a priori the desired number of classes g.

One might think that it is sufficient to enumerate all possible partitions of X and to select only the best one, but the combinatorial explosion of this approach makes this implementation impossible. The number of partitions in g classes of a set with n elements, which we note S_n^g is the Stirling number of the second kind. If $S_0^0 = 1$ and for all $n > 0$, $S_n^0 = S_0^n = 0$, then $S_n^g = S_{n-1}^{g-1} + gS_{n-1}^g$. And

$$S_n^g = \frac{1}{g!} \sum_{i=1}^{g} C_g^i (-1)^{g-i} i^n$$

and then $S_n^g \sim \frac{g^n}{g!}$ when $n \to \infty$. Using a computer calculating 10^6 partitions per second, it would take 126,000 years to compute all the partitions of a set with $n = 25$ elements!

Among the most commonly used cost functions in optimization-based *clustering* methods, we can mention:

- *k-means objective function*: in the corresponding algorithm, each class P_i is represented by a centroid $\mathbf{c_i}$. It is thus assumed that X is embedded in a metric space (X', d) with $\mathbf{c_i} \in X'$. The objective function of the *k-means* measures the squared distance between each $x_i \in X$ and the centroid of its class. Since

$$c_i = arg \min_{c \in X'} \sum_{x \in P_i} d(x, c_i)^2$$

the objective function is

$$f_{k-means} = \sum_{i=1}^{g} \sum_{x \in P_i} d(x, c_i)^2$$

and the optimization is related to the centroids and the memberships of the x to the classes.

- *k-medoids objective function*: similar to the previous one, this function requires that the class centers are elements of X.
- *k-median objective function*: here again, the formulation is the same, the distance is no longer squared:

$$f_{k-median} = \sum_{i=1}^{g} \sum_{x \in P_i} d(x, c_i)$$

These functions search for class centers c_i, and assign each point x_j to the nearest center. Other functions do not use class centers as a goal, such as:

- *the sum of inter-class distances* $f_{SOD} = \sum_{i=1}^{g} \sum_{x,y \in P_i} d(x, y)$

- *MinCut* $f_{cut} = \sum_{i=1}^{g} \sum_{x \in P_i, y \notin P_i} W_{x,y}$, where $W_{x,y}$ is a similarity measure between x and y.

As an example, we implement below the *k-means*, the feature space being $\mathbb{R}^2$, where each vector x_i describing the pixel i has for components:

- the mean gray level in a 5×5 neighborhood;
- the variance of gray levels in a 5×5 neighborhood.

Each feature is normalized to avoid differences in the components' amplitude. Code 7.6 describes how a set of features is computed. Of course, a relevant set of features is always defined according to the application considered.

> **Code 7.6 – Computing feature vectors.**

```
CImg<> Features(CImg<>& imgIn)
{
  int p = 2;
  CImg<> features(imgIn.width(),imgIn.height(),p);

  // For each pixel, mean and variance in a 5x5 neighborhood.
```

```
CImg<> N(5,5);
cimg_for5x5(imgIn,x,y,0,0,N,float)
{
  features(x,y,0) = N.mean();
  features(x,y,1) = N.variance();
}
features.get_shared_slice(0).normalize(0,255);
features.get_shared_slice(1).normalize(0,255);
return features;
}
```

The interest of this type of algorithm is that it makes it possible to do multithresholding, i.e., find g regions or classes in the image.

The exact minimization of $f_{k-means}$ is infeasible (*NP*-complete), and we prefer an algorithmic alternative [26] (Algorithm 4), converging to a local minimum of $f_{k-means}$.

Algorithm 4: *k-means* algorithm.

Input: X, g
Output: A partition P of X into g classes

Initialization: random draw of g points $\mathbf{c_1} \cdots \mathbf{c_g}$
while *non-convergence* **do**

$$(i)(\forall 1 \leq i \leq g) \quad P_i = \{\mathbf{x} \in X; i = \arg\min_j d(\mathbf{x}, \mathbf{c_j})^2\}$$

$$(ii)(\forall 1 \leq i \leq g) \quad \mathbf{c_i} = \frac{1}{|P_i|}\sum_{\mathbf{x} \in P_i}\mathbf{x}$$

Code 7.7 implements step (i), i.e., the assignment of points to classes. The Euclidean metric in $\mathbb{R}^2$ is used here.

Code 7.7 – Assigning points to classes.

```
float d2(CImg<>& g_i, CImg<>& data, int x, int y)
{
  float d = 0;
  cimg_forX(g_i,dim)
    d += cimg::sqr(data(x,y,dim) - g_i(dim));
  return d;
}

/*
  Assigment of points to classes
```

```
  data       : Feature vectors
  g          : Class centers
  label      : Classes of the points
*/
void F(CImg<>& data, CImgList<>& g, CImg<unsigned int>& label)
{
  float dist, min;
  unsigned int jmin;

  // For all feature vectors.
  cimg_forXY(data,x,y)
  {
    // Closest class center.
    min = d2(g[0],data,x,y);
    jmin = 0;

    for (int j = 1; j<g.size(); ++j)
    {
      dist = d2(g[j],data,x,y);
      if (dist<min)
      {
        min = dist;
        jmin = j;
      }
    }
    // Point assignment.
    label(x,y) = jmin;
  }
}
```

Code 7.8 implements step (ii), where new class centers are computed.

Code 7.8 – Computing class centers.

```
/*
  Computing class centers.

  data       : Feature vectors
  label      : Classes of the points
  g          : Class centers
*/
void G(CImg<>& data, CImg<unsigned int>& label, CImgList<>& g)
{
  CImg<int> npc(g.size());
  npc.fill(0);

  // Class centers initialization.
  cimg_forX(g,i)
```

```
   g[i].fill(0);

   // If (x,y) belongs to class k, the  center is modified
   cimg_forXY(label,x,y)
   {
     unsigned int icl = label(x,y);
     cimg_forX(g[icl],dim)
       g[icl](dim) += data(x,y,dim);
     ++npc(icl);
   }

   cimg_forX(g,i)
     g[i] /= npc(i);
}
```

The stopping criterion can take various forms, Code 7.9 proposes to compute the sum of the distances of the feature vectors to their assigned class center, whose small variation will serve as a stopping criterion.

Code 7.9 – Stopping criterion.

```
/*
  K-means stopping criterion.

  data        : Feature vectors
  g           : Class centers
  label : Classes of the points
*/
float W(CImg<>& data, CImgList<>& g, CImg<unsigned int>& label)
{
  float d = 0;

  cimg_forXY(data,x,y)
    d += d2(g[label(x,y)],data,x,y);

  return d;
}
```

Code 7.10 uses previous implementations to segment an image using *k-means* algorithm. The output image is the segmented one.

Code 7.10 – *k-means* algorithm.

```
/*
  K-means algorithm.

  imgIn  : Input image
```

```
  ncl      : Number of classes
*/
CImg<unsigned int> Kmeans(CImg<>& imgIn, int ncl)
{
  // Features.
  CImg<> attributs = Features(imgIn);

  CImg<unsigned int> imgOut(attributs.width(),attributs.height());
  float w0, w;

  // Class centers.
  CImgList<> g(ncl,attributs.depth());

  // Initialization.
  cimg_forX(g,i)
  {
    int
      x = (int)(rand()%attributs.width()),
      y = (int)(rand()%attributs.height());
    cimg_forX(g[i],dim)
      g[i](dim) = attributs(x,y,dim);
  }

  // Initial partition.
  F(attributs,g,imgOut);
  w = W(attributs,g,imgOut);

  float epsilon = 1e-3f;
  do
  {
    w0 = w;
    F(attributs,g,imgOut);
    G(attributs,imgOut,g);
    w = W(attributs,g,imgOut);
  }
  while ((cimg::abs(w - w0)/w0)>epsilon);

  return imgOut;
}
```

Figure 7.6 presents results with respect to the number of classes and the feature space. Three cases are considered:

- D_1: $\mathbf{x} = I(x,y)$, the pixel is described by its gray level;
- D_2: $\mathbf{x} = \left(\|\nabla I(x,y)\| \quad \phi(x,y) \right)^{\top}$, the pixel is described by the norm and phase of its gradient;
- D_3: $\mathbf{x} = \left(\bar{I}(x,y) \quad \sigma^2(I(x,y)) \right)^{\top}$, the pixel is described by the mean and variance of the gray levels in a 5×5 neighborhood.

For each image, the pixel value represents the class to which it has been assigned.

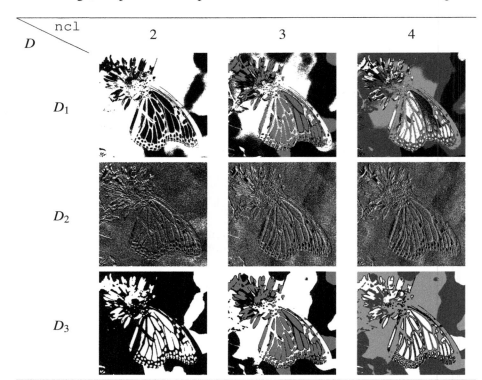

Figure 7.6 – *k-means* results with respect to the number of classes and the feature space.

7.2.4 Transformation of regions

Transformation methods are based on the notion of predicate. A predicate $\mathscr{P}$ is a logical proposition whose value depends on its argument. Here, the predicates concern the regions R_i of the image to be segmented, and the basic predicate in this case is $\mathscr{P}$: "the region R_i is homogeneous". To evaluate $\mathscr{P}$, several arguments are possible, among which:

- the contrast of R_i: ($\mathscr{P}$ is true) $\Leftrightarrow \left(\left[\max_{R_i} I(x,y) - \min_{R_i} I(x,y) \right] < \varepsilon \right)$

- the variance of R_i: ($\mathscr{P}$ is true) $\Leftrightarrow \left(\frac{1}{Card(R_i)} \sum_{R_i} (I(x,y) - \bar{I})^2 < \varepsilon \right)$

- the limited differences: ($\mathscr{P}$ is true) $\Leftrightarrow (\forall (x_1,y_1),(x_2,y_2))$ neighbors, $|I(x_1,y_1) - I(x_2,y_2)| < \varepsilon)$

When all the regions of an image verify $\mathscr{P}$, we say that the partition is verified. Of course, there is a very large number of partitions which verify this property (for example, it is enough to subdivide any region of a partition which verifies $\mathscr{P}$ to obtain a new valid partition), and we do not know how to find all these partitions, nor how to theoretically choose among the partitions verifying $\mathscr{P}$ the one which best solves the segmentation problem.

Empirical criteria are often used, such as the evaluation of the cardinal of the partition (to be minimized), the size of the smallest region (to be maximized), an inter-region distance... In the absence of a defined strategy, here are some general methods for region transformation.

1. **Region growing**: starting from seeds, we successively apply to the image predicates more severe than $\mathscr{P}$. Thus, we start to associate to the seeds only the pixels which are in very good agreement with the predicate. We reduce this severity progressively, and we get closer and closer to $\mathscr{P}$. The *CImg* method `CImg<T>::draw_fill()` implements this approach.

2. **Region splitting**: in a region splitting approach, we consider the whole image as a region R, to which we apply several divisions δ producing R_i^δ regions. We test $\mathscr{P}$ on the R_i^δ and retain the best subdivision, i.e., the one that leads to regions verifying all $\mathscr{P}$, or the one that gives the most regions verifying $\mathscr{P}$, or, if none of the R_i^δ verify $\mathscr{P}$, the one which will provide the best value to a criterion called failure criterion (measure of variance tested in predicates). The strategies of division δ are numerous and include divisions by image triangulation or quadtree decomposition. Chapter 2 shows how to implement such an algorithm.

3. **Region merging**: merging techniques are bottom-up methods during which all pixels are visited. For each pixel neighborhood, $\mathscr{P}$ is tested, and if so the corresponding pixels are grouped in a region. After the whole image has been browsed, the groups of neighborhoods are given the same test, and are joined together if $\mathscr{P}$ is verified. The process is iterated until stability is reached (i.e., when no region merges with another). The tests of union of regions are in general statistical tests. We often assume that there is Gaussian noise with constant mean and in this case the usual statistical tests are the χ^2, the Wilcoxon test, the Student or Fisher-Snedecor test.

4. *Split-and-merge* **approaches**: in order to benefit from the advantages of the region splitting and merging approaches, both techniques can be combined into a *split-and-merge* algorithm which, in a first phase, over-segments the image according to a very strict predicate and then clusters adjacent regions according to a smoother predicate.

7.2.5 Super-pixels partitioning

The *SLIC* (*Simple Linear Iterative Clustering*) method, proposed by R. Achanta et al. [1], defines an algorithm for partitioning color images into super-pixels. Super-pixels are clusters of neighboring pixels forming compact blocks of various shapes, interlocking with each other, while adapting to the local geometry of the image structures.

DESCRIPTION OF THE METHOD

The core of the *SLIC* method is based on a *k-means* classification of all the pixels of the image (Algorithm 4, Section 7.2.3), with the consideration of an objective function that depends on both the color difference between the pixels to be classified and the colors of the centroids, and their respective spatial distance. More precisely, the authors propose to compute the distance $D(\mathbf{x}_1,\mathbf{x}_2)$ between two points $\mathbf{x}_1$ and $\mathbf{x}_2$ by:

$$D(\mathbf{x}_1,\mathbf{x}_2) = \sqrt{d_c^2 + \left(\frac{d_s}{S}\right)^2 m^2} \quad \text{where} \quad d_c = \sqrt{(L_1 - L_2)^2 + (a_1 - a_2)^2 + (b_1 - b_2)^2}$$

and $d_s = \sqrt{(x_1 - x_2)^2 + (y_1 - y_2)^2}$.

The measure d_s corresponds to the *spatial* distance between the two measured points, and d_c to the *color* distance, where the color of each point is expressed in the *CIE* $L^*a^*b^*$ color space. The two constants $S, m \in \mathbb{R}$ are user-defined parameters, which indicate the approximate size of the resulting super-pixels and the regularity of their shape, respectively.

Code 7.11 implements the computation of this objective function.

Code 7.11 – Implementation of the objective function D for *SLIC*.

```
float D(float x1, float y1, float L1, float a1, float b1,
        float x2, float y2, float L2, float a2, float b2,
        float S, float m) {
  return std::sqrt(cimg::sqr(L1 - L2) +
                   cimg::sqr(a1 - a2) +
                   cimg::sqr(b1 - b2) +
                   m*m/(S*S)*(cimg::sqr(x1 - x2) +
                   cimg::sqr(y1 - y2)));
}
```

where the values $L_1, a_1, b_1, L_2, a_2, b_2$ come from the image `lab`, which is a copy of the input color image `img`, expressed in the *CIE* $L^*a^*b^*$ color space:

```
CImg<> lab = img.get_RGBtoLab(); // Conversion RGB -> Lab
```

CENTROID INITIALIZATION

Unlike the classical *k-means* algorithm, the position of the centroids c_i is not chosen randomly in the *SLIC* method, but initialized in multiple steps:

1. Centroids c_i are first set at the center of the rectangles that correspond to the subdivision of the image, as a grid of $S \times S$ cells.
2. The position of each c_i is then shifted toward the point having minimal gradient, in the neighborhood of size $S \times S$.
3. The *Lab* color of this point in the image is finally assigned to the centroid c_i. Each centroid is then defined by five feature values $c_i = (x, y, L, a, b)$.

In the proposed implementation, the set of the N centroids is stored in an image `CImg<float>` of size $N \times 1 \times 1 \times 5$ (i.e., an image organized "row by row," with pixels having five channels). This image is initialized by Code 7.12:

Code 7.12 – Initialization of the centroids for SLIC.

```
CImgList<> grad = lab.get_gradient("xy");
CImg<> grad_norm = (grad>'c').norm(); // Gradient norm
CImg<> centroids(cimg::round(img.width()/S),
cimg::round(img.height()/S),1,5);
int S1 = S/2, S2 = S - 1 - S1;

cimg_forXY(centroids,x,y) {
  int
    xc = x*S + S1,
    yc = y*S + S1,
    x0 = std::max(xc - S1,0),
    y0 = std::max(yc - S1,0),
    x1 = std::min(xc + S2,img.width() - 1),
    y1 = std::min(yc + S2,img.height() - 1);

  // Retrieve the position of the point with the minimal gradient
  // in a neighborhood of size SxS.
  CImg<> st = grad_norm.get_crop(x0,y0,x1,y1).get_stats();
  centroids(x,y,0) = x0 + st[4];
  centroids(x,y,1) = y0 + st[5];
  centroids(x,y,2) = lab(xc,yc,0);
  centroids(x,y,3) = lab(xc,yc,1);
  centroids(x,y,4) = lab(xc,yc,2);
}
// Unroll as an image of size Nx1x1x5.
```

```
centroids.resize(centroids.width()*centroids.height(),1,1,5,-1);
```

ASSIGNMENT OF THE CENTROIDS TO THE IMAGE PIXELS

Once the centroids are initialized, it is possible to assign to each pixel of the image a label i attaching it to the centroid c_i. We take advantage of the fact that the centroids are scattered in the image, not to test the attachment of each pixel to all the existing centroids, but only to those present in a neighborhood of this pixel (of size $2S \times 2S$). This greatly reduces the number of evaluations of the objective function to label these pixels. However, it happens that some pixels are outside these neighborhoods, and they are then labeled in a second step in a more conventional way, by testing them against all existing centroids (code 7.13).

> **Code 7.13 – Assignment of the centroids to the image pixels for SLIC.**

```
CImg<> get_labels(CImg<>& lab, CImg<>& centroids, float S, float m)
  {
  CImg<> labels(lab.width(),lab.height(),1,2,1e20);

  // Test neighbor pixels of each centroid,
  // in a neighborhood of size 2Sx2S.
  cimg_forX(centroids,k)
  {
    float
      xc = centroids(k,0), yc = centroids(k,1),
      Lc = centroids(k,2), ac = centroids(k,3), bc = centroids(k,4);
    int
      x0 = std::max((int)(xc - S),0),
      y0 = std::max((int)(yc - S),0),
      x1 = std::min((int)(xc + S - 1),lab.width() - 1),
      y1 = std::min((int)(yc + S - 1),lab.height() - 1);

    // Loop over the neighborhood (x0,y0)-(x1,y1) of size 2Sx2S.
    cimg_for_inXY(lab,x0,y0,x1,y1,x,y)
    {
      float dist = D(x,y,lab(x,y,0),lab(x,y,1),lab(x,y,2),
                     xc,yc,Lc,ac,bc,S,m);
      if (dist<labels(x,y,1))
      {
        labels(x,y,0) = k;
        labels(x,y,1) = dist;
      }
    }
  }

  // Label remaining pixels by testing them against all centroids.
```

```
cimg_forXY(labels,x,y) if (labels(x,y)>=centroids.width())
{
  // The pixel (x,y) is not assigned yet.
  float
    L = lab(x,y,0),
    a = lab(x,y,1),
    b = lab(x,y,2);
  float distmin = 1e20;
  int kmin = 0;

  // Test against all centroids.
  cimg_forX(centroids,k)
  {
    float
      xc = centroids(k,0),
      yc = centroids(k,1),
      Lc = centroids(k,2),
      ac = centroids(k,3),
      bc = centroids(k,4),
      dist = D(x,y,lab(x,y,0),lab(x,y,1),lab(x,y,2),
               xc,yc,Lc,ac,bc,S,m);
    if (dist<distmin)
    {
      distmin = dist;
      kmin = k;
    }
  }
  labels(x,y,0) = kmin;
  labels(x,y,1) = distmin;
}

return labels;
}
```

The resulting label map is a `CImg<float>` having two channels: the first one gives the centroid label associated to each pixel. The second one keeps the minimal cost D obtained for this pixel.

ITERATIVE UPDATE OF THE CENTROIDS

Once the image pixels have been labeled, the positions and colors of each centroid are updated, using the positions and colors of the pixels that make up the corresponding class. The residual error E, defined as the L_1 norm of the differences between the old centroids and the updated ones, is calculated and the *labeling/updating* process is repeated as long as the centroids change significantly (Code 7.14).

Code 7.14 – Iterative update of the centroids for SLIC.

```
float E = 0; // Residual error
do {
  // Assign a centroid to each image pixel.
  CImg<> labels = get_labels(lab,centroids,S,m);

  // Recompute the average positions and colors of each centroid.
  CImg<>
    next_centroids = centroids.get_fill(0),
    accu(centroids.width(),1,1,1,0);
  cimg_forXY(img,x,y)
  {
    int k = (int)labels(x,y);
    next_centroids(k,0) += x;
    next_centroids(k,1) += y;
    next_centroids(k,2) += lab(x,y,0);
    next_centroids(k,3) += lab(x,y,1);
    next_centroids(k,4) += lab(x,y,2);
    ++accu[k];
  }
  accu.max(1e-8f);
  next_centroids.div(accu);

  // Compute the residual error (using L1 norm).
  E = (next_centroids - centroids).norm(1).sum()/centroids.width();
  centroids.swap(next_centroids);
} while (E>0.25f);
```

At the end of this loop, we have a stable set of centers for the super-pixels of the image.

VISUALIZATION OF THE PARTITION

To visualize the resulting partition, we must recompute first the label map from the positions of the centroids:

```
CImg<> labels = get_labels(lab,centroids,S,m).channel(0);
```

Then, we generate a color rendering out of it, as a new image `visu`, by assigning to each pixel the average *RGB* color of its corresponding centroid (color that has been stored in the channels 2 to 4 of the image `centroids`):

```
CImg<unsigned char>
visu = labels.get_map(centroids.get_channels(2,4)).LabtoRGB();
```

The detection of neighboring pixels having different labels, in the image `labels`, allows to draw a black border around the countours of the super-pixels, in the image

```
visu.
```

```
CImg<> N(9);
cimg_for3x3(labels,x,y,0,0,N,float)
if (N[4]!=N[1] || N[4]!=N[3])
  visu.fillC(x,y,0,0,0,0);
```

Finally, we mark the center of each centroid in `visu` with a semi-transparent red dot:

```
unsigned char red[] = { 255,0,0 };
cimg_forX(centroids,k)
  visu.draw_circle((int)centroids(k,0),(int)centroids(k,1),
                   2,red,0.5f);
```

Figure 7.7 illustrates the partitioning into *SLIC* super-pixels, obtained from the 800×800 kingfisher color image, for two different values of the regularization parameter $m = 1$ and $m = 10$, and for $S = 30$.

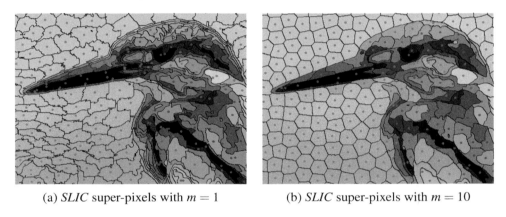

(a) *SLIC* super-pixels with $m = 1$ (b) *SLIC* super-pixels with $m = 10$

Figure 7.7 – Results of partitioning a color image with the *SLIC* algorithm, with different regularization values m.

8. Motion Estimation

Motion estimation is an important topic in image processing, especially in computer vision. Being able to estimate the motion between two images of a sequence opens a field of applications in object tracking, image registration, 3D reconstruction, or even video compression.

Motion analysis can be categorized into three different classes of methods:
- 3D-3D approaches, which involve computing 3D motion from a set of 3D correspondences. Generally, 3D data are difficult to obtain;
- 2D-3D approaches, which estimate the 3D motion from correspondences between a 3D model and 2D projections;
- 2D-2D approaches, which do not use a 3D model and just assume correspondences between 2D projections, from which the 3D motion can be reconstructed.

One of the critical points of motion estimation is therefore the search for correspondences in the frames of a sequence. This includes the correspondence between points (calculated for example by a point detector, cf. Section 6.1), lines or curves (cf. Section 6.2), or even regions (cf. Section 7.2). It is then a question of estimating first a *sparse* displacement field. On the other hand, these correspondences can be also considered pixelwise, in a dense approach of motion estimation.

8.1 Optical flow: dense motion estimation

In a sequence of 2D images, motion is perceptible through changes in the spatial distribution of pixel luminances. The motion perceived in this way is called "apparent" because it does not necessarily correspond to the projection, in the image plane, of the motion taking place in the 3D space (Fig. 8.1). Thus, for example, the apparent velocities of points located on a uniformly rotating sphere are zero, and therefore different from the projections of the true velocities of these points. The field of apparent velocities is called the optical flow. We will use the terms *optical flow* and *velocity field* interchangeably to designate the field of apparent velocities.

Figure 8.1 – Example of calculus of the optical flow. The points located on the rotating tray have zero velocity although they rotate in 3D.

The estimation of apparent motion in a sequence of images is necessarily based on an assumption of conservation of certain photometric properties of the imaged objects. The only basic property that can be attributed to a point in the image is its intensity (or its color). Many authors have shown that motion estimation that uses only the luminance conservation as a constraint is an underdetermined problem:

$$I(\mathbf{m},t) = I(\mathbf{m} - \mathbf{v}t, 0)$$

where $I(\mathbf{m},t)$ is the grayscale at the point $\mathbf{m} = (x,y)^\top$ at time $t > 0$, and $\mathbf{v}(\mathbf{m},t) = (u(\mathbf{m},t), v(\mathbf{m},t))^\top$ is the velocity vector. Under the assumptions of small displacements and spatiotemporal differentiability of luminance, the luminance conservation constraint is generally expressed by the first-order constraint of the motion equation [18]:

$$I_x \cdot u + I_y \cdot v + I_t = \nabla I^\top \mathbf{v} + I_t = 0$$

where I_x, I_y, I_t represent respectively the horizontal/vertical components of the spatial gradient of the luminance I and the temporal gradient of the luminance. This equation allows to uniquely determine the projection of the velocity vector into the direction of the luminance spatial gradient. This projection being locally orthogonal to the photometric boundaries, we name it normal component of the velocity vector. To find the second, tangential component, it is necessary to regularize the estimation, i.e., to reduce the space of solutions by introducing an additional constraint.

8.1.1 Variational methods

Variational methods for motion estimation aim at determining the field of displacement vectors $\mathbf{v} = (u \ v)^\top$ through a functional minimization

$$E(\mathbf{v}) = \int_D F(u, v, u_x, v_x, u_y, v_y, I, I_x, I_y, I_t) d\mathbf{m} \qquad (8.1)$$

where F is a real positive function, with value 0 when the optical flow constraints hold. $*_x$ (respectively $*_y$) indicates the partial derivative of $*$ along the axis x (resp. y). The minimization is performed by iterative schemes which are defined from the Euler-Lagrange equations related to the functional $E(\mathbf{v})$:

$$\frac{\partial F}{\partial u} - \frac{d}{dx}\frac{\partial F}{\partial u_x} - \frac{d}{dy}\frac{\partial F}{\partial u_y} = 0 \quad \text{and} \quad \frac{\partial F}{\partial v} - \frac{d}{dx}\frac{\partial F}{\partial v_x} - \frac{d}{dy}\frac{\partial F}{\partial v_y} = 0$$

HORN AND SCHUNCK METHOD

Horn and Schunck [18] combine the luminance conservation equation with a global regularization to estimate the velocity field $\mathbf{v}$, minimizing:

$$\int_D (\nabla I^T \mathbf{v} + I_t)^2 + \alpha(\|\nabla u\|^2 + \|\nabla v\|^2)d\mathbf{m}$$

defined on the domain D, where the constant α allows to adjust the influence of the regularization term. It is thus a special case of the functional (8.1), with

$$F(u,v,u_x,v_x,u_y,v_y,I,I_x,I_y,I_t) = (u\,I_x + v\,I_y + I_t)^2 + \alpha(u_x^2 + u_y^2 + v_x^2 + v_y^2)$$

Note also that Lucas and Kanade [24] propose a similar minimization, in a discretized and localized way, which will be discussed in Section 8.1.2.

The associated Euler-Lagrange equations are:

$$\begin{cases} (uI_x + vI_y + I_t)I_x + \alpha\nabla^2 u = 0 \\ \\ (uI_x + vI_y + I_t)I_y + \alpha\nabla^2 v = 0 \end{cases}$$

Horn and Schunck propose to re-write these equations with a discrete approximation of the Laplacians $\nabla^2 u = 4(\bar{u} - u)$ and $\nabla^2 v = 4(\bar{v} - v)$ with $\bar{u}$ and $\bar{v}$ being spatially averaged versions of u and v. This leads to a linear system of two equations with two unknowns u and v, at each point (x,y) of the field $\mathbf{v}$:

$$\begin{cases} u(I_x^2 + 4\alpha) + vI_xI_y + (I_xI_t - 4\alpha\bar{u}) = 0 \\ \\ v(I_y^2 + 4\alpha) + uI_xI_y + (I_yI_t - 4\alpha\bar{v}) = 0 \end{cases}$$

Solving this linear system gives the following expressions for u and v:

$$u = \bar{u} - \frac{I_x\left[I_x\bar{u} + I_y\bar{v} + I_t\right]}{I_x^2 + I_y^2 + 4\alpha} \quad \text{and} \quad v = \bar{v} - \frac{I_y\left[I_x\bar{u} + I_y\bar{v} + I_t\right]}{I_x^2 + I_y^2 + 4\alpha}$$

As this solution depends on $\bar{u}$ and $\bar{v}$ (thus the values of u and v in a neighborhood of (x,y)), one has to iterate this calculus, until convergence of the field $\mathbf{v}$, by choosing an initial estimate $\mathbf{v^0}$ that is zero everyhwere.

Code 8.1 proposes the implementation of this method. The input of the function is the initial estimate V of the displacement field (here, an image with two channels, with values set to 0), as well as a sequence seq of two images stacked together along the z-axis, in order to be able to easily estimate the temporal gradient with the function CImg<T>::get_gradient(). As an output, the image V is filled with the estimated displacement field.

Code 8.1 – Horn and Schunck method for estimating the displacement field.

```
/*
   Horn and Schunck method

   V       : Displacement field
   seq     : Sequence of two images, stacked along z
   nb_iters: Number of iterations for the numerical scheme
   alpha   : Regularization weight for the displacement field
*/
void HornSchunck(CImg<>& V, CImg<>& seq,
                 unsigned int nb_iters, float alpha)
{
  // Compute the gradient along the axes 'x','y' and 't'.
  CImgList<> grad = (seq.get_slice(0).get_gradient("xy"),
  seq.get_gradient("z",1));

  CImg<> avg_kernel(3,3,1,1,  // Mask for averaging
                   0., 0.25, 0.,
                   0.25, 0., 0.25,
                   0., 0.25,0.),
         denom = grad[0].get_sqr() + grad[1].get_sqr() + 4*alpha;

  // Iteration loop.
  for (unsigned int iter = 0; iter<nb_iters; ++iter)
  {
    CImg<> Vavg = V.get_convolve(avg_kernel);
    cimg_forXY(V,x,y) {
      float tmp = (grad[0](x,y)*Vavg(x,y,0) +
                   grad[1](x,y)*Vavg(x,y,1) +
                   grad[2](x,y))/denom(x,y);
      V(x,y,0) = Vavg(x,y,0) - grad[0](x,y)*tmp;
      V(x,y,1) = Vavg(x,y,1) - grad[1](x,y)*tmp;
    }
  }
}
```

DIRECT METHOD

A variant of the Horn and Schunck algorithm consists in solving the direct problem, rather than the linearized problem, i.e., minimizing the functional:

$$\int_D (I_{(x+u,y+v,t)} - I_{(x,y,t+dt)})^2 + \alpha(\|\nabla u\|^2 + \|\nabla v\|^2)d\mathbf{m}$$

which is actually a particular case of the functional (8.1) with:

$$F(u,v,u_x,v_x,u_y,v_y,I,I_x,I_y,I_t) = (I_{(x+u,y+v,t)} - I_{(x,y,t+dt)})^2 + \alpha(u_x^2 + u_y^2 + v_x^2 + v_y^2)$$

The associated Euler-Lagrange equations define the gradient descent which minimizes this functional:

$$\begin{cases} \frac{\partial u}{\partial k} = I_{x(x+u,y+v,t)}\delta I + \alpha \nabla^2 u \\[2mm] \frac{\partial v}{\partial k} = I_{y(x+u,y+v,t)}\delta I + \alpha \nabla^2 v \end{cases}$$

with $\delta I = I_{(x+u,y+v,t)} - I_{(x,y,t+dt)}$.

The discretization of this gradient descent by a semi-implicit scheme leads to the following iterative scheme:

$$\begin{cases} u^{k+1} = \frac{u^k + I_{x(x+u,y+v,t)}\delta I + 4\alpha \bar{u}}{1+4\alpha} \\[2mm] v^{k+1} = \frac{v^k + I_{y(x+u,y+v,t)}\delta I + 4\alpha \bar{v}}{1+4\alpha} \end{cases}$$

Code 8.2 shows the implementation of this variant.

Code 8.2 – Direct method for estimating the displacement field.

```
/*
  Direct method

  V       : Displacement field
  seq     : Sequence of two images, stacked along z
  nb_iters: Number of iterations for the numerical scheme
  alpha   : Regularization weight for the displacement field
*/
void DirectMotion(CImg<>& V, CImg<>& seq,
                  unsigned int nb_iters, float alpha)
{
  // Normalize the input sequence
  // (improve convergence of the numerical scheme).
  CImg<> nseq = seq.get_normalize(0,1);
```

```
// Define the spatial averaging mask.
CImg<> avg_kernel(3,3,1,1,
                  0.,  0.25, 0.,
                  0.25, 0.,  0.25,
                  0.,  0.25, 0.);

// Compute image gradient along axes 'x','y'.
CImgList<> grad = seq.get_slice(0).get_gradient("xy");

// Iteration loop.
float denom = 1 + 4*alpha;
for (unsigned int iter = 0; iter<nb_iters; ++iter)
{
  CImg<> Vavg = V.get_convolve(avg_kernel);
  cimg_forXY(V,x,y) {
    float
      X = x + V(x,y,0),
      Y = y + V(x,y,1),
      deltaI = nseq(x,y,0) - nseq.linear_atXY(X,Y,1);
    V(x,y,0) = (V(x,y,0) + deltaI*grad[0].linear_atXY(X,Y,0,0,0) +
               4*alpha*Vavg(x,y,0))/denom;
    V(x,y,1) = (V(x,y,1) + deltaI*grad[1].linear_atXY(X,Y,0,0,0) +
               4*alpha*Vavg(x,y,1))/denom;
  }
}
}
```

MULTI-SCALE RESOLUTION SCHEME

In practice, the determination of the velocity field using this kind of method does not allow to obtain a correct estimation in the case of large displacements. Indeed, the expressions to be iterated are based only on the first derivatives of the image, giving by nature a very local information of the intensity variations (and thus of the motion). It is then classical to use a multi-scale resolution scheme to get rid of this problem:

1. We define a number $N > 0$ of scales.
2. The displacement field **v** is estimated for images with spatial resolution $2^{-N}W \times 2^{-N}H$, where W and H are the width and height of the images.
3. We multiply the estimated vectors by 2 and double the spatial resolution of **v** (using bi-linear interpolation for instance).
4. If $N > 0$, we decrement N, and return to step (2) by considering the **v** estimated in the previous step as the initial displacement field estimate.

The multi-scale resolution scheme can be implemented as proposed in Code 8.3.

```
            Code 8.3 – Multi-scale resolution scheme for the variational methods.

CImg<> V;
for (int N = nb_scales - 1; N>=0; --N)
{
  float factor = (float)std::pow(2,(double)N);
  int
    s_width = std::max(1,(int)(seq.width()/factor)),
    s_height = std::max(1,(int)(seq.height()/factor));
  CImg<> scale_seq = seq.get_resize(s_width,s_height,-100,-100,2).
                     blur(N,N,0,true,false);
  if (V) (V *= 2).resize(s_width,s_height,1,-100,3);
  else V.assign(s_width,s_height,1,2,0);
  DirectMotion(V,scale_seq,nb_iters<<N,alpha);
}
```

The smaller the scale, the more iterations are performed, as this is less time consuming (fewer pixels to process). We also apply a Gaussian smoothing filter on the input images for each scale, with a standard deviation that is as high as the scale is small. This multi-scale resolution scheme is particularly efficient for minimizing the direct problem. And, moreover, it allows estimating motion with large displacement vectors.

ESTIMATION RESULTS

Figure 8.2 shows an application of these algorithms. In order to visualize a vector field, *CImg* proposes the method

```
CImg<T>& draw_quiver(CImg<t1>& flow, const t2 *color, float opacity
   =1, unsigned int sampling=25, float factor=-20,
                    bool is_arrow=true, unsigned int pattern=~0U)
```

which draws the vector field stored in the image flow (the components of each vector being stored as several channels in the image). The pixels for which the motion vectors are displayed, are sampled according to the parameter sampling. The length of the vectors is set by the parameter factor.

8.1.2 Lucas and Kanade differential method

Later, Lucas and Kanade [24] proposed a method based on a local regularization of the velocity field, minimizing:

$$\sum_{\mathbf{m} \in \Omega} W^2(\mathbf{m}) \left[\nabla I(\mathbf{m},t)^\top \mathbf{v} + I_t(\mathbf{m},t) \right]^2$$

where Ω is a spatial neighborhood of the image, $W(\mathbf{m})$ is a windowing function allowing to give more influence to the center of the neighborhood.

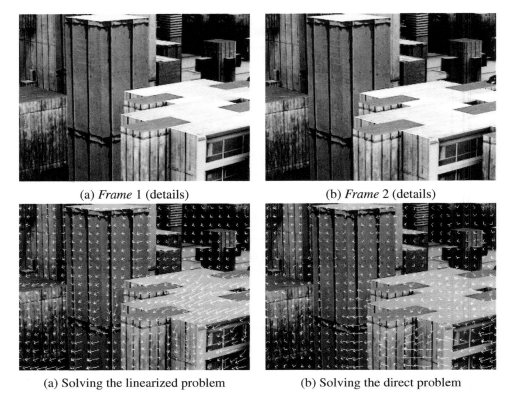

(a) *Frame* 1 (details)   (b) *Frame* 2 (details)

(a) Solving the linearized problem   (b) Solving the direct problem

Figure 8.2 – Results of motion estimation between two *frames* by the method of Horn and Schunck.

The solution of this weighted least square problem is the field $\mathbf{v}$ which verifies the normal equations system $\mathbf{A}^\top W^2 \mathbf{A} \mathbf{v} = \mathbf{A}^\top W^2 \mathbf{b}$, where, for the n points $\mathbf{m}_i \in \Omega$ at time t:

$$\mathbf{A} = [\nabla I(\mathbf{m}_1), \dots, \nabla I(\mathbf{m}_n)]^\top, \quad \mathbf{W} = diag\,[W(\mathbf{m}_1), \dots, W(\mathbf{m}_n)]$$

$$\mathbf{b} = -\left(I_t(\mathbf{m}_1), \dots, I_t(\mathbf{m}_n) \right)^\top$$

We note $\mathbf{B} = \mathbf{A}^\top W^2 \mathbf{A} = \begin{pmatrix} \sum W^2(\mathbf{m}) I_x^2(\mathbf{m}) & \sum W^2(\mathbf{m}) I_x(\mathbf{m}) I_y(\mathbf{m}) \\ \sum W^2(\mathbf{m}) I_y(\mathbf{m}) I_x(\mathbf{m}) & \sum W^2(\mathbf{m}) I_y^2(\mathbf{m}) \end{pmatrix}$.

Code 8.4 shows a basic implementation of this local algorithm.

An analysis of the eigenelements of $\mathbf{B}$ allows to characterize some particular cases. For the normal equations system to have a solution, the matrix $\mathbf{B}$ must be of rank 2. In this case, the solution of this equation is $\mathbf{v} = \mathbf{B}^{-1} \mathbf{A}^\top W^2 \mathbf{b}$. When both eigenvalues are close to zero, the matrix is almost defective and no motion can be estimated. This corresponds to the area of the image with uniform gray levels.

When a single eigenvalue is significantly different from 0 (**B** is almost a rank-1 matrix), the gradients of the luminance have a preferred spatial direction and only the normal velocity can be estimated (aperture problem).

Code 8.4 – Lucas and Kanade algorithm without eigenelement analysis.

```
CImg<> LucasKanade1(CImg<>& seq)
{
  CImg<>
    B(2,2),
    C(1,2),
    W(n,n);
  int
    n = 9,
    n2 = n/2;

  // Velocity field.
  CImg<> field(seq.width(),seq.height(),1,2,0);

  // Gradient of the image sequence.
  CImgList<> grad = seq.get_gradient("xyz",4);

  // Windowing function.
  float
    sigma = 10,
    color = 1;
  W.draw_gaussian(n2,n2,sigma,&color);

  cimg_for_insideXY(seq,i,j,n)
  {
    B.fill(0);
    C.fill(0);
    // Matrix computation.
    for (int k = -n2; k<=n2; ++k)
      for (int l = -n2; l<=n2;++l)
      {
        float temp = cimg::sqr(W(k + n2,l + n2));
        B(0,0) += temp*cimg::sqr(grad(0,i + k,j + l));
        B(1,1) += temp*cimg::sqr(grad(1,i + k,j + l));
        B(0,1) += temp*(grad(0,i + k,j + l)*grad(1,i + k,j + l));
        C(0) += temp*(grad(0,i + k,j + l)*grad(2,i + k,j + l));
        C(1) += temp*(grad(1,i + k,j + l)*grad(2,i + k,j + l));
      }
    B(1,0) = B(0,1);

    // Estimate velocity at (i,j).
    B.invert();
```

```
      CImg<> v = -B*C;
      field(i,j,0,0) = v(0);
      field(i,j,0,1) = v(1);
   }
   return field;
}
```

Code 8.5 shows the algorithm using the amplitudes of the eigenvalues of **B**. Incidentally, note the use of `CImg` instances as matrices in the calculation of eigenelements and in the matrix/vector product (`CImg<> C(1,2)` designates a one-column, two-row matrix [image notation], and thus the matrix product $B*C$ makes sense). Figure 8.3 compares the two displacement fields obtained, with and without the analysis of the spectrum of **B**.

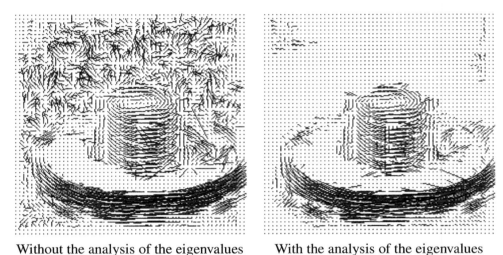

Without the analysis of the eigenvalues   With the analysis of the eigenvalues

Figure 8.3 – Displacement field with the method of Lucas and Kanade, estimated on the images of Fig. 8.1.

Code 8.5 – Lucas and Kanade algorithm with eigenelement analysis.

```
CImg<> LucasKanade2 (CImg<>& seq)
{
  CImg<> B(2,2), C(1,2), W(n,n);
  int n = 9, n2 = n/2;

  CImgList<> eig;

  // Boundaries for the eigenvalues.
  float
```

```
  epsilon = 1e-8f,
  tau_D = 300;

// Velocity field.
CImg<> field(seq.width(),seq.height(),1,2,0);

// Gradient of the image sequence.
CImgList<> grad = seq.get_gradient("xyz",4);

// Windowing function.
float
  sigma = 10,
  color = 1;
W.draw_gaussian(n2,n2,sigma,&color);

cimg_for_insideXY(seq,i,j,n)
{
  B.fill(0);
  C.fill(0);
  // Compute M and b in a neighborhood n*n.
  for (int k = -n2; k<=n2; ++k)
    for (int l = -n2; l<=n2; ++l)
      {
        float temp = cimg::sqr(W(k + n2,l + n2));
        B(0,0) += temp*cimg::sqr(grad(0,i + k,j + l));
        B(1,1) += temp*cimg::sqr(grad(1,i + k,j + l));
        B(0,1) += temp*(grad(0,i + k,j + l)*grad(1,i + k,j + l));
        C(0)   += temp*(grad(0,i + k,j + l)*grad(2,i + k,j + l));
        C(1)   += temp*(grad(1,i + k,j + l)*grad(2,i + k,j + l));
      }
  B(1,0) = B(0,1);

  // Analysis of the spectre of B.
  eig = B.get_symmetric_eigen();
  CImg<> &val = eig[0], &vec = eig[1];

  B.invert();

  // Eigenvalues of B are high.
  if (std::min(val(0),val(1))>=tau_D)
  {
    CImg<> v = -B*C;
    field(i,j,0,0) = v(0);
    field(i,j,0,1) = v(1);
  }
  // Only one eigenvalue is high, and B is not singular : Project
      v.
  else if (val(1)>=tau_D && cimg::abs(B.det())>epsilon)
  {
```

```
      CImg<> v = -B*C;
      const float tmp = v(0)*vec(1,0) + v(1)*vec(0,0);
      field(i,j,0,0) = -tmp*vec(1,0);
      field(i,j,0,1) = tmp*vec(0,0);
    }
  }
  return field;
}
```

8.1.3 Affine flow

The assumption of a constant flow in a neighborhood can be insufficient, especially when the objects to be tracked are large. In order to handle local deformations, an affine model may be more appropriate.

In the vicinity of a point $\mathbf{m_0} = (x_0, y_0)^\top$, the velocity field is assumed to be affine:

$$\mathbf{v} = \begin{pmatrix} a_1 & a_2 \\ a_3 & a_4 \end{pmatrix} (\mathbf{m} - \mathbf{m_0}) + \begin{pmatrix} a_5 \\ a_6 \end{pmatrix} = \mathbf{A}(\mathbf{m})\mathbf{a}$$

with

$$\mathbf{A}(\mathbf{m}) = \begin{pmatrix} x - x_0 & y - y_0 & 0 & 0 & 1 & 0 \\ 0 & 0 & x - x_0 & y - y_0 & 0 & 1 \end{pmatrix} \text{ and } \mathbf{a} = (a_i) \in \mathbb{R}^6$$

The equation of motion constraint is then $\nabla I^\top \mathbf{v} + I_t = \nabla I^\top \mathbf{A}\mathbf{a} + I_t = 0$ and as for Lucas and Kanade algorithm, the velocity field is given by the solution of $\mathbf{M}\mathbf{a} = \mathbf{b}$ with

$$\mathbf{M} = \sum_{\mathbf{m} \in \Omega} W^2(\mathbf{m})\mathbf{A}(\mathbf{m})^\top \nabla I(\mathbf{m}) \nabla I(\mathbf{m})^\top \mathbf{A}(\mathbf{m}) \text{ and } \mathbf{b} = -\sum_{\mathbf{m} \in \Omega} W^2(\mathbf{m})\mathbf{A}(\mathbf{m})^\top \nabla I(\mathbf{m}) I_t(\mathbf{m})$$

At a lower cost, this model can be used to search for similarities (uniform scale change α, rotation of angle θ and translation of vector $\mathbf{t}$). For this:

$$\mathbf{v} = \alpha \begin{pmatrix} cos(\theta) & -sin(\theta) \\ sin(\theta) & cos(\theta) \end{pmatrix} (\mathbf{m} - \mathbf{m_0}) + \mathbf{t} = \mathbf{A}\mathbf{a}$$

where $\mathbf{A} = \begin{pmatrix} x - x_0 & -y + y_0 & 1 & 0 \\ y - y_0 & x - x_0 & 0 & 1 \end{pmatrix}$ and $\mathbf{a} = (\alpha cos(\theta) \quad \alpha sin(\theta) \quad t_1 \quad t_2)^\top$.

This can be easily done with *CImg*, using here again images as matrices. Code 8.6 proposes, for a given point $\mathbf{m} = (x, y)^\top$, and a neighborhood of size n, the procedure to estimate the parameters of the similarity for a sequence of images seq.

Code 8.6 – **Calculus of the parameters of a similarity at a point m.**

```
CImg<> M(4,4), b(1,4), W(n,n);
int n = 9, n2 = n/2;

CImgList<> grad = seq.get_gradient("xyz",4);

// Windowing function.
float
  sigma = 10,
  color = 1;

W.draw_gaussian(n2,n2,sigma,&color);
M.fill(0);
b.fill(0);

for (int k = -n2; k<=n2; ++k)
  for (int l = -n2; l<=n2; ++l)
  {
    float temp = cimg::sqr(W(k + n2,l + n2));
    A(0,0) = k; A(1,0) = -1; A(2,0) = 1; A(3,0) = 0;
    A(0,1) = 1; A(1,1) = k;  A(2,1) = 0; A(3,1) = 1;
    CImg<> At = A.get_transpose();

    g(0,0) = grad(0,x + k,y + l);
    g(0,1) = grad(1,x + k,y + l);

    M += temp*At*g*g.get_transpose()*A;
    b += temp*At*g*grad(2,x + k,y + l);
  }

// Compute the solution of Ma = b.
CImg<> a = M.invert()*b;

// Compute the parameters of the similarity.
float
  theta = std::atan2(a(1),a(0)),
  alpha = a(0)/std::cos(theta);

CImg<> t = CImg<>::vector(a(2),a(3));
```

8.2 Sparse estimation

In the case of a sparse approach, we estimate the displacement field only at certain points corresponding to particular primitives (points, curves, objects, regions of interest...) detected in the input images. Also called "matching" techniques, we illustrate these methods in two cases:

1. In the case of two images only, the analysis consists in finding the disparities between two consecutive images in the sequence. For a sequence of several images, each pair is then considered.
2. Tracking the movement of a primitive through a sequence of images as a whole.

8.2.1 Displacement field using spatial correlation

Let $I(t_1)$ and $I(t_2)$ be two image frames taken at two distinct times t_1 and t_2, and $\mathcal{R}$ a region of $I(t_1)$. Under the assumption of small geometric deformations, the location of $\mathcal{R}$ in $I(t_2)$ can be found by computing the correlation between $\mathcal{R}$ and *patches* $\mathcal{P}$ (having the same size as $\mathcal{R}$) of the image $I(t_2)$.

Code 8.7 presents the calculation of the correlation between the *patches* extracted from the image $I(t_2) = $ I(1), in an area defined by the dimensions area, and a reference image T. The *patch* center which maximizes the correlation, as well as the corresponding correlation value, are used to display the optimal *patch* containing the object to track, having size size, initially located at coordinates pos in the image $I(t_1) = $ I(0). The method CImg<T>::draw_rectangle is used to draw the bounding rectangle on the image.

```
CImg<T>& draw_rectangle(int x0, int y0, int x1, int y1,
                        const tc *color, float opacity, unsigned int
                        pattern)
```

Figure 8.4 shows a result obtained from two non-consecutive images of a video sequence. The first cyclist, identified by its position pos in the initial image (arrow) is tracked in the image $I(t_2)$ by the search of the maximal correlation in a neighborhood of size area centered around the initial position. A bounding box is used to identify the tracked object. Figure 8.5 shows the result of the tracking on nine consecutive images.

Code 8.7 – Estimate the object position by correlation.

```
/*
  Object tracking by cross-correlation.

  I    : Image sequence
  pos  : Initial position of the object to track
  size : Size of the template window around p
  area : Size of the lookup window
*/
CImg<> SuiviCC(CImgList<>& I, CImg<int>& pos,
               CImg<int>& size, CImg<int>& area)
{
  CImg<int>
```

```
      prevPos(pos),
      currPos(1,2);

   // Normalized reference.
   CImg<> T = I[0].get_crop(pos(0) - size(0),pos(1) - size(1),
                            pos(0) + size(0),pos(1) + size(1));
   int
     w = T.width(),
     h = T.height();
   T -= T.sum()/(w*h);
   float
     norm = T.magnitude(),
     correlation,
     corr = -1;

   // Max correlation in the region 'area'.
   for (int x = prevPos(0) - area(0); x<=prevPos(0) + area(0); ++x)
   {
     for (int y = prevPos(1) - area(0); y<=prevPos(1) + area(1); ++y)
     {
       CImg<> u = I[1].get_crop(x - w/2,y - h/2,x + w/2,y + h/2);
       u -= u.sum()/(u.width()*u.height());
       correlation = u.dot(T)/(u.magnitude()*norm);
       if (correlation>corr)
       {
         corr = correlation;
         currPos(0,0) = x;
         currPos(0,1) = y;
       }
     }
   }

   // Region of interest.
   unsigned char red [3] = {255,0,0};
   CImg<> imgOut(I[1]);
   imgOut.draw_rectangle(currPos(0) - size(0),currPos(1) - size(1),
                         currPos(0) + size(0),currPos(1) + size(1),
                         red,1,~0U);
   return imgOut;
}
```

If, instead of $\mathscr{R}$, n points are to be matched (e.g., corners detected by Harris, cf. Section 6.1), the idea is to find a function to match the n points in $I(t_1)$ with the n points of $I(t_2)$, so that no two points in the initial image are matched with the same point in $I(t_2)$.

Depending on the difference $t_2 - t_1$, the matches can be anywhere in $I(t_2)$, which makes the problem combinatorial in complexity. For example, if $n = 5$, the number of

| Image $I(t_1)$ | Image $I(t_2)$ | Detected object in $I(t_2)$ |

Figure 8.4 – Object tracking by searching for maximal correlation.

possible matches is $5! = 120$. To reduce this complexity, we use physical or heuristic constraints, such as:

- maximum displacement constraints: the point **m** can only have moved in a ball of radius R, depending on an assumption of maximum speed;
- model constraints: we assume a certain type of displacement model, parametric for example;
- joint motion constraints: the n points are assumed to move in the same way (rigidity constraint).

The difficulty lies in the translation of these heuristics into quantitative expressions allowing to mathematically solve the problem. As a result, we often use dynamic programming to solve these optimization tasks.

While these methods are easy to implement and effective on well-detected regions or points, they rely on an assumption of regularity that is ill-suited to track multiple objects, especially since these objects may overlap. In the case of false detection, moreover, the tracking may have difficulties in re-aligning with the object of interest (Fig. 8.6).

8.2.2 Displacement field using phase correlation

The technique of image registration by phase correlation allows to estimate a shift between two images, thanks to a frequency analysis in the Fourier domain.

Let I_1 and I_2 be two images, of identical size, acquired with the same acquisition system. We are looking for two images that, after registration, will have the same gray levels for an identical position. We are therefore looking for a translation, noted $\mathbf{t} = (t_x, t_y)^\top$, verifying the relation $I_2(x,y) = I_1(x + t_x, y + t_y)$ for all (x, y).

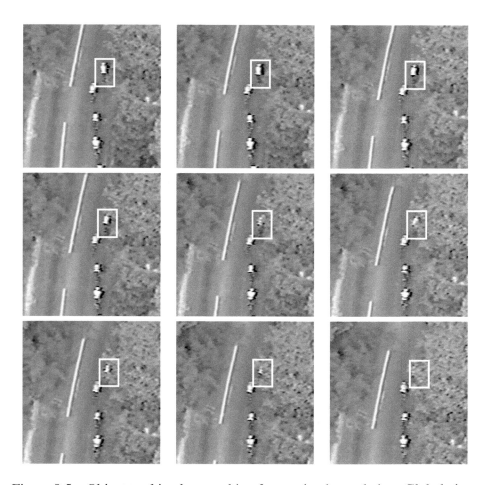

Figure 8.5 – Object tracking by searching for maximal correlation. Global view.

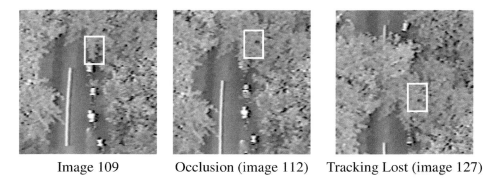

Image 109   Occlusion (image 112)   Tracking Lost (image 127)

Figure 8.6 – Tracking lost due to occlusion.

ANALYSIS IN THE FOURIER SPACE

Using the properties of the Fourier space (Section 5.3.2), this relation can be written as:

$$\hat{I}_2(f_x, f_y) = \hat{I}_1(f_x, f_y) \times e^{-j2\pi(f_x t_x + f_y t_y)}$$

The Fourier transforms of both images have the same modulus but above all have a phase difference directly related to the translation. This change in phase allows to estimate the translation, hence the name of the method.

The use of the cross-power spectrum isolates this phase difference. It is calculated from the two images I_1 and I_2 by:

$$R(f_x, f_y) = \frac{\hat{I}_1(f_x, f_y)\overline{\hat{I}_2(f_x, f_y)}}{\|\hat{I}_1(f_x, f_y)\hat{I}_2(f_x, f_y)\|}.$$

We have then

$$
R(f_x, f_y) = \frac{\hat{I}_1(f_x, f_y)\overline{\hat{I}_2(f_x, f_y)}}{\|\hat{I}_1(f_x, f_y)\hat{I}_2(f_x, f_y)\|} = \frac{\hat{I}_1(f_x, f_y)\overline{\hat{I}_1(f_x, f_y) \times e^{-j2\pi(f_x t_x + f_y t_y)}}}{\|\hat{I}_1(f_x, f_y)\hat{I}_1(f_x, f_y) \times e^{-j2\pi(f_x t_x + f_y t_y)}\|}
$$

$$
= \frac{\|\hat{I}_1(f_x, f_y)\|^2 \times e^{+j2\pi(f_x t_x + f_y t_y)}}{\|\hat{I}_1(f_x, f_y)\|^2} = e^{j2\pi(f_x t_x + f_y t_y)}
$$

Here, the cross-power spectrum has a very interesting form since it is a pure monochromatic wave in Fourier space. Then, the inverse Fourier transform will be a Dirac distribution localized to the value of the corresponding shift. The inverse Fourier transform of the cross-power spectrum is called the phase correlation, denoted by r where $\hat{r}(f_x, f_y) = R(f_x, f_y)$. Thus, we obtain:

$$r(x, y) = \delta(x + t_x, y + t_y).$$

Finally, to estimate the translation between two images, it is sufficient to search for the maximum of their phase correlation. Algorithm 5 summarizes this method.

Code 8.8 implements the calculation of the phase correlation for the estimation of the translation between two images.

Code 8.8 – Estimation of a translation by phase correlation.

```
/*
   Image registration by phase correlation

   IS : Source image
```

Algorithm 5: Displacement field using phase correlation.

Data: Two images I_1 and I_2
Result: The translation $\mathbf{t} = (t_x, t_y)^\top$
Compute the Fourier transform of I_1: $\hat{I}_1(f_x, f_y)$;
Compute the Fourier transform of I_1: $\hat{I}_2(f_x, f_y)$;
Compute the cross-power spectrum: $R(f_x, f_y)$;
Compute the phase correlation by inverse Fourier transform of R: $r(x, y)$;
return $(t_x, t_y) = \underset{(x,y)}{\arg\max}\, r(x, y)$

```
  IC : Target image
  tx : Horizontal component of the translation (output)
  ty : Vertical component of the translation (output)
*/
void CorrelationPhase(CImg<>& IS, CImg<>& IC, int& tx, int& ty)
{
  float eps = 1.0e-8f;
  // Compute the Fourier transform of the images.
  CImgList<>    fft_S = IS.get_FFT("xy"),
                fft_T = IC.get_FFT("xy");

  // Compute the cross-power spectrum:
  CImg<>
    r_R = fft_S(0).get_mul(fft_T(0)) + fft_S(1).get_mul(fft_T(1)),
    i_R = fft_T(0).get_mul(fft_S(1)) - fft_S(0).get_mul(fft_T(1)),
    deno_R = (r_R.get_mul(r_R) + i_R.get_mul(i_R)).get_sqrt();
  r_R.div(deno_R + eps);
  i_R.div(deno_R + eps);
  // Compute the phase correlation (r = TF-1(R)).
  CImg<>::FFT(r_R,i_R,true);
  CImg<> r = (r_R.get_mul(r_R) + i_R.get_mul(i_R)).get_sqrt();

  // Look for the maximum of the phase correlation.
  float r_max = 0;
  int   w = IS.width(),
        h = IS.height();

  cimg_forXY(r,x,y)
  {
    if (r(x,y)>r_max) {
      r_max = r(x,y);
      tx = -((x - 1 + (w/4))%(w/2) - (w/4) + 1);
      ty = -((y - 1 + (h/4))%(h/2) - (h/4) + 1);
    }
  }
}
```

a) Extraction of images I_1 and I_2 with $\mathbf{t} = (-120, 117)^{\top}$

b) Result of the registration by phase correlation, by merging the image I_2 with input image I_1

c) Image I_1 (noisy)   d) Image I_2 (noisy)

e) Phase correlation: the maximum gives the translation between the two images

Figure 8.7 – Image registration by phase correlation, on a synthetic displacement, by extracting regions of interest for images I_1 and I_2.

In Fig. 8.7, Code 8.8 is first tested for synthetic displacements. We extract two images (Fig. 8.7a) from an input image, then we add noise (Fig. 8.7c and 8.7d) to show the good performances of this approach even for noisy images. Indeed, the phase is less sensitive to noise in an image than the previous correlation techniques seen in Section 8.2.1. In Fig. 8.7e we can observe that the phase correlation has a sharp maximum. Figure 8.7b illustrates the final result, with images I_1, I_2, the displacement estimated by the method as well as the starting image merged on the three color channels of an image.

REPRESENTATION CHANGES

The previous technique estimates a translation between two images, but it is also possible to use it for other transformations. Using variable substitution, we can convert for example a rotation or a similarity into a translation:

- Rotation: we consider that the image I_2 is a rotation of angle θ_0 of the image I_1. By changing the variable from a cartesian space to a polar space, we get the following relation: $I_2(\rho, \theta) = I_1(\rho, \theta - \theta_0)$. With this new representation, estimating a rotation is equivalent to estimating a translation vector $(0, \theta_0)$ in the polar space;
- Similarity: we consider that I_2 is a scaling of factor (s_x, s_y) of the image I_1. By changing the variable from a cartesian space to a logarithmic space, we have $I_2(\log(x), \log(y)) = I_1(\log(x) + \log(s_x), \log(y) + \log(s_y))$. With this new representation, estimating the scaling is equivalent to estimating a translation vector $(s_x, s_y)^\top$ in the logarithmic space.

OBJECT TRACKING

Image registration by phase correlation can be used for sparse motion estimation. Code 8.9 shows how to perform object tracking using *CImg*.

Code 8.9 – Object tracking by phase correlation.

```
/*
  Object tracking by phase correlation.
*/
int main(int argc, const char **argv)
{
  cimg_usage("Object tracking by image registration (phase
     correlation)");
  int
    roi_x0 = cimg_option("-x",102,"X-coordinate of the ROI"),
    roi_y0 = cimg_option("-y",151,"Y-coordinate of the ROI"),
    roi_w  = cimg_option("-w",64,"Width or the ROI"),
    roi_h  = cimg_option("-h",64,"Height of the ROI");
  bool save = cimg_option("-o",1,"Save (0 or 1)");

  // Read an image sequence.
  CImg<> img = CImg<>("frame_0000.bmp").channel(0);
  img.append(CImg<>("frame_0005.bmp").channel(0),'z');
  img.append(CImg<>("frame_0010.bmp").channel(0),'z');
  ...;
  img.append(CImg<>("frame_0135.bmp").channel(0),'z');
```

```
img.append(CImg<>("frame_0140.bmp").channel(0),'z');

int
  tx,ty,          // Translation
  x0 = roi_x0,    // Object position (X-coordinate)
  y0 = roi_y0;    // Object position (Y-coordinate)

for (int f = 0; f<img.depth() - 1; ++f)
{
  CImg<>
    IS = img.get_slice(f).
             crop(x0,y0,x0 + roi_w - 1,y0 + roi_h - 1),
    IC = img.get_slice(f + 1).
             crop(x0,y0,x0 + roi_w - 1,y0 + roi_h - 1);

  // Motion estimation by phase correlation.
  PhaseCorrelation(IS,IC,tx,ty);

  // Update object position.
  x0 -= tx;
  y0 -= ty;

  // Save object tracking.
  if (save)
  {
    CImg<unsigned char> out(img.width(),img.height(),1,3,0);
    unsigned char mycolor[] = { 243,102,25 };

    out.draw_image(0,0,0,0,img.get_slice(f + 1),1).
      draw_image(0,0,0,1,img.get_slice(f + 1),1).
      draw_image(0,0,0,2,img.get_slice(f + 1),1).
      draw_rectangle(x0,y0,
                     x0 + roi_w - 1,y0 + roi_h - 1,mycolor,0.5f);

    std::string fileName = "Tracking_" + std::to_string(f + 1) + "
      .png";
    out.normalize(0,255).save_png(fileName.c_str());
  }
}
  return 0;
}
```

Figure 8.8 shows the results obtained using Code 8.9. This approach has several limitations. In order to robustly estimate the translation of the object, the background of the object must be uniform. Otherwise, there would be two moving areas (the object and the background) and therefore the theoretical results previously given are no longer valid. Finally, if the object is occluded, this tracking method can "lose" the object, because the method does not take into account the dynamics of the object. This type of information can be integrated in the tracking, thanks to Kalman filtering.

Figure 8.8 – Object tracking using image registration based on phase correlation.

8.2.3 Kalman filtering

The Kalman filter [21] is an infinite impulse response filter that estimates the states
of a dynamic system from a series of incomplete or noisy measurements. It has
many applications in various domains. Here we are interested in its application to the
tracking of objects in image sequences.

Let $(I_0, I_1 \cdots I_T)$ be an image sequence acquired at different times $t_0 = 0 \cdots t_T = T$,
by assuming that the temporal discretization step $\Delta t = t_{i+1} - t_i$ is small enough to
consider that the motion is linear from one image to another.

Let $\mathbf{m}_i = (x_i \ y_i)^\top$ be a point of interest detected in the ith frame, moving with a
speed of $\mathbf{v}_i = (u_i \ v_i)^\top$ (e.g., estimated by the optical flow). In the image plane, one
can describe the motion of a point by a state vector $\mathbf{s}_i = \begin{pmatrix} x_i & y_i & u_i & v_i \end{pmatrix}^\top$. We will
denote by $\mathbf{z}_i$ the *measure* of the position of the point of interest in the image i.

The goal of the Kalman filter is to compute $\mathbf{s}_i$, knowing $\mathbf{s}_{i-1}$ and $\mathbf{z}_i$. Under the
assumption of a Gaussian noise, the prediction of the current state $\mathbf{s}_i \sim \mathcal{N}(\mathbf{D}_i\mathbf{s}_{i-1}; \Sigma_{d,i})$
where $\mathbf{D}_i$ is a dynamical model of its evolution state. Similarly, we suppose that the
measure $\mathbf{z}_i \sim \mathcal{N}(\mathbf{M}_i\mathbf{s}_i; \Sigma_{m,i})$, where $\mathbf{M}_i$ is a precision model of the measures.

$\mathbf{s}_0$ and $\Sigma_{d,0}, \Sigma_{m,0}$ are assumed to be known. We denote by Σ_i the a priori estimation
of the error.

The Kalman filter works in two steps:
1. A *prediction* step:

$$\mathbf{s}_i = \mathbf{D}_i\mathbf{s}_{i-1}$$
$$\Sigma_i = \Sigma_{d,i} + \mathbf{D}_i\Sigma_{i-1}\mathbf{D}_i^{\top}$$

2. A *correction* step:

$$\mathbf{K}_i = \Sigma_i\mathbf{M}_i^{\top}\left(\mathbf{M}_i\Sigma_i\mathbf{M}_i^{\top} + \Sigma_{m,i}\right)^{-1}$$
$$\mathbf{s}_i = \mathbf{s}_i + \mathbf{K}_i(\mathbf{z}_i - \mathbf{M}_i\mathbf{s}_i)$$
$$\Sigma_i = (I - \mathbf{K}_i\mathbf{M}_i)\Sigma_i$$

The prediction step derives an estimate of the state at time i from the prediction at time $i-1$, as well as the error covariance matrix based on the error covariance matrix of the system at the previous time. The correction step corrects the estimate provided by the prediction step.

Typically, we choose $\mathbf{D_i} = \mathbf{D}$ and $\mathbf{M_i} = \mathbf{M}$. In prediction, the uncertainty increases with time, and these error models can be used to state whether one should rely more on the measurements made in the image or the calculations made. The gain $\mathbf{K}_i$ specifies how strongly the current state $\mathbf{s}_i$ tends toward the measurements $\mathbf{z}_i$ with time, and also how much the accuracy of the estimate of $\mathbf{s}_i$ will be reduced with time.

In the case we are interested in (the state is described by the positions and the speed of the tracked object), we have in particular

$$\mathbf{M} = \begin{pmatrix} 1 & 0 & 0 & 0 \\ 0 & 1 & 0 & 0 \end{pmatrix} \text{ and } \mathbf{D} = \begin{pmatrix} 1 & 0 & \Delta t & 0 \\ 0 & 1 & 0 & \Delta t \\ 0 & 0 & 1 & 0 \\ 0 & 0 & 0 & 1 \end{pmatrix}$$

Code 8.10 proposes the implementation of linear Kalman filtering. Figure 8.9 illustrates the fact that the Kalman filtering manages to recover the object to be tracked, even after an occultation (see Figure 8.6 for comparison). The image on the right, much further in the sequence, illustrates the fact that the cyclist was found after occultation by the trees.

Code 8.10 – Kalman filter.

```
/*
  Linear Kalman filter.

  I      : List of images
  pos    : Initial position of the tracked object
  size   : Size of the window surrounding the object
```

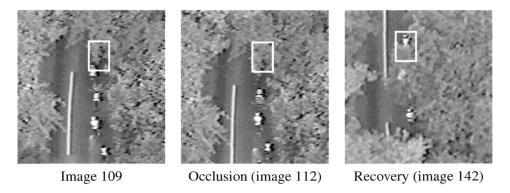

Image 109   Occlusion (image 112)   Recovery (image 142)

Figure 8.9 – Post-occlusion tracking recovery by Kalman filtering.

```
*/
void Kalman(CImgList<>& I, CImg<int>& pos, CImg<int>& size)
{
  CImg<>
    prevState(1,4),
    currState(1,4);
  CImg<int>
    prevPos(pos),
    currPos(1,2),
    estimPos(1,2);

  prevState(0,0) = pos(0);
  prevState(0,1) = pos(1);
  prevState(0,2) = 0;
  prevState(0,3) = 0;

  CImg<> T = I[0].get_crop(pos(0) - size(0), pos(1) - size(1),
                           pos(0) + size(0), pos(1) + size(1));

  // Matrix D, constant speed model and Delta t = 1.
  CImg<> D = CImg<>::identity_matrix(4);
  D(2,0) = D(3,1) = 1;

  // Matrix M.
  CImg<> M(4,2,1,1,0);
  M(0,0) = M(1,1) = 1;
  CImg<> Mt = M.get_transpose();

  // Covariance of the model.
  CImg<> SigmaD = CImg<>::identity_matrix(4)*5;
  SigmaD(2,2) = SigmaD(3,3) = 1;

  // Covariance of the measure.
```

```
CImg<> SigmaM = CImg<>::identity_matrix(2)*50;

// A priori estimation of the error.
CImg<> PkPrevious(4,4,1,1,0);

// A posteriori estimation of the error.
CImg<> PkCurrent(4,4);
for (int i = 1; i<I.size(); ++i)
{
  // Prediction.
  currState = D*prevState;
  PkCurrent = SigmaD + D*PkPrevious*D.get_transpose();

  // Correction.
  CImg<> Kt = PkCurrent*Mt*((M*PkCurrent*Mt+ SigmaM).get_invert())
     ;
  currState = currState + Kt*(estimPos - M*currState);
  CImg<> I = CImg<>::identity_matrix(PkCurrent.width());
  PkCurrent = (I - Kt*M)*PkCurrent;

  // Update of the position.
  currPos(0) = (int)currState(0);
  currPos(1) = (int)currState(1);
  prevPos(0) = (int)currState(0);
  prevPos(1) = (int)currState(1);
  prevState = currState;
  PkPrevious = PkCurrent;
}
}
```

In general, the Kalman filter quantifies the uncertainty in the state estimate. This information allows the point detector to automatically size the region of interest for the primitive in the next image. This region is centered on the best estimated position and its width is proportional to the uncertainty. In a properly designed filter, the value of this uncertainty decreases rapidly with time and the region shrinks accordingly.

Two problems arise for the actual implementation of this algorithm:
- missing data: filtering relies on prior knowledge of s_0 and $\Sigma_{d,0}, \Sigma_{m,0}$;
- the data association problem: in the presence of several primitives of interest (points, curves) and several measurements, which measurement should be associated with which primitive?

To better manage occlusions, it is possible to modify the algorithm, by varying $\Sigma_{m,i}$ according to the maximum correlation found: if the latter is low, then the diagonal terms can be set to very large values.

9. Multispectral Approaches

A multispectral image is an image that captures data in specific wavelength ranges across the electromagnetic spectrum. When acquiring such an image, wavelengths are separated by filters, or detected via the use of instruments sensitive to particular wavelengths, including light from frequencies beyond the visible light range (infrared, ultraviolet). By extension, the term *multispectral* is also used for acquisitions of objects made by imagers that use particular techniques (diffusion MRI for example), and which lead to images having multiple channels.

Multispectral imaging allows the extraction of additional information that the human eye cannot necessarily capture. It permits the exploitation of redundancies and complementarities between the acquisition channels, and in addition to the extraction of relevant information, the analysis of these images can lead to a reduced and synthetic representation of the information contained in the whole set of channels. Numerous applications are concerned ranging from satellite imagery to astronomy, including military applications, medicine or art.

Generally speaking, *multispectral* imaging refers to data with a low (two to ten) number of acquisition channels. *Hyperspectral* imaging is dedicated to studies where the number of channels is higher (sometimes several hundreds). Color images (three or four channels) are of course part of multispectral images.

CImg library can handle multispectral images through the fourth dimension (spectral dimension, named `spectrum`) objects of type `CImg<T>`. A 2D multispectral image with p channels will thus be defined as a `CImg<>(w,h,1,p)`. Various *CImg* methods allow to recover the number of channels (`CImg<T>::spectrum()`), to assign or retrieve images to channels (`CImg<T>::get_[shared_]channel()`), etc. There is no hard limit on the number of possible channels, except the memory.

9.1 Dimension reduction

A multi-spectral image is thus a 3D array (or 4D for volume images), of size $w \times h \times p$, where (w,h) is the size of an image and p is the number of acquisition channels.

It can be interesting for the analysis:
- to transform the data to match to the algorithms that will be used;
- to reduce the time complexity of these algorithms;
- to reduce the spatial complexity of the problem;
- to disentangle variables and look for dependencies;
- to introduce a priori or important properties for the algorithms (normalized data, sparse features...);
- to allow a more intuitive and/or graphical interpretation by representing the information in a reduced way, in the form of an image $w \times h \times k$, $k << p$ (generally $k = 2$ or 3), in order to visualize the essential information directly on the screen.

Two approaches are then classically used: select from the initial pixel features (the p values measured in the channels) those judged to be the most relevant and eliminate the others (this is called variable selection); or construct, from these quantitative values, new features by linear or non-linear transformations (this is called feature extraction).

In this context, dimension reduction methods are often applied [25]. We propose in the following a simple example of linear dimension reduction in multi-spectral imaging, and its implementation in *CImg*.

9.1.1   Principal component analysis

Factorial methods aim at processing and visualizing multi-dimensional data. The simultaneous consideration of all the variables is a difficult problem, sometimes made easier because the information provided by the variables is redundant. The factorial methods then aim at exploiting this redundancy to try to replace the initial variables by a reduced number of new variables, preserving the initial information at best.

For quantitative data, *Principal Component Analysis* (*PCA*) [19] is one of the most widely used methods. It considers that the new variables are linear combinations and uncorrelated variables of the initial ones.

In the following, the data will be arrays $\mathcal{M}_{np}(\mathbb{R})$ of quantitative variables, a row being a pixel of the image, and the columns describing the measured parameters (the channels) on this pixel.

PRINCIPLE

PCA often works on centered and/or standardized variables. Let $\mathbf{g} \in \mathbb{R}^p$ note the vector of arithmetic means of each channel:

$$\mathbf{g} = \mathbf{X}^\mathbf{T}\mathbf{D}\mathbf{1}$$

where $\mathbf{D}$ is a diagonal matrix, each d_{ii} giving the importance of the individual i in the data (most often $\mathbf{D} = \frac{1}{n}\mathbb{I}$, which we will assume in the sequel), and $\mathbf{1}$ is the vector of $\mathbb{R}^n$ whose components are all equal to 1. The matrix $\mathbf{Y} = \mathbf{X} - \mathbf{1}\mathbf{g}^T$ is the centered array associated to $\mathbf{X}$.

If $\mathbf{D}_{1/\sigma}$ is the diagonal matrix of the inverses of the standard deviations of the variables, then $\mathbf{Z} = \mathbf{Y}\mathbf{D}_{1/\sigma}$ is the matrix of standardized centered data and

$$\mathbf{R} = \mathbf{Z}^{\mathbf{T}}\mathbf{Z}$$

is the correlation matrix of the standardized centered data (up to the p coefficient) and summarizes the structure of the linear dependencies between the p variables (the *PCA* can also reason on the variance/covariance matrix $\mathbf{R} = \mathbf{Y}^{\mathbf{T}}\mathbf{Y}$.)

Using `CImg<>` as matrices, and assuming that the p channel multispectral image is contained in a `CImg<>` of size `(w, h, 1, p)`, then the matrix $\mathbf{R}$ is computed by:

```
CImg<> mean(p,1), var(p,1);
cimg_forC(imgIn,c)
{
  mean(c) = imgIn.get_channel(c).mean();
  var(c)  = 1./std::sqrt(imgIn.get_channel(c).variance());
}

// Data matrix.
CImg<> X(p,imgIn.width()*imgIn.height());
cimg_forXYC(imgIn,x,y,c)
  X(c,x + y*imgIn.width()) = imgIn(x,y,0,c);

// Centered/standardized data.
CImg <> ones(1,imgIn.width()*imgIn.height());
var.diagonal();
CImg<> Z = (X - ones*mean)*var;

// Correlation matrix (up to p).
CImg<> R = Z.get_transpose()*Z;
```

PCA aims at obtaining an approximate representation of the cloud of n individuals (pixels) in a k low-dimensional subspace $\mathscr{F}_k$. This is done by a projection mechanism. The choice of the projection space is driven by the following criterion, which aims at distorting the distances in projection as little as possible: the subspace of dimension k is such that the average of the squares of the distances between projections is the largest possible. By defining the inertia of a point cloud as the weighted average of the squares of the distances to the center of gravity, the criterion then aims at maximizing the inertia of the cloud projected on $\mathscr{F}_k$.

Let $\mathbf{u} \in \mathbb{R}^p$. The projection of the standardized centered individuals on the line generated by $\mathbf{u}$ is $\mathbf{P}_u = \mathbf{Z}\mathbf{u}$. The empirical variance (inertia) on the line is therefore

$$\mathbf{P}_u^T \mathbf{P}_u = \mathbf{u}^T \mathbf{Z}^T \mathbf{Z}\mathbf{u}$$

The matrix $\mathbf{Z}^T\mathbf{Z}$ being symmetric $\mathbf{Z}^T\mathbf{Z} = \mathbf{Q}^T\Lambda\mathbf{Q}$, and

$$\mathbf{P}_u^T \mathbf{P}_u = \mathbf{u}^T \mathbf{Q}^T \Lambda \mathbf{Q}\mathbf{u} = \mathbf{v}^T \Lambda \mathbf{v} \quad \text{where} \quad \mathbf{v} = \mathbf{Q}\mathbf{u}$$

Seeking to maximize the inertia on the line $\mathscr{F}_1$, the vector $\mathbf{u}_1$ to choose is the eigenvector of $\mathbf{Z}^T\mathbf{Z}$ associated to the largest eigenvalue λ_1. For this vector, $\mathbf{v}^T\Lambda\mathbf{v} = \lambda_1$ is the inertia of individuals on the line generated by $\mathbf{u}_1$. If this variance is not large enough (we do not explain enough of the initial variation of $\mathbf{X}$), then we start the procedure again in the space orthogonal to $\mathbf{u}_1$. We obtain a second line, generated by $\mathbf{u}_2$, which explains part of the variation of the initial data. And we iterate possibly in the orthogonal of $(\mathbf{u}_1, \mathbf{u}_2)\ldots$ until we obtain a sufficient amount of explained variance. This finally aims to search for $\mathscr{F}_k$, the eigensubspace of $\mathbf{Z}^T\mathbf{Z}$, generated by the first k eigenvectors, defining the principal axis (or principal components - *PC*). The inertia explained by this subspace is $\sum_{i=1}^k \lambda_i$.

Using `CImg<T>::get_symmetric_eigen()`, the projection is implemented as follow:

```
CImgList<> eig = R.get_symmetric_eigen();
CImg<>  &val = eig[0],
        &vec = eig[1];

CImg<> Xpca = X*vec;
```

INTERPRETATION

The primary goal of *PCA* is to reduce the dimension to allow an efficient visualization of the data, while preserving the information (here represented by the inertia). Therefore, we need tools to answer the question: what dimension for $\mathscr{F}_k$? There is no universal theoretical answer, the main thing being to have a sufficiently expressive representation to allow a correct interpretation of the variation of the data. Commonly used criteria include:

- the total percentage of explained variance, expressed on the first k axis by $\frac{\sum_{j=1}^k \lambda_j}{\sum_{j=1}^p \lambda_j}$.
  A threshold (e.g., 90%) of the total explained inertia gives a corresponding value of k. However, the percentage of inertia must take into account the number of initial variables;

- if we work on standardized centered data, we retain the PC corresponding to eigenvalues greater than 1 (Kaiser criterion).

The first criterion is for example written:

```
float s = 0.9*val.sum(), inertia = val[0];
int nb_pca = 1;
while (inertia<s)
    inertia   += val[nb_pca++];
```

9.1.2 Example

As an illustration, we propose to process images of the Sun, from the *Solar Dynamics Observatory*[1] project [33], whose main objective is the understanding and prediction of solar variations that influence life on Earth and technological systems. The mission includes three scientific investigations (*Atmospheric Imaging Assembly* (*AIA*), *Extreme Ultraviolet Variability Experiment* (*EVE*) and *Helioseismic and Magnetic Imager* (*HMI*)), giving access to $p = 19$ solar images under different wavelengths (Fig. 9.1).

Applying the previous method, three components capture more than 90% of the initial variation of the data. The code

```
CImgList<> imgOut(nb_pca,256,256);
cimg_forXYC(imgIn,x,y,c)
if (c<nb_pca) imgOut(c,x,y) = Xpca(c,x + y*imgIn.width());
imgOut.display();
```

allows to display the corresponding PC (Fig. 9.2).

9.2 Color imaging

Color images are an integral part of our daily lives. Not surprisingly, they represent multi-spectral images that are most frequently encountered when one is interested in digital image processing. The processing of color images can often be carried out channel by channel, while being thus brought back to the scalar processings, such as those described in the previous chapters. But it can sometimes be interesting to develop dedicated processing methods, by generalizing the grayscale techniques. As an illustration, we propose here to study two variations of classical algorithms, for color imaging: median filtering and an algorithm for edge detection. As an introduction, we present the main existing color spaces managed by the *CImg* library. A broader overview of the aspects of color image processing is proposed in [23].

---

[1] https://sdo.gsfc.nasa.gov/

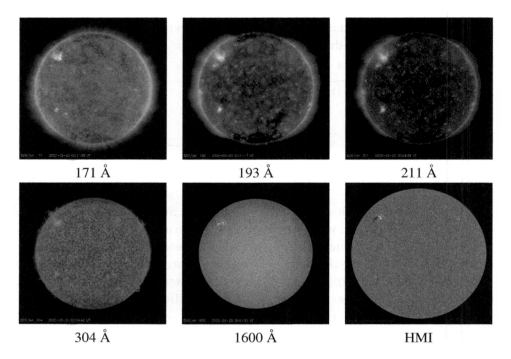

171 Å	193 Å	211 Å

304 Å	1600 Å	HMI

Figure 9.1 – Example of solar images from the Solar Dynamics Observatory.

9.2.1   Colorimetric spaces

RGB SPACE

RGB is an additive color space, which remains by far the most used color space for digital images. Each color is coded by a triplet of values (most often in the integer range $[\![0,255]\!]$), representing the quantities of red, green and blue which make up the color. The storage and the display of the color images use most of the time a coding of the pixel values in the *RGB* space. It is "the default color space" in image processing.

XYZ AND *xyY* SPACES

The *XYZ* color space was defined in order to correct certain defects of the *RGB* space. This space consists of three primary colors *X*, *Y* and *Z*, known as virtual, obtained by linear transformations of the (R, G, B) triplet. According to the International

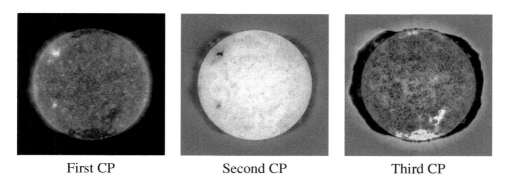

First CP   Second CP   Third CP

Figure 9.2 – PC images explaining 90% of the total initial inertia.

Commission on Illumination (ICI) norm:

$$\begin{pmatrix} X \\ Y \\ Z \end{pmatrix} = \begin{pmatrix} 2.7689 & 1.7517 & 1.1302 \\ 1.0000 & 4.5907 & 0.060100 \\ 0.0000 & 0.056508 & 5.5943 \end{pmatrix} \begin{pmatrix} R \\ G \\ B \end{pmatrix}$$

The Y component represents the *luminance* of the incident spectrum. From XYZ, the xyY space (chromatic coordinates + luminance) is defined by $x = \frac{X}{X+Y+Z}$ and $y = \frac{Y}{X+Y+Z}$.

   CImg proposes
`CImg<T>::RGBtoXYZ()`, `CImg<T>::XYZtoRGB()`, `CImg<T>::XYZtoxyY()`, `CImg<T>::xyYtoXYZ()` (and their `get_*` version) to convert *RGB* images into XYZ and xyY ones (and vice versa).

$L^*a^*b^*$ SPACE

RGB and *XYZ* spaces are perceptually non-uniform spaces, in the sense that the value of the Euclidean distance between two colors in these spaces is not necessarily characteristic of the perception of these colors by the human visual system: two colors distant in the *RGB* space can be perceived as close to the eye (and vice versa).

   The $L^*a^*b^*$ space is a system created in 1976 by the *ICI*, which seeks to be perceptually uniform, obtained by non-linear relations computed in the XYZ space. Components are computed from a reference white (X_0, Y_0, Z_0), by:

$$L^* = 116 f(Y/Y_0) - 16$$

$$a^* = 500 \left[f(X/X_0) - f(Y/Y_0) \right] \quad \text{with } f(x) = \begin{cases} x^{1/3} & \text{if } x > \left(\frac{6}{29}\right)^3 \\ \frac{1}{3}\left(\frac{29}{6}\right)^2 x + \frac{4}{29} & \text{otherwise} \end{cases}$$

$$b^* = 200 \left[f(Y/Y_0) - f(Z/Z_0) \right]$$

Luminance L^* represents the clarity of the color, components a^* and b^* represent respectively the opposition of green/red color and the opposition of blue/yellow color (the chromaticities of the color). Calculating brightness by a cube root was suggested by psychovisual experiments conducted on the appreciation of distances between monochromatic stimuli. The threshold value $\left(\frac{6}{29}\right)^3$ is chosen in order to suppress the too abrupt variations of $x^{1/3}$ around 0. This cube root is interesting in the search for the approximation of how the human eye works, even if it has been shown since, that the Euclidean norm in this space is not a totally reliable measure to discriminate colors from a perceptual point of view.

Methods `CImg<T>::RGBtoLab()`, `CImg<T>::LabtoRGB()`, `CImg<T>::XYZtoLab()`, `CImg<T>::LabtoXYZ()` and their `get_*` versions convert color images to and from the $L^*a^*b^*$ space.

YUV SPACE

Introduced by the German *PAL* standard, this system is based on a transformation of *RGB* components:

$$\begin{pmatrix} Y \\ U \\ V \end{pmatrix} = \begin{pmatrix} 0.299 & 0.587 & 0.114 \\ -0.147 & -0.289 & 0.436 \\ 0.615 & -0.515 & -0.1000 \end{pmatrix} \begin{pmatrix} R \\ G \\ B \end{pmatrix}$$

Y represents the *luma* (luminance with gamma correction), U and V represent color chrominance. *CImg* proposes the following methods `CImg<T>::RGBtoYUV()`, `CImg<T>::YUVtoRGB()` (and the `get_*` versions), `CImg<T>::load_yuv()` and `CImg<T>::save_yuv()` to manipulate color images in the YUV color space.

$YCbCr$ SPACE

The $YCbCr$ space is the international standard for the coding of digital television images. It is currently part of the *JPEG* standard, for the lossy compression of color images. It is conceptually very close to YUV. The associated mathematical transformation is:

$$\begin{pmatrix} Y \\ Cb \\ Cr \end{pmatrix} = \begin{pmatrix} 0.299 & 0.587 & 0.114 \\ -0.169 & -0.331 & 0.500 \\ 0.500 & -0.419 & -0.081 \end{pmatrix} \begin{pmatrix} R \\ G \\ B \end{pmatrix}$$

Methods `CImg<T>::RGBtoYCbCr()`, `CImg<T>::YCbCrtoRGB()` (and their `get_*` versions) convert *RGB* color images to $YCbCr$ space. (and vice versa).

REPRESENTATION USING TRIANGULAR *HSI* COORDINATES

HSI representation (*Hue, Saturation, Intensity*) is derived from the transformation of *RGB* values:

$$H = \arccos\left(\frac{0.5(R-G) + (R-B)}{\sqrt{(R-G)^2 + (R-B)(G-B)}}\right), \quad S = 1 - 3\frac{min(R,G,B)}{R+G+B}, \quad I = \frac{R+G+B}{3}$$

and `CImg<T>::RGBtoHSI()` and `CImg<T>::HSItoRGB()` (and their `get_*` versions) allow to compute these components. This representation is based on the psychology of visual perception, which is used mainly in the field of computer graphics.

HEXAGONAL CONE REPRESENTATION *HSV*

Similar to *HSI*, the *HSV* (*Hue, Saturation, Value*) model is built upon *RGB* values: if $M = max(R,G,B)$ and $m = min(R,G,B)$, then

$$S = 1 - \frac{m}{M}, \quad V = M \quad \text{and} \quad H = \begin{cases} \left(60\frac{G-B}{M-m} + 360\right) \bmod 360 & \text{if } M = R \\ 60\frac{B-R}{M-m} + 120 & \text{if } M = G \\ 60\frac{R-G}{M-m} + 240 & \text{if } M = B \end{cases}$$

Methods `CImg<T>::RGBtoHSV()` and `CImg<T>::HSVtoRGB()` (and their `get_*` versions) give access to the conversion of color images in the *HSV* color space.

HSL REPRESENTATION

Like *HSI* and *HSV*, *HSL* (*Hue, Saturation, Lightness*) representation is built from the *RGB* values: if $M = max(R,G,B)$ and $m = min(R,G,B)$, then

$$L = \frac{M+m}{2}, S = \begin{cases} \frac{M-m}{2L} & \text{if } L < 0.5 \\ \frac{M-m}{2-2L} & \text{otherwise} \end{cases}, \quad H = \begin{cases} \left(60\frac{G-B}{M-m} + 360\right) \bmod 360 & \text{if } M = R \\ 60\frac{B-R}{M-m} + 120 & \text{if } M = G \\ 60\frac{R-G}{M-m} + 240 & \text{if } M = B \end{cases}$$

Methods `CImg<T>::RGBtoHSL()` and `CImg<T>::HSLtoRGB()` (and their `get_*` versions) handle images in *HSL* color space.

CMY AND $CMYK$ SPACES

CMY (*Cyan, Magenta, Yellow*) is the space dedicated to the printing of digital color images on paper. It results from a subtractive synthesis of the colors and is represented by the inverse cube of the *RGB* space: the origin $(0,0,0)$ color is white, and it has cyan, magenta and yellow as axes. Assuming that an *RGB* color has components coded in the interval $[0,1]$, then:

$$C = 1 - R, \quad M = 1 - G \quad \text{and} \quad Y = 1 - B$$

For material needs (mainly for the printers), this space was extended by adding a fourth component, K (for *Key black*), which, on the one hand, comes to fill the difficulty for a printer to restore correctly gray levels by mixing cyan, magenta and yellow inks (which are in practice imperfect), and on the other hand, makes it possible to minimize the quantity of ink necessary to print gray levels (colors very frequently met in printing). For this reason, printers have a black ink cartridge, in addition to the cyan, magenta and yellow ink cartridges. The *CMYK* components are calculated as follows:

$$K = min(C, M, Y), \quad C' = \frac{C - K}{1 - K}, \quad M' = \frac{C - K}{M - K} \quad \text{and} \quad Y' = \frac{C - K}{Y - K}$$

Methods `CImg<T>::RGBtoCMY()`, `CImg<T>::CMYtoRGB()`, `CImg<T>::RGBtoCMYK()`, `CImg<T>::CMYKtoRGB()`, `CImg<T>::CMYtoCMYK()`, `CImg<T>::CMYKtoCMY()` and the `get_*` versions allow to handle these spaces.

Figures 9.3 and 9.4 illustrate the values of the various color channels obtained in these colorimetric spaces, for the kingfisher image, originally coded by *RGB* values (first row of the first figure). All channels have been normalized for visualization.

9.2.2 Median filtering in color imaging

If the concept of median value is clearly defined in $\mathbb{R}$, generalizing this notion in $\mathbb{R}^d$ is much easier, since there is no order relation in this space. However, it is possible to specify an equivalent formulation that will allow to define a median filtering algorithm for multi-spectral images.

Let $X = (x_1 \cdots x_n)$ be a set of n real values. The median of X can be defined as the value $x_m \in X$ such that:

$$(\forall j \in [\![1, n]\!]) \ \sum_{i=1}^{n} |x_m - x_i| \leq \sum_{i=1}^{n} |x_j - x_i|$$

Following this definition, the transposition to the vector case is then immediate: if $\mathbf{X} = (\mathbf{x}_1 \cdots \mathbf{x}_n)$ is a set of vectors of $\mathbb{R}^d$ (in our case, $d = 3$ for a color image, or $d = 4$ for the *CMYK* case), then we can define the median element $\mathbf{x}_m$ of $\mathbf{X}$ as the one satisfying:

$$(\forall j \in [\![1,n]\!]) \sum_{i=1}^{n} \|\mathbf{x}_m - \mathbf{x}_i\| \leq \sum_{i=1}^{n} \|\mathbf{x}_j - \mathbf{x}_i\|$$

where $\|.\|$ is a vectorial norm.

Code 9.1 implements this filter for the L_2 norm. Note that, in the basic version presented here, the complexity of the algorithm is significant: for a neighborhood of size p, computing distances requires $\mathcal{O}(p^2)$ and the search for the smallest distance is in $\mathcal{O}(p)$, thus a complexity of $\mathcal{O}(p^3)$ for each point processed.

Code 9.1 – Median filtering in color imaging.

```
CImg<> ColorMedianFiltering(CImg<> imgIn)
{
  // Transformation into a perceptually uniform space
  imgIn.RGBtoLab();

  CImg<>
    imgOut(imgIn),
    V(5,5,1,3), // 5x5 color neighbor
    vL = V.get_shared_channel(0),
    va = V.get_shared_channel(1),
    vb = V.get_shared_channel(2);


  cimg_for5x5(imgIn,x,y,0,0,vL,float)
  {
    cimg_get5x5(imgIn,x,y,0,1,va,float);
    cimg_get5x5(imgIn,x,y,0,2,vb,float);

    // Distance to the central pixel.
    float dmin = 0;
    CImg<> z = V.get_vector_at(2,2);
    cimg_forXY(V,i,j)
    {
      CImg<> zi = V.get_vector_at(i,j);
      dmin += (zi -= z).magnitude();
    }

    cimg_forXY(V,i,j)
    {
      float d = 0;
      CImg<> z = V.get_vector_at(i,j);
```

```
      cimg_forXY(V,u,v)
      {
        CImg<> zi = V.get_vector_at(u,v);
        d += (zi -= z).magnitude();
      }
      if (d<dmin)
      {
        dmin = d;
        imgOut(x,y,0,0) = V(i,j,0);
        imgOut(x,y,0,1) = V(i,j,1);
        imgOut(x,y,0,2) = V(i,j,2);
      }
    }
  }
}
  return imgOut.LabtoRGB();
}
```

Figure 9.5 shows a median filtering result of a color image. A salt and pepper noise (b) is added to color test pattern (a). The resulting image is filtered by the multispectral median filter (d) and by a more classical median filtering applied channel by channel (c) (see Section 5.1.2). We can clearly see on details (e) and (f) that the median filtering designed specifically for the color image minimizes the appearance of "false colors" (the only false colors being from the noise), unlike the filtering applied on each channel independently, and also generates less geometric distortions (see white and black grid).

Let us note finally that, since this filtering depends on the definition of a distance in the color space, we preferentially use the perceptually uniform space $L^*a^*b^*$.

9.2.3   Edge detection in color imaging

To be able to detect contours by using the color information, one can process the image as a vector field.

A 2D color image $\mathbf{I}(\mathbf{x}) = (I_R(\mathbf{x}), I_G(\mathbf{x}), I_B(\mathbf{x}))^\top$ can be considered as a vector field of $\mathbb{R}^2$ in $\mathbb{R}^3$, which associates to a pixel $\mathbf{x}$ the vector of its values on the three RGB channels. We can then calculate the Jacobian of $\mathbf{I}$ in $\mathbf{x}$, defined by

$$J_{\mathbf{I}}(\mathbf{x}) = \begin{pmatrix} \frac{\partial I_R}{\partial x}(\mathbf{x}) & \frac{\partial I_R}{\partial y}(\mathbf{x}) \\ \frac{\partial I_G}{\partial x}(\mathbf{x}) & \frac{\partial I_G}{\partial y}(\mathbf{x}) \\ \frac{\partial I_B}{\partial x}(\mathbf{x}) & \frac{\partial I_B}{\partial y}(\mathbf{x}) \end{pmatrix} = \begin{pmatrix} \nabla I_R^\top(\mathbf{x}) \\ \nabla I_G^\top(\mathbf{x}) \\ \nabla I_B^\top(\mathbf{x}) \end{pmatrix} = \begin{pmatrix} \mathbf{I}_x(\mathbf{x}) & \mathbf{I}_y(\mathbf{x}) \end{pmatrix}$$

where the second part involves in row the gradients of the R, G, B channels, and where the last part presents in column the vectors of $\mathbb{R}^3$ composed of the partial derivatives with respect to the components. To calculate the color gradient in any θ direction, we use the definition of the directional derivative:

$$\nabla_\theta \mathbf{I}(\mathbf{x}) = J_{\mathbf{I}}(\mathbf{x}) \begin{pmatrix} cos(\theta) \\ \end{pmatrix} = \mathbf{I}_x(\mathbf{x})cos(\theta) + \mathbf{I}_y(\mathbf{x})sin(\theta)$$

The norm of this vector is called the *local contrast* and is denoted $S_\theta(\mathbf{I}, \mathbf{x})$.

Directions maximizing $S_\theta(\mathbf{I}, \mathbf{x})$ can be searched by zeroing the partial derivative of the local contrast with respect to θ (di Zenzo gradient [12]). It is also possible to compute the maximum local contrast as the root of the largest eigenvalue of the symmetric matrix $\mathbf{M}(\mathbf{x}) = J_\mathbf{I}^\top(\mathbf{x}) J_\mathbf{I}(\mathbf{x})$:

$$\mathbf{M}(\mathbf{x}) = \begin{pmatrix} \mathbf{I}_x^2(\mathbf{x}) & \mathbf{I}_x(\mathbf{x}) \mathbf{I}_y(\mathbf{x}) \\ \mathbf{I}_x(\mathbf{x}) \mathbf{I}_y(\mathbf{x}) & \mathbf{I}_y^2(\mathbf{x}) \end{pmatrix} = \begin{pmatrix} \mathbf{A}(\mathbf{x}) & \mathbf{B}(\mathbf{x}) \\ \mathbf{B}(\mathbf{x}) & \mathbf{C}(\mathbf{x}) \end{pmatrix}$$

It is the equivalent in color imaging of the *structure tensor*, already met in Section 6.1. The largest eigenvalue of $\mathbf{M}(\mathbf{x})$, giving the maximum local contrast, is then computed by

$$\lambda_1(\mathbf{x}) = \frac{\mathbf{A}(\mathbf{x}) + \mathbf{B}(\mathbf{x}) + \sqrt{(\mathbf{A}(\mathbf{x}) - \mathbf{B}(\mathbf{x}))^2 + 4\mathbf{C}^2(\mathbf{x})}}{2}$$

and the corresponding eigenvector is $\mathbf{q}_1(\mathbf{x}) = \begin{pmatrix} \mathbf{A}(\mathbf{x}) - \mathbf{B}(\mathbf{x}) + \sqrt{(\mathbf{A}(\mathbf{x}) - \mathbf{B}(\mathbf{x}))^2 + 4\mathbf{C}^2(\mathbf{x})} \\ 2\mathbf{C}(\mathbf{x}) \end{pmatrix}$

The other eigenvector of $\mathbf{M}(\mathbf{x})$ is orthogonal to $\mathbf{q}_1(\mathbf{x})$ ($\mathbf{M}(\mathbf{x})$ is symmetric), and is therefore tangent to the contour at the point $\mathbf{x}$. The phase of the gradient in $\mathbf{x}$ is:

$$\tan(\theta(\mathbf{x})) = \frac{2\mathbf{C}(\mathbf{x})}{\mathbf{A}(\mathbf{x}) - \mathbf{B}(\mathbf{x}) + \sqrt{(\mathbf{A}(\mathbf{x}) - \mathbf{B}(\mathbf{x}))^2 + 4\mathbf{C}^2(\mathbf{x})}}$$

that can be written as $\tan(2\theta(\mathbf{x})) = \frac{2\mathbf{C}(\mathbf{x})}{\mathbf{A}(\mathbf{x}) - \mathbf{B}(\mathbf{x})}$, and then, if $\mathbf{A}(\mathbf{x}) \neq \mathbf{B}(\mathbf{x})$ and $\mathbf{C}(\mathbf{x}) \neq 0$

$$\theta(\mathbf{x}) = \frac{1}{2} \arctan\left(\frac{2\mathbf{C}(\mathbf{x})}{\mathbf{A}(\mathbf{x}) - \mathbf{B}(\mathbf{x})} \right)$$

Code 9.2 illustrates the application of the previous method, and Fig. 9.6 shows a result. Instead of using the explicit calculation of λ_1 described above, we use `CImg<T>::get_symmetric_eigen()`.

Code 9.2 – Local contrast and gradient orientation in color imaging.

```
/*
   Gradient of a color image.

   imgIn : Input image
   E     : Local contrast image
   Phi   : Gradient orientation image
*/
void ColorGradient(CImg<>& imgIn, CImg<>& E, CImg<>& Phi)
{
   CImgList<> eig;
```

```
// Gradients.
CImgList<> grad = imgIn.get_gradient();

cimg_forXY(imgIn,x,y)
{
  CImg<>
    Ix = grad[0].get_vector_at(x,y),
    Iy = grad[1].get_vector_at(x,y),
    M(2,2);
  M(0,0) = Ix.dot(Ix);
  M(1,1) = Iy.dot(Iy);
  M(0,1) = M(1,0) = Iy.dot(Ix);
  eig = M.get_symmetric_eigen();
  E(x,y) = std::sqrt(eig[0](0));
  Phi(x,y) = std::atan2(M(0,0) - M(1,1),2*M(0,1));
}
}
```

If only the norm of the gradient matters in the calculations related to a processing algorithm, then applying a gradient on the vector field or channel to channel is almost equivalent. On the other hand, if the phase (contour orientation) plays an important role, then the multi-spectral approach gives a generally more consistent and reliable result.

Figure 9.3 – Representation of an image in different color spaces.

Figure 9.4 – Representation of an image in different color spaces.

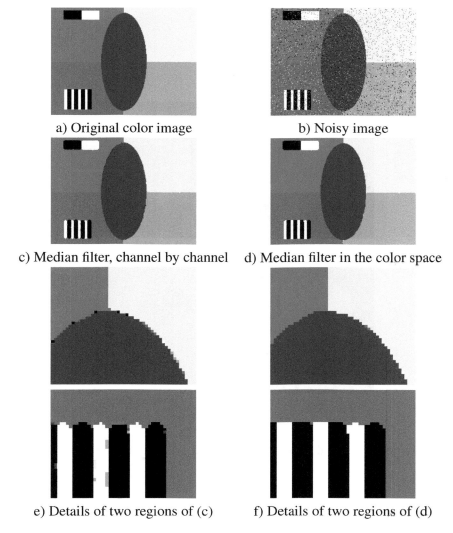

a) Original color image   b) Noisy image

c) Median filter, channel by channel   d) Median filter in the color space

e) Details of two regions of (c)   f) Details of two regions of (d)

Figure 9.5 – Comparison of monochromatic and color median filters.

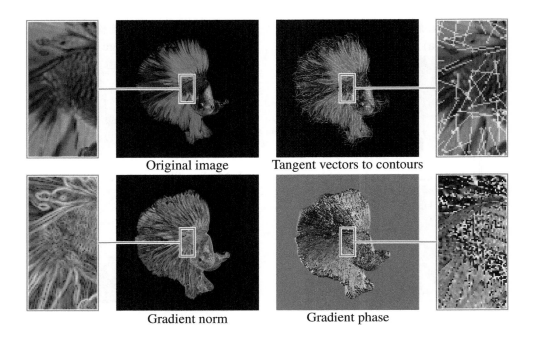

Figure 9.6 – Local contrast and gradient orientation in color imaging.

10. 3D Visualisation

The *CImg* library has basic capabilities for visualizing and rendering 3D mesh objects, which can help the developer represent complex image data. In this chapter, we propose a quick tour of these possibilities, first describing the general principles governing the creation of 3D mesh objects, and then detailing the way these objects are internally represented in the library. Several examples are proposed to illustrate different practical use cases.

10.1 Structuring of 3D mesh objects

A 3D mesh object is completely defined with *CImg* by the union of four distinct structures:

1. A set of **3D points**, defining the N vertices of the object. The 3D coordinates of these points are stored in a `CImg<T>` image of size $N \times 3$, where type `T` is most often `float` (the coordinates of 3D vertices being generally decimal numbers).

2. A set of P **primitives**, composing the object. Each primitive can be a: quadrangle, triangle, segment, point, sphere (perfect sphere) or sprite (small image). Segments, triangles and quadrangles can be textured. This set of primitives is stored as a `CImgList<T>` of P images, each representing a single primitive of the object. The type `T` is usually `unsigned int`, because each of these images contains the set of indices of the 3D vertices composing the primitive.

3. A set of P **materials**, defining either the color or the texture of each primitive. This set is stored as a list of `CImgList<T>` images, each representing the material of a single primitive. The type `T` is usually `unsigned char`, because 3D objects are drawn or visualized most often in 8-bit per component `CImg<unsigned char>` images.

4. A set of P **opacities**, defining the transparency level of each primitive in the object. This set is stored as an image `CImg<T>` of size $1 \times P$, or as a list of

images `CImgList<T>`. The type `T` is usually `float`, as opacities have values between 0 (fully transparent) and 1 (fully opaque).

With these four datasets defined, it is possible to interactively view the corresponding 3D object directly via the `CImg<T>::display_object3d()` method or to draw it in an image, via the `CImg<T>::draw_object3d()` method. In addition, there is a set of `CImg<T>` methods returning pre-defined 3D mesh objects, such as parallelepipeds (`CImg<T>::box3d()`), spheres (`CImg<T>::sphere3d()`), torus (`CImg<T>::torus3d()`), cylinders (`CImg<T>::cylinder3d()`), etc. Two separate 3D objects can be merged into one, with the `CImg<T>::append_object3d()` method. Note that the sets of materials and opacities do not appear as arguments in the signature of these functions, since they only participate in the decoration of the 3D object, not in the definition of its structure per se.

Code 10.1 illustrates the use of these different functions for the creation and visualization of a compound 3D mesh object (a chain, with a ball), obtained by concatenating several simple 3D primitives (deformed and rotated torii and a sphere).

Code 10.1 – Creation and visualization of a simple 3D object.

```
// Structures of the 3D object to be generated.
CImg<> g_points;
CImgList<unsigned int> g_primitives;

// Add torii in chain.
CImgList<unsigned int> primitives;
CImg<> points;
for (unsigned int k = 0; k<8; ++k) {
  points = CImg<>::torus3d(primitives,100,30);
  points.resize_object3d(240,160,60).shift_object3d(130.f*k,0.f,0.f)
    ;
  if (k%2) points.rotate_object3d(1,0,0,90);
  g_points.append_object3d(g_primitives,points,primitives);
}

// Add a sphere at the end of the chain.
points = CImg<>::sphere3d(primitives,150).shift_object3d(1000,0,0);
g_points.append_object3d(g_primitives,points,primitives);

// Create a 800x600 background image, with color gradients.
CImg<unsigned char> background(1,2,1,3,
                     "y?[64,128,255]:[255,255,255]",false)
    ;
background.resize(800,600,1,3,3);
```

```
// Launch the 3D interactive viewer.
background.display_object3d("3D Object",g_points,g_primitives);
```

The resulting 3D object, as displayed in the 3D mesh viewer of *CImg*, is illustrated in Figure 10.1.

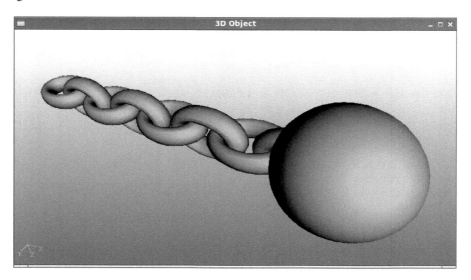

Figure 10.1 – Result of Code 10.1: Creation and visualization of a simple 3D mesh object.

10.2 **3D plot of a function** $z = f(x,y)$

Without going further into the details of the implementation of 3D mesh objects in *CImg*, we can already use the few notions discussed to build an interesting application for visualizing a function f of two variables, in the form of a 3D elevation, namely $z = f(x,y)$. The idea is to allow the user to indicate to the program a mathematical formula $f(x,y)$ and to create a visualization in the form of a 3D surface.

First, we retrieve the different values of the parameters passed on the command line (by defining default values for the parameters not specified by the user), and we initialize the minimum and maximum bounds $(x_0, y_0) - (x_1, y_1)$ of the evaluation domain of the function f:

Code 10.2 – Retrieve parameters from the command line.

```
const char
  *expr = cimg_option("-z",
                      "sinc(sqrt(x^2+y^2)/4)*abs(sin(x/2)*cos(y/2))"
                      ,
                      "Expression of f(x,y)"),
  *xyrange = cimg_option("-xy",
                         "-30,-30,30,30",
                         "Definition domain");
int
  resolution = cimg_option("-r",256,"3D plot resolution");
float
  sigma = cimg_option("-s",0.0f,"Smoothness of the function f"),
  factor = cimg_option("-f",150.0f,"Scale factor");

// Initialize the evaluation domain of the function.
float x0, y0, x1, y1;
if (std::sscanf(xyrange,"%g,%g,%g,%g",&x0,&y0,&x1,&y1)!=4)
throw CImgArgumentException("3D Plotter: "
                            "The domain '%s' is invalid.",
                            xyrange);
if (x0>x1) cimg::swap(x0,x1); // We ensure that x0<x1...
if (y0>y1) cimg::swap(y0,y1); // ... and that y0<y1
if (resolution<8) resolution = 8; // Be sure the resolution is large
    enough
```

The evaluation of the function $f(x, y)$ on the whole domain $(x_0, y_0) - (x_1, y_1)$ is done thanks to the following version of the constructor of `CImg<T>`:

```
CImg(unsigned int size_x, unsigned int size_y,
     unsigned int size_z, unsigned int size_c,
     const char *values, bool repeat_values);
```

This overloading of the constructor allows to specify as an argument a string `values` containing the values you wish to give to the pixels of the image. This string can be a list of values separated by commas as well as a mathematical expression that will be evaluated for each pixel of the image under construction.

The string we are going to pass here to the constructor will consist of the concatenation of three formulas, the first two lines setting new values for the pre-defined variables x and y so that they become linearly normalized in the intervals $[x_0, x_1]$ and $[y_0, y_1]$, respectively. The last row is just the function $f(x, y)$ to evaluate. We also allow to smooth the resulting image and normalize its values:

Code 10.3 – Generate the elevation map $z = f(x, y)$.

```
CImg<char> s_expr(1024);
std::sprintf(s_expr,"x = lerp(%g,%g,x/(w-1));"
                    "y = lerp(%g,%g,y/(h-1));"
                    "%s",
                    x0,x1,y0,y1,expr);
CImg<> elevation(resolution,resolution,1,1,s_expr,true);
elevation.blur(sigma).normalize(0,factor);
```

In a second step, we use this same constructor to generate a gradient color palette built by linear interpolation of four basic colors (red, orange, yellow and white) (Code 10.4).

Code 10.4 – Create a color gradient (red, orange, yellow, white).

```
CImg<unsigned char>
  lut(4,1,1,3,"!x?[255,79,106]:"        // Red
             "x==1?[196,115,149]:"      // Orange
             "x==2?[231,250,90]:"       // Yellow
             "[255,255,255]",true);     // White
lut.resize(256,1,1,3,3);

// Generate a color representation of 'elevation'.
CImg<unsigned char>
  c_elevation = elevation.get_normalize(0,255).map(lut);
```

At this point, we have a 2D scalar image `elevation`, which gives the value of the function $f(x, y)$ at each point, as well as a colored version `c_elevation`, (Fig. 10.2), which we will use afterwards to color the 3D object.

The mesh corresponding to the 3D elevation of $z = f(x, y)$ can now be generated in color, thanks to the `CImg<T>::get_elevation3d()` method:

Code 10.5 – Generate a colored 3D elevation.

```
CImgList<unsigned int> primitives;
CImgList<unsigned char> colors;
CImg<> points = c_elevation.get_elevation3d(primitives,colors,
                                            elevation);

// Apply a 3D rotation such that the z-axis of the object
// points upward (i.e. along the y-axis).
points.rotate_object3d(1,0,0,100);
```

The only thing left to do is to build a background image, with a color gradient, and call the `CImg<T>::display_object3d()` method to visualize f in 3D (Code 10.6).

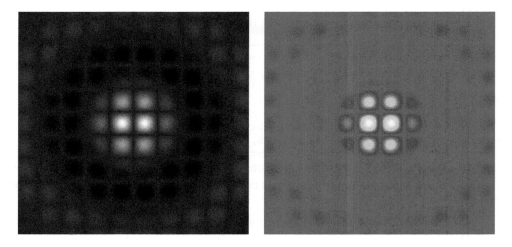

Figure 10.2 – Result of Codes 10.3 and 10.4: Images `elevation` (scalar, left), and `c_elevation` (color, right), for the expression defined by default as $f(x,y) = \text{sinc}\left(\frac{\sqrt{x^2+y^2}}{4}\right) \text{abs}\left(\sin(\frac{x}{2})\cos(\frac{y}{2})\right)$.

Code 10.6 – Create a background and start the 3D viewer.

```
CImg<unsigned char> background(1,2,1,3,
                        "y?[64,128,255]:[255,255,255]",false);
background.resize(800,600,1,3,3);
const unsigned char black[] = { 0,0,0 };
background.draw_text(2,2,"f(x,y) = %s",black,
                    (unsigned char*)0,1.0f,24U,expression);

// Start the interactive 3D viewer.
background.display_object3d("3D Plotter",points,primitives,colors);
```

The rendering of this code can be seen in Fig. 10.3, with different functions $f(x,y)$ and different evaluation ranges passed as parameters. The first image (top left) corresponds to the function defined by default in the program (i.e., the elevation illustrated in Fig. 10.2). The second row of Fig. 10.3 illustrates the evaluation results of the Mandelbrot fractal function, and shows that the mathematical function evaluator integrated in *CImg* is actually able to evaluate complex expressions, which are programs in their own (here, a program evaluating the convergence of a series of complex numbers).

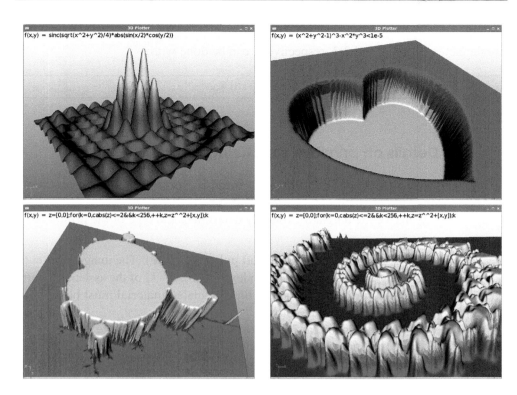

Figure 10.3 – Result of our program for plotting functions $z = f(x, y)$, as 3D elevation maps.

10.3 Creating complex 3D objects

Let's now go into more detail on how the data of vertices, primitives, materials and opacities are interpreted in practice, when displaying 3D mesh objects with the *CImg* library.

10.3.1 Details on vertex structuring

Each vertex n (for $n \in [\![1, N]\!]$) of a 3D object is a point with coordinates (x_n, y_n, z_n). The set of vertices composing a 3D object is stored as an image `CImg<float>` of size $N \times 3$, which is the horizontal concatenation of all vectors $(x_n, y_n, z_n)^\top$. This representation allows to have an easily manipulated matrix of vertex coordinates. In particular, we can apply a rotation to the points of a 3D object in the following way :

```
points = CImg<>::rotation_matrix(ax,ay,az,angle)*points;
```

where (a_x, a_y, a_z) are the coordinates of the desired rotation axis.

Similarly, the dilation of the 3D coordinates along each of the axes x, y and z, with scale factors 0.2, 1.2 and 2.3, respectively, can be done with:

```
points = CImg<>::diagonal(0.2,1.2,2.3)*points;
```

10.3.2 Details on primitive structuring

Each primitive p (for $p \in [\![1, P]\!]$) of a 3D mesh is stored as a `CImg<unsigned int>` `img_p` image with size $1 \times S$, in an image list `CImgList<unsigned int>`. The choice of the height S explicitly determines the type of the primitive:

- When $S = 1$: the primitive is a **colored point** (or **sprite**). The image $img_p = (i_1)$ contains a single value which is the index $i_1 \in [\![0, N-1]\!]$ of the associated vertex. In order to display a *sprite* instead, the associated material must be an image (rather than a simple color vector).
- When $S = 2$: the primitive is a **colored segment**. The image $img_p = (i_1, i_2)$ contains the two indices of the starting and ending vertices.
- When $S = 3$: the primitive is a **colored triangle**. The image $img_p = (i_1, i_2, i_3)$ contains the three indices of the triangle vertices.
- When $S = 4$: the primitive is a **colored quadrangle**. The image $img_p = (i_1, i_2, i_3, i_4)$ contains the four indices of the quadrangle vertices.
- When $S = 5$: the primitive is a **colored sphere**. The image $img_p = (i_1, i_2, 0, 0, 0)$ contains two indices of vertices that define the diameter of the sphere.
- When $S = 6$: the primitive is a **textured segment**. The image $img_p = (i_1, i_2, tx_1, ty_1, tx_2, ty_2)$ contains the two indices of the segment vertices, followed by the coordinates of the corresponding texture (the texture being given as the material associated to this primitive).
- When $S = 9$: the primitive is a **textured triangle**. The image $img_p = (i_1, i_2, i_3, tx_1, ty_1, tx_2, ty_2, tx_3, ty_3)$ contains the three indices of the triangle vertices, followed by the coordinates of the corresponding texture (the texture being given as the material associated to this primitive).
- When $S = 12$: the primitive is a **textured quadrangle**. The image $img_p = (i_1, i_2, i_3, i_4, tx_1, ty_1, tx_2, ty_2, tx_3, ty_3, tx_4, ty_4)$ contains the four indices of the quadrangle vertices, followed by the coordinates of the corresponding texture (the texture being given as the material associated to this primitive).

The set of these primitives, associated to the set of vertices, entirely define the 3D structure of the mesh object.

10.3.3 Details on material structuring

Each material p (for $p \in [\![1, P]\!]$) of a 3D mesh object is also stored as a `CImg<unsigned char>` `img_p` image, in an image list `CImgList<unsigned char>`.

- When the primitive is colored, img_p is an image having three values that encode the color components (R, G, B) of the primitive.
- When the primitive is textured, img_p is directly the image of the considered texture. When several primitives share the same texture, it is strongly recommended to associate the texture to the first primitive, then use shared memory images associated to the initial texture, to define the materials of the other primitives, so that having multiple copies of the same texture in memory is avoided. It is indeed easy to insert shared copies of an image into an image list, by using for instance the method `CImgList<T>::insert()`, with the argument `is_shared = true`.

```
CImgList<T>& insert(CImg<t>& img,
                    unsigned int pos=~0U,
                    bool is_shared=false);
```

- When the primitive is a *sprite*, img_p is the sprite image to draw. If we are looking for a sprite with transparent pixels, we must associate a corresponding image of opacity, with same dimensions, to the list of primitive opacities.

10.3.4 Details on opacity structuring

Each opacity p (for $p \in [\![1, P]\!]$) follows a similar pattern, when using a list of images `CImgList<T>` to store them. In this case, the opacity of a primitive will typically be represented by a 1×1 image whose single value indicates the transparency level of the primitive. A value of 0 indicates that the primitive is completely transparent, a value of 1 that it is completely opaque. Only in the special case where the primitive is a *sprite*, the corresponding opacity will be specified as a transparency image, with pixel values between 0 and 1. This case happens only rarely, and if the object contains no *sprite*, then it is allowed to define the set of opacities as a `CImg<float>` image of size $1 \times P$, containing the opacity values of each primitive p.

The knowledge of these few rules that define the set of possible properties of 3D vector objects with *CImg* allows to build complex objects in a procedural way: by iteratively adding in `CImgList<T>` new vertices, associated primitives and colored or textured materials, we can easily create elaborated 3D visualizations. This is what we illustrated in the next section, with an application to cardiac image segmentation.

10.4 Visualization of a cardiac segmentation in *MRI*

We aim here to use the capabilities of *CImg* in 3D visualization to generate a 3D view of the inner side of one of the heart's ventricles and its estimated motion between two instants t_1 and t_2.

10.4.1 Description of the input data

The input data are three volume images of size $100 \times 100 \times 14$, stored as `CImg<float>`. The first two (Figures 10.4 (a) and (b)), named respectively `frame1` and `frame2` are two scalar images, extracted from a sequence of cardiac *MRI* images, from the database [9]. The left ventricle can be seen as a bright circular spot in the center of both images.

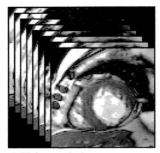 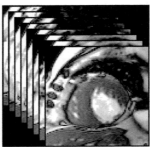 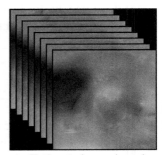

a) Volumetric image at $t = t_1$ (`frame1`) b) Volumetric image at $t = t_2$ (`frame2`) c) Estimated motion between t_1 and t_2 (`motion`)

Figure 10.4 – Input data.

The third image, `motion`, is a volumetric image of 3D vectors representing the displacement of voxels in `frame1` between times t_1 and t_2 (shown in Fig. 10.4 (c), as an *RGB* color image). This last image does not come from an acquisition: it has been estimated from `frame1` and `frame2`, by a 3D extension of the motion estimation methods discussed in Chapter 8.

The visualization of dense volumetric images such as these is never easy: the number of points is often too large for the simultaneous display of all the voxels in 3D to visually highlight the relevant structures of the images. Here, we therefore propose to extract and display three features of interest:

1. The 3D surface corresponding to the inner side of the ventricle, to be extracted from `frame1`.
2. The estimated motion vectors, displayed for the side points.
3. One of the full *XY* slice planes of `frame1`, allowing to locate the side of the ventricle with respect to the original image data.

A 3D vector object will be constructed for each of these features. The union of these objects will constitute the complete visualization.

10.4.2 Extraction of the 3D surface of the ventricle

As before, we start by initializing the four structures that will define the global 3D object:

```
CImg<> g_points;
CImgList<unsigned int> g_primitives;
CImgList<unsigned char> g_colors;
CImgList<> g_opacities;
```

The extraction of the 3D surface of the ventricle is performed in two steps: the ventricle is first segmented in a purely volumetric way, by the region growth algorithm implemented by the `CImg<T>::draw_fill()` method. This function starts from a point in the image, with coordinates specified by the user, and fills all surrounding pixels whose values are sufficiently close to the value of the initial point. This method is usually called for filling shapes in classical 2D images, but it can be used for volumetric images as well.

Here we choose an origin point of coordinates $(55, 55, 7)$, located in the bright structure from which we want to extract the shape. We call one of the versions of `CImg<T>::draw_fill()` allowing a `region` image to be passed as an argument. This method will construct the set of voxels visited during the region growth. When returning from `CImg<T>::draw_fill()`, the image `region` is a binary volumetric image with all voxels defining the interior of the 3D segmented region set to 1 (0 everywhere else).

In a second step, the call to `CImg<T>::get_isosurface3d()` on the image `region` (previously blurred then re-binarized) allows to extract the 3D surface referring to the 0.5 isovalue in this binary image. The assignment of colors and opacities associated with this 3D surface is then performed by adding as many color and opacity vectors as there are primitives to the lists `g_colors` and `g_opacities` (Code 10.7). The `CImg<T>::get_isosurface3d()` method actually implements the so-called *marching cubes* technique, in order to transform a dense volumetric image into a 3D mesh.

Code 10.7 – Ventricular side extraction by region growth.

```
CImg<> region;
float value = 0;
```

```
(+frame1).draw_fill(55,55,7,&value,1,region,40,true);
g_points = region.blur(1.f,1.f,3.f).threshold(0.5f).
                get_isosurface3d(g_primitives,0.5f);
g_colors.insert(g_primitives.size(),
                CImg<unsigned char>::vector(255,128,0));
g_opacities.insert(g_primitives.size(),
                CImg<>::vector(1));
```

10.4.3 Adding 3D motion vectors

The addition of the 3D motion vectors is in fact the most difficult part of the implementation. There is no ready-made method in *CImg* to convert the vector field `motion` into a 3D vector object, so we will have to build this object by hand.

As we only want to display these motion vectors for the voxels of the ventricle side, the first thing to do is to isolate them. For that purpose, we use the binary image `region`, whose voxels of value 1 define the interior of the segmented area. Then, to extract the surface contour of this region, it is sufficient to detect the voxels with value 1 having at least one of their neighbors set to 0. A simple way of doing this is to compute a morphological dilation of the image `region`, from which we subtract the image `region` itself (this is also called a dilation gradient, see Section 4 of Chapter 4).

```
region = region.get_dilate(3) - region;
```

To symbolize a displacement vector in 3D, we use a colored segment, terminated by a sphere giving the direction of the vector. So we just have to go through each voxel of the image `motion`, and add the vertices corresponding to each displacement vector that we want to visualize, into the lists `g_points` and `g_primitives`. This is what Code 10.8 does:

> **Code 10.8 – Adding the 3D motion vectors.**

```
CImgList<> points; // List of vertices for the motion vectors
int ind = g_points.width(); // Index of the next vertex to add
cimg_forXYZ(motion,x,y,z) if (region(x,y,z))
{
  float
     u = motion(x,y,z,0),
     v = motion(x,y,z,1),
     w = motion(x,y,z,2),
     norm = cimg::hypot(u,v,w);
  if (norm>0.5) { // The motion vector is long enough

     // Add a new primitive, of type 'segment'.
```

```
CImg<>::vector(x,y,z).move_to(points);
CImg<>::vector(x + u, y + v, z + w).move_to(points);
CImg<unsigned int>::vector(ind,ind + 1).
  move_to(g_primitives);

// Add a new primitive, of type 'sphere'.
CImg<>::vector(x + u - 0.2, y + v, z + w).move_to(points);
CImg<>::vector(x + u + 0.2, y + v, z + w).move_to(points);
CImg<unsigned int>::vector(ind + 2,ind + 3,0,0,0).
  move_to(g_primitives);

// Add the same color/opacity for both primitives.
CImg<unsigned char> color = motion.get_vector_at(x,y,z).
  normalize(0,255);
g_colors.insert(2,color);
g_opacities.insert(2,CImg<>::vector(0.7f));

ind += 4; // Update the index of the next vertex
  }
}

// Insert motion vectors vertices into the global list.
g_points.append(points.get_append('x'),'x');
```

10.4.4   Adding cutting planes

Finally, we add a cutting plane to the global 3D object, that allows to visualize the location of the ventricular surface in the environment of the original volumetric image. The input images, of dimensions $100 \times 100 \times 14$, having a relatively low depth, we limit ourselves to the addition of a single *XY* slice: the *XZ* and *YZ* slices being very thin, do not add anything interesting to the visualization.

A simple way to create a textured plane is to generate a 3D elevation of a texture (here the image `frame1`), via the method `CImg<T>::get_elevation3d()`, by passing a constant elevation map, as realized in Code 10.9:

Code 10.9 – Adding a cutting plane *XY*.

```
CImgList<unsigned int> c_primitives;
CImgList<unsigned char> c_colors;
frame1.normalize(0,255).resize(-100,-100,-100,3,1);

// Compute a textured 3D elevation from a constant elevation map.
CImg<> c_points = frame1.get_slice(2*frame1.depth()/3).
                    get_elevation3d(c_primitives,c_colors,
CImg<>(frame1.width(),frame1.height(),1,1,2*frame1.depth()/3));

// Add the textured plane to the global 3D object.
```

```
g_points.append_object3d(g_primitives,c_points,c_primitives);
g_colors.insert(c_colors);
g_opacities.insert(c_primitives.size(),CImg<>::vector(1));
```

10.4.5 Final result

The 3D object is now complete and ready to be visualized. Note that since image voxels are not cubic (voxel size is $1 \times 1 \times 2.5$), it is appropriate to apply a 3D scale correction, by multiplying the z-coordinates of each vertex:

```
g_points.get_shared_row(2) *= 2.5f;
```

All that remains is to generate a colored background, and launch *CImg*'s interactive 3D viewer using the `CImg<T>::display_object3d()` method, exactly as we did in previous examples (Code 10.6). The final visualization is displayed in Figure 10.5.

It is thus possible to create 3D views of relatively complex objects thanks to the integrated 3D rendering engine of *CImg* and this, without the need of third-party libraries or specific rendering software. Note however that the implementation of the *CImg* 3D engine is done purely with the *CPU* (no hardware acceleration using graphic cards is used). Thus, 3D rendering with *CImg* is somehow limited to the visualization of medium-sized objects (a few hundred thousand primitives). On the contrary, real-time visualization of larger 3D objects (several million primitives) would require to use specific 3D rendering libraries (*GPU*-accelerated). Anyway, this is still one of the nice features of *CImg*, which can help prototyping algorithms and applications that require simple and quick 3D visualization.

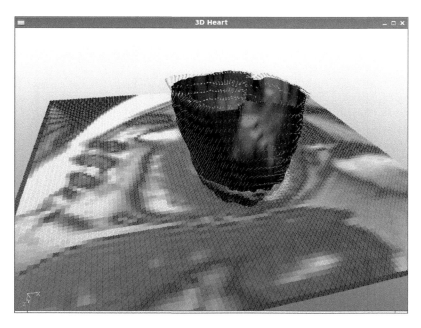

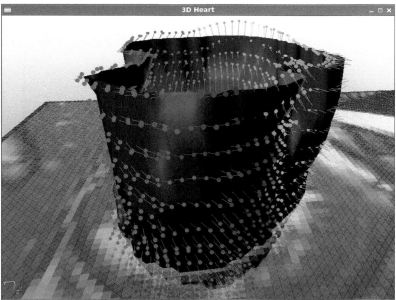

Figure 10.5 – 3D visualization of one ventricular side of the heart, from a sequence of *MRI* volumetric images.

11. And So Many Other Things...

The field of digital image processing is so large that it is actually impossible to embrace all its aspects exhaustively in a single book. In this last chapter, we therefore propose some other possible applications, more original or more rarely discussed, and which point out once again the flexibility and genericity of the *CImg* library to deal with various problems. Thus, we will illustrate here how to efficiently compress an image, how to reconstruct an object from its tomographic projections, how to recover the 3D geometry of a scene from a pair of stereographic images, or how to develop an original user interface allowing to warp images (e.g., portraits) from the webcam. Afterwards, we trust you to invent or discover other aspects of image processing that have not been covered in this book!

11.1 Compression by transform (*JPEG*)

11.1.1 Introduction - Compression by transform

Two main approaches exist for compressing data:

- *Lossless compression* or *coding* which minimizes the size of the data by reducing the redundancy of its code. During the decompression phase, or decoding, the data is found exactly as it was at the beginning;
- *Lossy compression* which suppresses information in the signal considered irrelevant for the subsequent use of the data. Generally, this type of compression is used to compress sound, image and video data. When decompressing the data, we obtain a signal different from the original one, but with a difference that is hopefully imperceptible for a given use case (listening to the music, viewing the image, etc.).

Lossy methods are often based on *compression by transform*. The idea is to apply a mathematical transform to the original signal, then quantize the coefficients of the resulting representation in the transformed space.

Several arguments justify this approach:
- The transform, which is mathematically equivalent to a change in the encoding

basis of the signal, often makes it possible to obtain an alternative representation which highlights its important content and thus the relevant information to be recorded or transmitted;

- The transform allows to concentrate the energy of the signal only on a few coefficients, obtaining a *sparse* representation, which implies less data to be recorded, by suppressing the coefficients of low values in the transformed representation;
- The transform reduces the correlation of the data, and thus decreases the source entropy. Shannon's information theory [38] links the source's entropy to the capacity of coding, and therefore of the compression.

Figure 11.1 shows the general idea of compression by transform. Quantizing the coefficients of the transform reduces their number because those close to zero will not be stored.

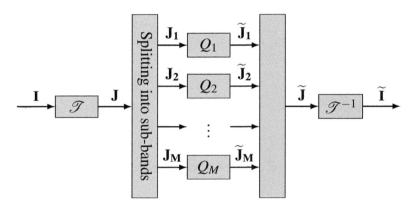

Figure 11.1 – Principle of compression by transform: following a transform $\mathscr{T}$, sub-bands are quantized to make the information sparse and thus to reduce the quantity of data $\left\{ \widetilde{\mathbf{J}_i} \right\}_{i=1..M}$ to be recorded.

11.1.2 *JPEG* Algorithm

The *JPEG*[1] standard defines the format and decoding algorithm for lossy compressed images. *JPEG* stands for *Joint Photographic Experts Group*, a group of experts working on these topics. The official and definitive standard for *JPEG* compression of images was adopted in 1992. The *JPEG* compression and decompression process consists of six main steps shown in Figure 11.2:

---

[1] ISO/CEI 10918-1 | UIT-T Recommendation T.81

1. **Color transformation**: *JPEG* works on the luminance/chrominance color space *YCbCr* (see Section 9.2);
2. **Chrominance sub-sampling**: To take advantage of the low sensitivity of the human eye to the chrominance, we subsample the chrominance signal. The idea is to reduce the size of the chrominance blocks (decimation) without altering the size of the luminance blocks (blocks *Y*) (different possibilities are offered: `4:4:4, 4:2:0, 4:2:2, ...`) ;
3. **Split into blocks**: The *JPEG* format splits the image into 8×8 square blocks ;
4. *DCT*: The *DCT* (*Discrete Cosine Transform*) is a variant of the Fourier transform (Section5.3.2) for a real-valued signal (rather than complex-valued). Each block is converted into a map of frequencies and amplitudes rather than light intensities and color coefficients. The value of a frequency in a block reflects the size and speed of change in a cosine base, while the amplitude value corresponds to the deviation associated with each color change. The *DCT* is invertible, therefore lossless;
5. **Quantization**: Quantization is the step in the *JPEG* compression algorithm where most of the information loss (and therefore visual quality) occurs. It is also the step that compresses the signal the most. Quantization consists in dividing the matrix resulting from the *DCT* with another matrix, namely the *quantization matrix*, which contains 8×8 coefficients specifically defined by the standard. Here the goal is to attenuate the very high frequencies in each block, i.e., those to which the human eye is the less sensitive. These high frequencies initially have low amplitudes, which are further attenuated by quantization (corresponding coefficients may even reduce to 0);
6. **RLE and Huffman coding**: The coding of the *DC* (i.e., *DCT* value in zero = average value) and *AC* coefficients (other coefficients) are different. The *AC* coefficients are scanned and encoded in zigzag, then compressed by a *RLE* algorithm (*Run Length Encoding*) and finally by an entropic coding (Huffman or arithmetic coding). These first two steps make it possible to reduce the entropy of the source and thus make encoding more efficient.

11.1.3 Discrete cosine transform and quantization

The discrete cosine transform, denoted *J*, of a digital image *I* of size $N \times N$ pixels is defined for all $(u,v) \in [\![0, N-1]\!]^2$ by:

$$J[u,v] = \frac{2}{N} C[u] C[v] \sum_{i=0}^{N-1} \sum_{j=0}^{N-1} I[i,j] \cos\left[\frac{(2i+1)u\pi}{2N}\right] \cos\left[\frac{(2j+1)v\pi}{2N}\right]$$

$$\text{where } C[u] = \begin{cases} \frac{1}{\sqrt{2}} & \text{for } u = 0 \\ 1 & \text{for } u > 0 \end{cases}$$

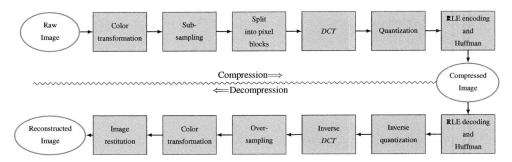

Figure 11.2 – General principle of the *JPEG* compression and decompression pipelines.

Code 11.1 computes the discrete cosine transform of a square image of size $N \times N$.

Code 11.1 – Discrete cosine transform of a square image.

```
/*
  JPEG_DCT: Compute the discrete cosine transform (DCT)

  block     : Input image
  cosvalues : Pre-calculation of the cosine values for DCT
  return    : DCT of the input image
*/
CImg<> JPEG_DCT(CImg<>& block, CImg<>& cosvalues)
{
  unsigned int N = 8; // Resolution of a block

  CImg<> dct(N,N,1,1,0);
  cimg_forXY(dct,i,j)
  {
    float
      ci = i==0 ? 1/sqrt(2.0f) : 1,
      cj = j==0 ? 1/sqrt(2.0f) : 1;

    cimg_forXY(block,x,y)
      dct(i,j) += block(x, y)*cosvalues(x,i)*cosvalues(y,j);

    dct(i,j) *= 2.0f/N*ci*cj;
  }
  return dct;
}
```

The inverse transform (Code 11.2) is defined for all $(i, j) \in [\![0, N-1]\!]^2$ by:

$$I[i,j] = \frac{2}{N} \sum_{u=0}^{N-1} \sum_{v=0}^{N-1} C[u]\,C[v]\,J[u,v] \cos\left[\frac{(2i+1)u\pi}{2N}\right] \cos\left[\frac{(2j+1)v\pi}{2N}\right]$$

The implementation of the inverse transform is done by Code 11.2:

Code 11.2 – Inverse discrete cosine transform of a square image.

```
/*
  JPEG_IDCT: Compute the inverse discrete cosine transform (iDCT).

  dct        : DCT <=> input data
  cosvalues  : Pre-calculation of the cosine values for DCT
  return     : Output image
*/
CImg<> JPEG_IDCT(CImg<>& dct, CImg<>& cosvalues)
{
  unsigned int N = 8;  // Resolution of a block

  CImg<> img(N,N,1,1,0);
  cimg_forXY(img,x,y)
  {
    cimg_forXY(dct,i,j)
    {
      float
        ci = (i==0) ? 1/std::sqrt(2) : 1,
        cj = (j==0) ? 1/std::sqrt(2) : 1;
      img(x,y) += ci*cj*dct(i,j)*cosvalues(x,i)*cosvalues(y,j);
    }
    img(x,y) *= 2.0f/N;
  }
  return img;
}
```

The quantization step is computed with:

$$\forall (u,v) \in [\![0, N-1]\!]^2, \ \widetilde{J}[u,v] = \text{round}\left(\frac{J[u,v]}{\gamma \times Q[u,v]}\right).$$

where the quantization matrix (defined by the *JPEG* standard) is given by:

$$\mathbf{Q} = \begin{bmatrix} 16 & 11 & 10 & 16 & 24 & 40 & 51 & 61 \\ 12 & 12 & 14 & 19 & 26 & 58 & 60 & 55 \\ 14 & 13 & 16 & 24 & 40 & 57 & 69 & 56 \\ 14 & 17 & 22 & 29 & 51 & 87 & 80 & 62 \\ 18 & 22 & 37 & 56 & 68 & 109 & 103 & 77 \\ 24 & 35 & 55 & 64 & 81 & 104 & 113 & 92 \\ 49 & 64 & 78 & 87 & 103 & 121 & 120 & 101 \\ 72 & 92 & 95 & 98 & 112 & 100 & 103 & 99 \end{bmatrix}.$$

The γ parameter adjusts the compression ratio (or the quality of the reconstructed image). The larger γ is, the more loss the image will suffer, thus leading to a better compression ratio. The implementation of the quantization step in the transformed space is given by Code 11.3.

Code 11.3 – Quantization of the *DCT* coefficients.

```
/*

    JPEGEncoder: Compute the DCT transform + Quantization

    image      : Input image
    quality    : Quality factor / Compression ratio ( low = higher
        quality )
    cosvalues : Pre-calculation of the cosine values for DCT
    return     : Image of the quantized DCT

*/
CImg<> JPEGEncoder(CImg<>& image, float quality, CImg<>& cosvalues)
{
  unsigned int N = 8; // Resolution of a bloc

  // Quantization matrix from the JPEG standard.
  int dataQ[] = { 16,11,10,16,24,40,51,61,
                  12,12,14,19,26,58,60,55,
                  14,13,16,24,40,57,69,56,
                  14,17,22,29,51,87,80,62,
                  18,22,37,56,68,109,103,77,
                  24,35,55,64,81,104,113,92,
                  49,64,78,87,103,121,120,101,
                  72,92,95,98,112,100,103,99 };
  CImg<>
    Q = CImg<>(dataQ,N,N)*quality,
    comp(image.width(),image.height(),1,1,0),
```

```
   block(N,N), dct(N,N);

  for (int k = 0; k<image.width()/N; ++k)
    for (int l = 0; l<image.height()/N; ++l)
    {
      block = image.get_crop(k*N,l*N,(k + 1)*N-1,(l + 1)*N - 1);
      block -= 128;

      dct = JPEG_DCT(block,cosvalues);
      cimg_forXY(dct,i,j)
        comp(k*N + i,l*N + j) = cimg::round(dct(i,j)/Q(i,j));
    }

  return comp;
}
```

Code 11.4 then illustrates the coefficient reconstruction. Of course, there is a loss of information between the quantization and reconstruction steps.

Code 11.4 – Compute the *DCT* coefficient in the reconstruction step.

```
/*
  JPEGDecoder: Compute the reconstructed image from the quantized
      DCT

  img_dct    : Quantized DCT <=> Input data
  quality    : Quality factor / Compression ratio ( low = higher
      quality )
  cosvalues : Pre-calculation of the cosine values for DCT
  return     : Reconstructed image
*/
CImg<> JPEGDecoder(CImg<>& img_dct, float quality, CImg<>& cosvalues
    )
{
  unsigned int N = 8; // Resolution of a bloc

  // Quantization matrix, from the JPEG standard.
  int dataQ[] = { 16,11,10,16,24,40,51,61,
                  12,12,14,19,26,58,60,55,
                  14,13,16,24,40,57,69,56,
                  14,17,22,29,51,87,80,62,
                  18,22,37,56,68,109,103,77,
                  24,35,55,64,81,104,113,92,
                  49,64,78,87,103,121,120,101,
                  72,92,95,98,112,100,103,99 };
  CImg<>
    Q = CImg<>(dataQ,N,N)*quality,
    decomp(img_dct.width(),img_dct.height(),1,1,0),
    dct(N,N), blk(N,N);
```

```
for (int k = 0; k<img_dct.width()/N; ++k)
  for (int l = 0; l<img_dct.height()/N; ++l)
  {
    dct = img_dct.get_crop(k*N,l*N,(k + 1)*N - 1,(l + 1)*N - 1);
    dct.mul(Q);
    blk = JPEG_IDCT(dct,cosvalues) + 128;

    cimg_forXY(blk,i,j)
      decomp(k*N + i,l*N + j) = blk(i,j);
  }
return decomp;
}
```

11.1.4 Simplified *JPEG* algorithm

The information loss in the compressed image can be evaluated by the distortion $\varepsilon = \frac{1}{N \times M} \sum_{i=0}^{N-1} \sum_{j=0}^{M-1} \left(\widetilde{I}[i,j] - I[i,j] \right)^2$, which is the average quadratic error between the reconstructed and the initial images (Code 11.5).

Code 11.5 – Compute the distortion due to the compression by transform.

```
/*
  distortionRate : Compute the quadratic deviation.

  image      : Original image
  comp_image : "Compressed" image (DCT + quantization)
  return     : Quadratic deviation
*/
float distortionRate(CImg<>& image, CImg<>& comp_image)
{
  float rate = (image - comp_image).sqr().sum();
  return rate /= image.width()*image.height();
}
```

To illustrate the compression by transform, we implement a simplified version of the *JPEG* compression algorithm. We will only implement the *DCT* transform of 8×8 pixel blocks, as well as the quantization step and the reconstruction of the image. These different steps are represented in Fig. 11.3.

The corresponding algorithm is given in Code 11.7, and uses a function (Code 11.6) that precomputes the cosine values.

Code 11.6 – Tabulation of cosine values.

```
CImg<> genCosValues()
{
  CImg<> cosinusvalues(N,N);
  cimg_forXY(cosinusvalues,i,x)
    cosinusvalues(x,i) = std::cos(((2*x+1)*i*cimg::PI)/(2*N));
  return cosinusvalues;
}
```

Code 11.7 – Compression by transform - Simplified version of the *JPEG* algorithm.

```
int main(int argc,char **argv)
{
  // Passing parameters by command line.
  cimg_usage("Simplified JPEG compression");
  const char
    *input_f = cimg_option("-i","lena.bmp","Input image"),
    *output_f = cimg_option("-o",(char*)0,"Output image");
  float quality = cimg_option("-q",1.0,"Quality factor");

  // Read input image.
  CImg<> imgIn(input_f);
  imgIn.channel(0);

  // Pre-compute cosine values.
  CImg<> cos_values = genCosValues();

  // Compute DCT + quantization.
  CImg<> dct_image = JPEGEncoder(imgIn,quality,cos_values);

  // Image reconstruction.
  CImg<> comp_image = JPEGDecoder(dct_image,quality,cos_values);

  // Display quadratic deviation between the images.
  float dist = distortionRate(imgIn,comp_image);
  std::cout << "Distortion Rate : " << dist << std::endl;

  // Display images.
  (imgIn,dct_image,comp_image).display("Input image - "
                                        "Image of the DCT blocks - "
                                        "Decompressed image");

  // Save output image (if filename specified).
  if (output_f)
    comp_image.save(output_f);
}
```

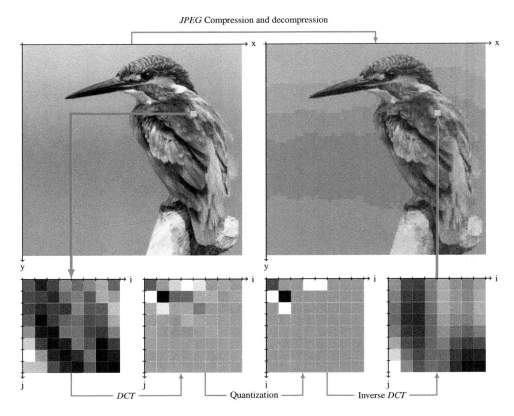

Figure 11.3 – Processing of a block by the *DCT* for the *JPEG* compression.

Figure 11.4 illustrates the compression by the *DCT* transform. The algorithm is a simplified version of the *JPEG* compression where the entropy coding, i.e., the Huffman coding step, is not implemented. The compression ratio can be overestimated by the number of the non-zero coefficients in the *DCT* space, divided by the number of coefficients. The loss of quality is not proportional to the reduction in the size of the compressed information.

11.2   Tomographic reconstruction

11.2.1   Introduction

Tomography (Greek roots, *tomos*: " slice " and *graphia*: " writing ") makes it possible to map the internal parameters of an object, according to one or more section planes, from external measurements and calculations. It is a technique that probes the material. The applications are numerous such as non-destructive testing, geophysics (ocean

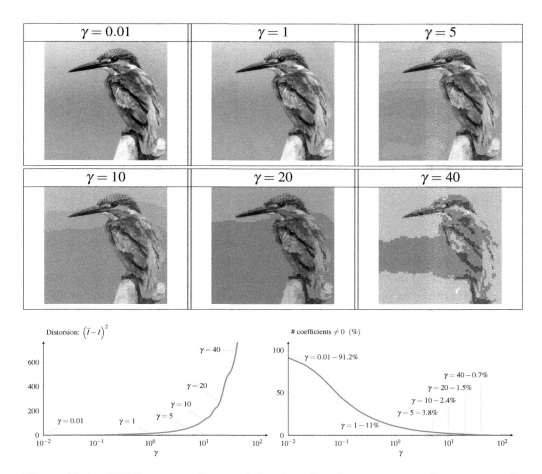

Figure 11.4 – *JPEG* compression result by changing the γ parameter. Reconstructed images for different values of γ. Evolution of the distortion and the proportion of non-zero coefficients in the *DCT* space as a function of γ.

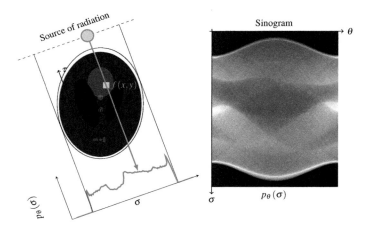

Figure 11.5 – Geometric modeling in analytical tomographic reconstruction, illustrated with a phantom.

probing, geological layers), astrophysics or medical imaging. There are several possible approaches that can be grouped into two main classes:
- *Analytical* reconstruction, based on a *continuous* representation of the problem;
- *Algebraic* reconstruction, based on a *discrete* representation of the problem.

11.2.2 Analytical tomographic reconstruction

The idea is to have external measurements of an object called projections. Depending on the application, these projections are obtained with different physical radiations. For example, in the case of a medical scanner, the radiation used are X-rays and the projections are related to the density of the material crossed by the rays.

GEOMETRIC MODELING - SINOGRAM

Figure 11.5 illustrates the geometric modeling in an analytical approach. We consider an unknown object (thus to be reconstructed) which will correspond to an image $f(x,y)$. The projections, which correspond to the input data, are obtained by "summation" (to simplify the problem and to detach from physical phenomena such as absorption or diffusion) along the rays which form an angle θ with the reference frame $(O;x;y)$ associated with the object to be reconstructed. The projection obtained along the angle θ is noted $p_\theta(\sigma)$.

The measurements are performed for $\theta \in [0, \pi[$. The *sinogram* is the set of measurements and corresponds to an image which is formed of the set of projections

$p_\theta(\sigma)$.

RADON TRANSFORM

The link between the image $f(x,y)$ and the projections $p_\theta(\sigma)$ is defined by the Radon transform (RT):

$$f(x,y) \overset{RT}{\leftrightarrow} p_\theta(\sigma) = \int_{\mathbb{R}} f(\sigma, \tau)\, \mathrm{d}\tau$$

Code 11.8 allows to simulate/compute the Radon transform of an image `imgIn` according to `nb_proj` projections.

Code 11.8 – Calculation of projections (Radon transform).

```
/*
   RadonTransform: Calculation of projections (<=> Radon transform).

   imgIn   : Input image
   nb_proj : Number of projections
*/
CImg<> RadonTransform(CImg<>& imgIn, int nb_proj)
{
  CImg<> sinogram(nb_proj,img.width(),1,1,0);
  for (int o = 0; o<nb_proj; ++o)
  {
    float
      orient = o*180.0f/nb_proj,
      xc = imgIn.width()/2.0f,
      yc = imgIn.height()/2.0f;
    CImg<> rot_img = imgIn.get_rotate(orient,xc,yc,2);
    cimg_forXY(rot_img,x,y)
      sinogram(o,x) += rot_img(x,y);
  }
  return sinogram;
}
```

The main problem of tomographic reconstruction in an analytical approach is therefore to invert the Radon transform.

INVERSE RADON TRANSFORM

To do this, a first step is to establish a link between the different projections and the image so we place ourselves in the Fourier space on the projections.

$$P_\theta(q) = \int_{-\infty}^{+\infty} p_\theta(\sigma) e^{-j2\pi\sigma q} d\sigma \quad \text{(definition via the 1D Fourier transform.)}$$

$$= \int_{-\infty}^{+\infty} \left(\int_{-\infty}^{+\infty} f(\sigma,\tau) d\tau \right) e^{-j2\pi\sigma q} d\sigma$$

$$= \iint_{\mathbb{R}^2} f(\sigma,\tau) e^{-j2\pi\sigma q} d\sigma d\tau \quad \text{(substitution } (\sigma,\tau) \Rightarrow (x,y))$$

$$= \iint_{\mathbb{R}^2} f(x,y) e^{-j2\pi(xq\cos(\theta)+yq\sin(\theta))} dx dy$$

$$= F(u,v)\Big|_{\begin{cases} u = q\cos(\theta) \\ v = q\sin(\theta) \end{cases}}$$

where $F(u,v)$ is the 2D Fourier transform of $f(x,y)$.

This result is known as the *Fourier-Slice Theorem*. Thanks to this theorem, we can build an algorithm to reconstruct the image from the projections, working in the Fourier space of the image. We can also build an algorithm using the notion of linear filtering, called filtered back projection algorithm.

TOMOGRAPHIC RECONSTRUCTION BY FILTERED BACK PROJECTION

Simple back projection is defined by: $g(x,y) = \int_0^\pi p_\theta(\sigma) d\theta$, and Code 11.9 implements this operation.

Code 11.9 – Simple back projection.

```
/*
   BackProjTransform: Calculation of a simple back projection.

   sinog : Sinogram <=> input datas
   bp    : Simple back-projection of "sinog" input data
*/
CImg<> BackProjTransform(CImg<>& sinog)
{
  float orient_step = 180.0f/sinog.width();
  CImg<> bp(sinog.height(),sinog.height(),1,1,0);

  for (int o = 0; o<sinog.width(); ++o)
  {
    cimg_forXY(bp_sinog,x,y)
       bp(x,y) += sinog(o,x);
    bp.rotate(orient_step,sinog.height()/2.0f,sinog.height()/2.0f,2)
       ;
  }
  bp.rotate(180,sinog.height()/2.0f,sinog.height()/2.0f,2);
```

```
    return bp;
}
```

The simple back projection is not the solution to the inverse Radon transform. On the other hand, we can show that:

$$p_\theta\left(\sigma\right) \overset{RT^{-1}}{\leftrightarrow} f\left(x,y\right) = \int_0^\pi \left(\int_{-\infty}^{+\infty} P_\theta\left(q\right)|q|e^{j2\pi q\sigma}\mathrm{d}q\right)\mathrm{d}\theta = \int_0^\pi h_\theta\left(\sigma\right)\mathrm{d}\theta$$

with $h_\theta\left(\sigma\right) \overset{FT_{1D}}{\longleftrightarrow} |q|P_\gamma\left(q\right)$. The image to be reconstructed $f\left(x,y\right)$ is thus the back projection of a quantity noted $h_\theta\left(\sigma\right)$. From the definition of $h_\theta\left(\sigma\right)$, we notice that it is a filtered version of the projections $p_\theta\left(\sigma\right)$. The filter to be used has a frequency response which is a ramp $G\left(q\right) = |q|$. This equation allows to propose a reconstruction algorithm (Algorithm 6).

Algorithm 6: Filtered back projection reconstruction algorithm.

Input: Acquisitions: projections $p_\theta\left(\sigma\right)$
Result: Reconstructed image: $f\left(x,y\right)$
Computation of the FT$_{1D}$ of $p_\theta\left(\sigma\right) \overset{FT_{1D}}{\longleftrightarrow} P_\theta\left(q\right)$

High-pass filtering via the ramp filter $|q|P_\theta\left(q\right) \overset{FT_{1D}^{-1}}{\longleftrightarrow} h_\theta\left(\sigma\right)$

Calculation of the back projection $f\left(x,y\right) = \int_0^\pi h_\theta\left(\sigma\right)\mathrm{d}\theta$

The filtering of the projections, arranged in the sinogram, is performed by Code 11.10. The whole algorithm of tomographic reconstruction by filtered back projection is then given in Code 11.11.

Code 11.10 – Filtering of the projections by the ramp filter.

```
/*
  SinogramFiltering: Projection filtering ( sinogram )

  sinog  : Sinogram <=> input data
  return : Sinogram filtered by the ramp filter
*/
CImg<> SinogramFiltering(CImg<>& sinog)
{
  // Calculation of the Fourier transform in 1D.
  CImgList<> FFTy_sinog = sinog.get_FFT('y');

  // Filtering with the ramp filter.
```

```
cimg_forX(FFTy_sinog[0],o)
{
  for (int sigma = 0; sigma<sinog.height()/2; ++sigma)
  {
    float coeff = xi/sinog.height()/2.0f;
    FFTy_sinog[0](o,sigma) *= coeff;
    FFTy_sinog[0](o,sinog.height() - 1 - sigma) *= coeff;
    FFTy_sinog[1](o,sigma) *= coeff;
    FFTy_sinog[1](o,sinog.height() - 1 - sigma) *= coeff;
  }
}
// Calculation of the 1D inverse Fourier transform.
CImgList<> iFFTy_sinog = FFTy_sinog.get_FFT('y',true);
return iFFTy_sinog[0];
}
```

Code 11.11 – Tomographic reconstruction by filtered back projection.

```
/*
  Main function for analytical tomographic reconstruction
*/

int main(int argc, const char * argv[])
{
  cimg_usage("Tomographic Reconstruction by "
             "filtered back projection");
  const char *file = cimg_option("-i","phantom.bmp",
                                 "Input : Name of the 2D input image
                                  (square image)");
  int nbProj = cimg_option("-np",50,
                           "Number of projections for the
                            calculation "
                           "of the Radon transform");
  CImg<>
    image(file),
    radon_img = RadonTransform(image,nbProj),
    fsin_img = SinogramFiltering(radon_img),
    fbp_img = BackProjTransform(fsin_img);

  (image,radon_img,fdb_img).display("Original image - "
                                    "Sinogram - "
                                    "Reconstructed Image");
  return 0;
}
```

In Fig. 11.6, the results for the analytical tomographic reconstruction are shown for a number of projections. Theoretically, it is necessary to have a number of projections (thus measurements) of the same order of magnitude as the size of the image. One of the particularities of this reconstruction is the presence of artifacts due to the use of back projection.

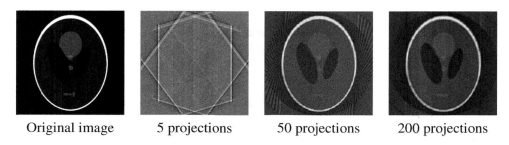

Original image   5 projections   50 projections   200 projections

Figure 11.6 – Results on analytical tomographic reconstruction by the filtered back projection algorithm.

11.2.3 Algebraic tomographic reconstruction

Analytical tomographic reconstruction techniques model the problem in continuous form as opposed to algebraic techniques which approach the problem directly in numerical form.

GEOMETRIC MODELING - MATRIX FORMULATION

The modeling of the problem can be written directly in matrix form:

$$\mathbf{p} = \mathbf{A}\mathbf{f} \text{ where } \begin{cases} \mathbf{p} = \begin{pmatrix} p_1, & \cdots, & p_M \end{pmatrix}^\top \\ \mathbf{f} = \begin{pmatrix} f_1, & \cdots, & f_N \end{pmatrix}^\top \\ \mathbf{A} = \begin{pmatrix} a_{11}, & \cdots, & a_{1N} \\ \vdots & & \vdots \\ a_{M1}, & \cdots, & a_{MN} \end{pmatrix} \end{cases} \tag{11.1}$$

In Equation 11.1, the values of the N pixels of the image to be reconstructed are stored in the vector $\mathbf{f}$. They are linked to the M measurements which are stored in the vector p through the projection matrix $\mathbf{A}$.

The projection matrix allows to model the acquisition system: the coefficient $a_{i,j}$ gives the contribution of the pixel j in the measurement i. This modeling is illustrated in Fig. 11.7. The major interest of this modeling concerns the beams where we can take into account the geometry (non-parallel geometries), the physical phenomena (attenuation, scattering, ...) and the response of the acquisition system.

These different elements are illustrated in Fig. 11.8: the vector **p** which corresponds to the measurements (in vectorized form), the projection matrix **A** which shows the link between the pixels and the measurements and finally the image to be reconstructed **f** which must be as close as possible to the original image.

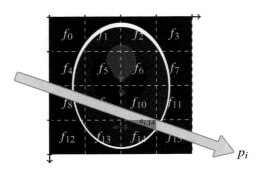

Figure 11.7 – Geometric modeling in algebraic tomographic reconstruction. For an image of N = 16 pixels, p_i is the ith measurement over the M available and $a_{i,14}$ corresponds to the share of the indexed pixel 14 in the ith measurement.

The objective is therefore to calculate **f** from Equation 11.1, which is an over-determined linear system. The classical methods of resolution (pseudo-inverse for example) cannot be used because the dimensions of the **A** matrix are too large. We therefore turn to iterative methods, such as the *Algebraic Reconstruction Technique (ART)* algorithm.

ART ALGORITHM - *Algebraic Reconstruction Technique*

The *Algebraic Reconstruction Technique (ART)* method described by Algorithm 7 and Code 11.12 allows to reconstruct the image by a rather simple iterative method. At iteration n we randomly choose a projection i. Then we compute the projection of the current image $\mathbf{f^{(n)}}$ and finally update it by taking into account the difference between this projection $\mathbf{a_i f^{(n)}}$ and the measurement p_i. This update takes into account the contribution of the pixels in this projection/measurement by the vector $\mathbf{a_i}$.

Code 11.12 – *ART* algorithm.

```
/*
  ART algorithm for algebraic tomographic reconstruction.

  A        : Projection matrix
  p        : Measurements (or projections)
  nbiter   : Number of iterations
```

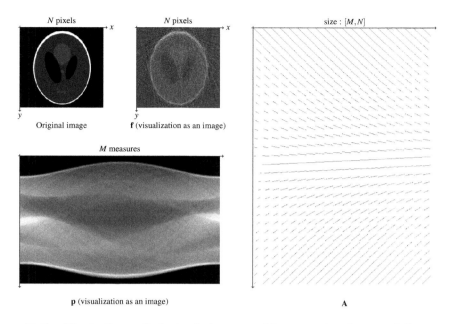

Figure 11.8 – Illustrations of algebraic tomographic reconstruction modeling: projection matrix **A**, measurements **p** and reconstruction **f**.

```
*/
CImg<> ART(CImg<>& A,CImg<>& p, int nbiter)
{
  float eps = 1e-8f;
  CImg<> f(1,A.width(),1,1,0);

  for (int k = 0; k<nbiter; ++k)
  {
    // Random drawing of a value of the measurement.
    int i = cimg::round(cimg::rand(p.height() - 1));

    // Extraction of the projection vector of the measure i.
    CImg<> ai = A.get_row(i),aiT = ai.get_transpose();

    // Calculation of the squared norm of ai.
    float norm2_ai = (ai*aiT)[0];

    // Update of the image.
    if (norm2_ai>eps) f -= (((ai*f)(0,0) - p(0,i))/norm2_ai)*aiT;
  }
  return f;
}
```

Algorithm 7: *ART* - Algebraic Reconstruction Technique.

Input: Projections: $\mathbf{p}$

Data: Projection matrix: $\mathbf{A}$

Result: Reconstructed image: $\mathbf{f}$

Initialization: $\mathbf{f}^{(0)} = (0, \cdots, 0)^T$

for $n = 0$ *to* n_{max} **do**

    Randomly draw a projection $i \in [\![1, M]\!]$

    Calculate this projection with the current image: $\mathbf{a_i}\mathbf{f}^{(\mathbf{n})}$

    Correct the image with the help of the projection error:

    $\mathbf{f}^{(\mathbf{n+1})} = \mathbf{f}^{(\mathbf{n})} - \frac{\mathbf{a_i}\mathbf{f}^{(\mathbf{n})} - p_i}{\mathbf{a_i}\mathbf{a_i^T}}\mathbf{a_i^T}$ où $\mathbf{a_i} = (a_{i1}, \cdots, a_{iN})$

To test this code, it is necessary to simulate the data acquisition process. Code 11.13 allows to calculate the projections of the image to be reconstructed. This code is almost identical to Code 11.8, except that the data are vectorized in the vector $\mathbf{p}$.

Code 11.13 – Simulation of the measurements for the *ART* algorithm.

```
/*
  Simulation of p projections (ART algorithm)
      imgIn    : Original image
      nbProj   : Number of projection orientations
*/
CImg<> Projections(CImg<> img, int nbProj)
{
  int size = imgIn.width();
  CImg<> p(1,nbProj*size,1,1,0);

  for (int o = 0; o<nbProj; ++o)
  {
    float orient = o*180.0f/nbProj;
    CImg<> rot_img = imgIn.get_rotate(orient,size/2.0f,size/2.0f,3);
    cimg_forXY(rot_img,x,y)
      p(0,x + o*size) += rot_img(x,y);
  }
  return p;
}
```

The projection matrix $\mathbf{A}$ is a matrix that characterizes the acquisition system and can be calculated with Code 11.14. For its estimation, we start from an image with a single pixel with the value 1, then we calculate all its projections to assess its contribution for all measurements. This process is repeated for all the pixels.

Code 11.14 – Computation of the projection matrix for the *ART* algorithm.

```
/*
  Simulation of the projection matrix A (ART algorithm).

  size    : Width of the image ( square )
  nbProj : Number of projection orientations
*/
CImg<> MatriceProjection(int size, int nbProj)
{
  CImg<> A(size*size,nbProj*size,1,1,0),
         imgPixel(size,size,1,1,0);

  cimg_forXY(imgPixel,x,y)
  {
    imgPixel(x,y) = 1;
    for (int o = 0; o<nbProj; ++o)
    {
      float orient = o*180.0f/nbProj;
      CImg<> rot_img = imgPixel.get_rotate(orient,
                                      size/2.0f,size/2.0f,3);
      cimg_forXY(rot_img,i,j)
        A(x + y*size,i + o*size) += rot_img(i,j);

    imgPixel(x,y) = 0;
  }
  return A;
}
```

The main program is finally provided by Code 11.15.

Figure 11.9 shows the evolution of the *ART* algorithm over the iterations. On the image reconstructed after 0.1% of the total number of iterations, we can see the update of the pixels on the first projections that have been processed by the algorithm. The image then tends iteratively towards the starting image.

Code 11.15 – Computation of the projection matrix for the *ART* algorithm.

```
/*
  Main program (ART algorithm)
*/
int main(int argc, const char * argv[])
{
  cimg_usage("ART algorithm (tomographic reconstruction)");
  char *file = cimg_option("-i","phantom.bmp","Input image");
  int
```

```
      size = cimg_option("-s",50,"Size of the resized image"),
    nbProj = cimg_option("-np",100,"Number of orientations"),
    scaleIt = cimg_option("-n",2,"Iteration number factor");

  CImg<> img = CImg<>(file).get_resize(size,size).channel(0);

  // Simulation of measurements.
  CImg<> p = Projections(img,nbProj);

  // Computation of the projection matrix (machine parameters).
  CImg<> A = MatriceProjection(size,nbProj);

  // ART reconstruction algorithm.
  CImg<> f = ART(A,p,scaleIt*nbProj*size);

  // Resize an image and save it.
  f.resize(size,size,1,1,-1);
  f.normalize(0,255).save_png("art.png");

  return 0;
}
```

11.3 Stereovision

Stereovision is a set of image analysis techniques aiming at retrieving information about the 3D structure and depth information of the real world from two (or more) images acquired from different points of view (parallax). Far from being exhaustive, we address two classical problems: the search for matching points between two images and the estimation of the depth of objects.

11.3.1 Epipolar geometry

Epipolar geometry (Fig. 11.10) models the geometric relationships of different images of the same scene, taken from different observation points. It allows to describe the dependencies between the pixels in correspondence, i.e., those formed by a single point of the 3D scene observed on each of the images.

Let I_1 and I_2 be two images from two perspective cameras $\mathbf{C_1}$ and $\mathbf{C_2}$ observing the same scene. Let $\mathbf{P_1}$ and $\mathbf{P_2}$ be the projection matrices corresponding to these two images. A point $\mathbf{m} \in \mathbb{R}^3$ of the 3D scene is projected in $\mathbf{m_1} = P_1\mathbf{m}$ on I_1 and $\mathbf{m_2} = P_2\mathbf{m}$ on I_2, where $\mathbf{m_1}$ and $\mathbf{m_2}$ are expressed in homogeneous coordinates. In the following, we are interested in the links between $\mathbf{m_1}$ and $\mathbf{m_2}$. These links are characterized by the epipolar geometry which follows from the epipolar constraint.

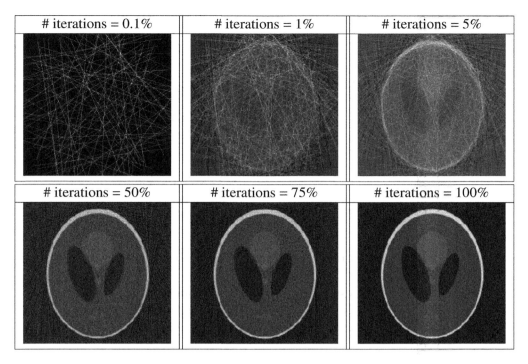

| # iterations = 0.1% | # iterations = 1% | # iterations = 5% |
| # iterations = 50% | # iterations = 75% | # iterations = 100% |

Figure 11.9 – Reconstruction of an image by the *ART* algorithm - Evolution of the reconstruction with respect to the number of iterations.

EPIPOLAR CONSTRAINT

The epipolar constraint characterizes the fact that the corresponding $\mathbf{m_2}$ of a point $\mathbf{m_1}$ lies on a line $\ell_{\mathbf{m_1}}$ in I_2. Indeed, $\mathbf{m_2}$ necessarily belongs to the plane defined by $\mathbf{m_1}$, $\mathbf{C_1}$ and $\mathbf{C_2}$. The line $\ell_{\mathbf{m_1}}$ is called the epipolar line of the point $\mathbf{m_1}$ in I_2. This constraint is symmetrical. The epipolar lines of an image all intersect at a point $\mathbf{e}$ called epipole, which corresponds to the projection of the center of projection of the other image. Thus $\mathbf{e_1} = \mathbf{P_1 C_2}$ and $\mathbf{e_2} = \mathbf{P_2 C_1}$.

FUNDAMENTAL MATRIX

This constraint can be expressed in an algebraic form, through the fundamental matrix, verifying the epipolar relation:

$$\mathbf{m_2^T \top F m_1} = 0$$

Then $\ell_{\mathbf{m_1}} = \mathbf{F m_1}$, and symmetrically $\ell_{\mathbf{m_2}} = \mathbf{F^\top m_2}$. This rank 2 matrix ($\mathbf{F e_1} = 0$) characterizes all the geometry between two images, excluding intrinsic parameters

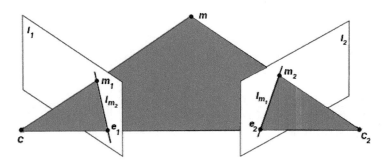

Figure 11.10 – Epipolar geometry.

(focal length, scale factors, optical axis) of the cameras. It is defined up to a scale factor.

The matrix $\mathbf{F}$ can be estimated from at least 8 point matches between images I_1 and I_2. These points can be obtained automatically (using a point of interest detector for example, see Section 6.1), or clicked by the user.

We provide here a simple interactive program, implemented in Code 11.16, which allows to click on n pairs of points, alternatively on the two images, and to return a CImgList of size $n \times 2 \times 3$, where each element of the list is an image whose columns are the coordinates of the clicked points $\mathbf{m}_i^k$.

Let $\mathbf{F} = (f_{ij})_{1 \leq i,j \leq 3}$ and $\mathbf{f} = \begin{pmatrix} f_{11} & f_{12} & f_{13} & f_{21} & f_{22} & f_{23} & f_{31} & f_{32} & f_{33} \end{pmatrix}^{\top}$.
For $(\mathbf{m}_1^k, \mathbf{m}_2^k), k \in [\![1,n]\!]$, n pairs of corresponding points in I_1 and I_2, the relation $\mathbf{m}_2^{k\top} \mathbf{F} \mathbf{m}_1^k = 0$ is valid. If $\mathbf{m}_i^k = \begin{pmatrix} x_i^k & y_i^k & 1 \end{pmatrix}^{\top}, i \in [\![1,2]\!]$, then

$$\begin{pmatrix} x_2^1 x_1^1 & x_2^1 y_1^1 & x_2^1 & y_2^1 x_1^1 & y_2^1 y_1^1 & y_2^1 & x_1^1 & y_1^1 & 1 \\ \vdots & \vdots & \vdots & \vdots & \cdots & \vdots & \vdots & \vdots & \vdots \\ x_2^n x_1^n & x_2^n y_1^n & x_2^n & y_2^n x_1^n & y_2^n y_1^n & y_2^n & x_1^n & y_1^n & 1 \end{pmatrix} \mathbf{f} = \mathbf{0} \quad \text{thus } \mathbf{Af} = \mathbf{0}$$

Code 11.16 – Manual selection of interest point pairs.

```
/*
    Manual selection of interest point pairs on stereo images

    I1,I2 : Stereo images
    n      : Number of points
*/
CImgList<> SelectPoints(CImg<>& I1, CImg<>& I2, int n)
```

```
{
  CImgList<> m(n,2,3);
  int DG = 1, i = 0;
  unsigned char red[] = { 255,0,0 }, gre[] = { 0,255,0 };
  CImgDisplay Dis1(I1,"I1"), Dis2(I2,"I2");

  while (!Dis1.is_closed() && !Dis2.is_closed() && i<n)
  {
    switch (DG)
    {
    case 1 :
      Dis2.set_title("I2");
      Dis1.set_title("Click here");
      Dis1.wait();
      if (Dis1.button() && Dis1.mouse_y()>=0)
      {
        m(i,0,0) = Dis1.mouse_x();
        m(i,0,1) = Dis1.mouse_y();
        m(i,0,2) = 1;
        I1.draw_circle(m(i,0,0),m(i,0,1),5,red,1.0,1).display(Dis1);
        DG = 2;
      } break;
    case 2 :
      Dis1.set_title("I1");
      Dis2.set_title("Click here");
      Dis2.wait();
      if (Dis2.button() && Dis2.mouse_y()>=0)
      {
        m(i,1,0) = Dis2.mouse_x();
        m(i,1,1) = Dis2.mouse_y();
        m(i,1,2) = 1;
        I2.draw_circle(m(i,1,0),m(i,1,1),5,gre,1.0,1).display(Dis2);
        DG = 1;
        ++i;
      } break;
    default : break;
    }
  }
  return m;
}
```

Algorithm 8 and its implementation (Code 11.17) allow to find **F**.

Code 11.17 – 8-points algorithm.

```
/*
  8-points algorithm.

  m : List of points to match
```

Algorithm 8: 8-point algorithm.

Input: $n \geq 8$ pairs of matching points between I_1 and I_2

Output: F

Build **A**

Compute a Singular Value Decomposition of **A**: $\mathbf{A} = \mathbf{U}\Sigma\mathbf{V}^\top$

Elements of **F** =elements of **V** corresponding to the smallest singular value

---

```
    n : Number of points
*/
CImg<> FundamentalMatrix(CImgList<>& m, int n) {
  CImg<> F(3,3),
         A(9,n);
  // Matrix A.
  for (int i = 0; i<n; ++i)
  {
    A(0,i) = m(i,1,0)*m(i,0,0);
    A(1,i) = m(i,1,0)*m(i,0,1);
    A(2,i) = m(i,1,0);
    A(3,i) = m(i,1,1)*m(i,0,0);
    A(4,i) = m(i,1,1)*m(i,0,1);
    A(5,i) = m(i,1,1);
    A(6,i) = m(i,0,0);
    A(7,i) = m(i,0,1);
    A(8,i) = 1;
  }

  // SVD.
  CImg<> U, S, V;
  A.SVD(U,S,V);

  //  F = last column of V.
  CImg<> f = V.get_column(8);
  F(0,0) = f(0);   F(1,0) = f(1);   F(2,0) = f(2);
  F(0,1) = f(3);   F(1,1) = f(4);   F(2,1) = f(5);
  F(0,2) = f(6);   F(1,2) = f(7);   F(2,2) = f(8);

  return F;
}
```

F is generally not a rank 2 matrix (it would be of rank 2 if there were no measurement, model or computational error). To impose the rank, we go again through the singular value decomposition. Let **F** be the matrix previously computed. We look for the matrix $\hat{\mathbf{F}}$ of rank 2 closest to **F** by computing $\mathbf{F} = \mathbf{U}$, by imposing to the smallest singular value to be null, and by reconstructing $\hat{\mathbf{F}} = \mathbf{U}\hat{\Sigma}\mathbf{V}^\top$ where $\hat{\Sigma}$ differs from Σ by the last null column.

The implementation is simply

```
CImg<> U, S, V;
F.SVD(U,S,V);
S(2) = 0;
F = U*S.diagonal()*V.transpose();
```

The epipolar line in I_2 of a point $\mathbf{m_1} \in I_1$ is then given by $\ell_{\mathbf{m_1}} = \mathbf{F}\mathbf{m_1}$, and the equation of the line in the image plane is $\ell_{\mathbf{m_1}}^{\top}\begin{pmatrix} x & y & 1 \end{pmatrix}^{\top} = 0$ (Fig. 11.11), that is:

```
CImgDisplay Disp2(I2,"I2");
CImg<> l = F*m1;
float
   l1x = -1(2)/1(0),
   l1y = 0,
   l2x = 0,
   l2y = -1(2)/1(1);
I2.draw_line(l1x,l1y,l2x,l2y,red,1.0).display(Disp2);
```

(R) It is easy, knowing $\mathbf{F}$, to find the epipoles: from a decomposition $\mathbf{F} = \mathbf{U}^{\top}$, $\mathbf{e_1}$ (respectively $\mathbf{e_2}$) is the column of $\mathbf{U}$ (resp. $\mathbf{V}$) corresponding to the null singular value.

I_1 and the clicked point $\mathbf{m_1}$ $\quad\quad$ I_2 and the corresponding epipolar line

Figure 11.11 – Epipolar line computed using the fundamental matrix. (Source of the original image: [34].)

MATCHING

A possible use of the epipolar line is the matching of points detected on images I_1 and I_2.

Let's suppose that we have n_i points of interest detected on the image I_i, $1 \le i \le 2$ by a dedicated algorithm (Harris and Stephens detector type, see Section 6.1). Among these points we assume to know at least eight correspondences, so that the fundamental matrix $\mathbf{F}$ can be estimated. The question that arises is the following: for a point of interest P_1^j detected on I_1, is it possible to find its corresponding point on I_2, if it has indeed been detected?

A simple solution to this matching problem is to look for the point on the epipolar line associated with P_1^j with maximum correlation. For this purpose, we define around P_1^j a neighborhood of size t, and we look for the window of the same size, centered at a point on the epipolar line, having a maximum correlation. This technique, similar to motion estimation by correlation (see Section 8.2.1), is very simple to implement and is robust to errors in the estimation of $\mathbf{F}$. It assumes a conservation of luminance, and no geometrical deformation of the two images.

Other methods exist, not discussed here, such as the *RANSAC* algorithm, the phase shift approach or methods based on dynamic programming.

 Epipolar lines have no reason to be parallel. But this makes it easier to find the corresponding image and to estimate the depth. We can rectify the images, i.e., have parallel epipolars, if we know how to compute the images corresponding to the scene with parallel image planes. For this, we can generate an image of the scene by rotation around the optical center without knowing the scene. It is a question of projecting the images on a plane parallel to the baseline (the line passing through C_1 and C_2) in order to have rectified views.

11.3.2 Depth estimation

Once the $\mathbf{m_1} - \mathbf{m_2}$ mapping is done, it is possible to retrieve the depth information using the disparity d of the two points. We assume in the following, for simplicity, that the images are rectified, so the epipolar lines are parallel. The depth information of a point $\mathbf{m}$ can be calculated by a simple geometrical consideration (Fig. 11.12).

If b is the distance between the two cameras and f the focal length (assumed equal) of the two sensors, then the depth z of the point $\mathbf{m}$ in the scene can be estimated by

$$\frac{z}{f} = \frac{x}{x_1} = \frac{x-b}{x_2} = \frac{y}{y_1} = \frac{y}{y_2} \quad \text{thus } z = \frac{bf}{d} \text{ with } d = x - b$$

The matching can be done by epipolar matching, as we have seen. It is also possible to generate dense disparity maps, by computing the disparity of each pixel using its

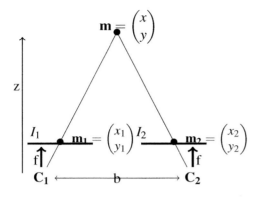

Figure 11.12 – Calculating the depth z of point $\mathbf{m}$ as a function of the geometry. b is the distance between the two optical centers of the cameras, f is their focal length.

neighborhood. The matching costs of each pixel with each disparity level in a given interval (disparity interval) are calculated. These costs determine the probability of a good matching, with these two quantities being inversely proportional. The costs are then aggregated into a neighborhood of a given size. The best match for each pixel is then sought by selecting the minimum cost match, independently of the other pixels.

Different measures are classically defined to measure matching costs, the most used being the Sum of Absolute Differences (*SAD*), the Sum of Squared Differences, (*SSD*), the Normalized Cross-Correlation (*NCC*) and the Sum of Hamming Distances (*SHD*). Code 11.18 implements the calculation of the disparity by sum of the square differences, for disparity values in the range [-dbound, dbound] and a neighborhood of size h.

Figure 11.13 shows as a result of this algorithm the estimation of the depth, knowing b and f.

Code 11.18 – Computing the disparity using SSD.

```
/*
  Computing the disparity using SSD.

  I1,I2    : Stereo images
  h        : Size of the neighborhood
  dbound   : Bound for the disparity
*/
CImg<> computeSSDDisparity(CImg<>& I1, CImg<>& I2,int h, int dbound)
{
  CImg<int> disparityMap(I1.width(),I1.height(),1,1,0);
  int arg, h2 = h/2;
  CImg<> patch1, patch2, val;

  cimg_forXY(I1,x,y)
```

```
{
  patch1 = I1.get_crop(x - h2, y - h2,x + h2, y + h2);
  float min = 1e8f;
  for (int dx = -dbound; dx<=dbound; ++dx)
  {
    patch2 = I2.get_crop(x + dx - h2,y - h2,x + dx + h2,y + h2);
    float ssd = (patch1 - patch2).get_sqr().sum();
    if (ssd<min)
    {
      min = ssd;
      arg = dx;
    }
  }
  disparityMap(x,y) = arg;
}
return disparityMap;
}
```

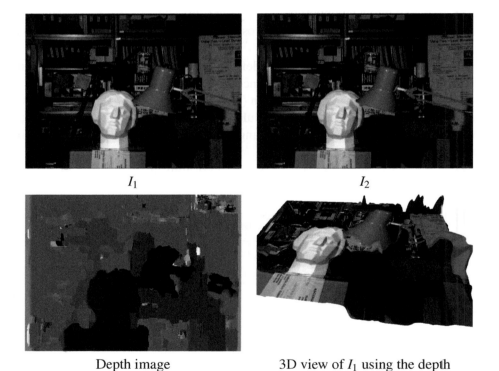

I_1 I_2

Depth image   3D view of I_1 using the depth

Figure 11.13 – Depth map calculated on two rectified images. (Source of the original images: [34].)

11.4 **Interactive deformation using *RBF***

11.4.1 **Goal of the application**

The goal of this last section is to develop an interactive "deforming mirror" application, allowing the user to visualize and modify, in real time, images coming from his *webcam*. The idea is to allow the addition and displacement of keypoints that model the desired local deformation, as illustrated in Figure 11.14.

 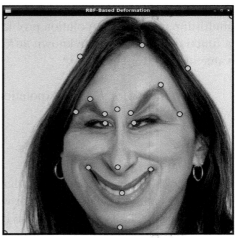

a) Image from the *webcam*, and interactive placement of keypoints

b) Image deformation obtained after moving the keypoints

Figure 11.14 – Goal: Develop an interactive deforming mirror application, getting images from the *webcam*.

To implement this application, three main components are required:

1. The ability to access the image stream from the *webcam*. With *CImg*, this is made easy by using the `CImg<T>::load_camera()` method, which internally uses functions of the *OpenCV* library to access the image stream. When compiling the program, all you need to do is enable the `cimg_use_opencv` macro, and link the executable with the *OpenCV* libraries to make use of this functionality.

2. The implementation of a function to generate a dense displacement field - of the size of the image - from a list of user-defined keypoints. The theoretical description and implementation of such a function are described in Sections 11.4.2 and 11.4.3.

3. A rudimentary graphical interface displaying a visualization of the *webcam* stream in a window, that lets the user place keypoints and move them to generate an image deformation accordingly. Here we will use the display capabilities of the *CImg* library (via the `CImgDisplay` class), and its user event handler, as already presented in the tutorial (Chapter 2).

11.4.2 The *RBF* interpolation

RBFs (*Radial Basis Functions*) are real functions used, among other things, to solve multi-dimensional interpolation problems from sparse data: assuming the values of a function $f : \mathbb{R}^n \to \mathbb{R}$ are known at K points $\mathbf{x}_k$, we try to estimate an interpolated value of $f(\mathbf{x})$, for any $\mathbf{x} \in \mathbb{R}^n$.

The principle of *RBF* interpolation is based on the assumption that f can be written:

$$\forall \mathbf{x} \in \mathbb{R}^n, \quad f(\mathbf{x}) = \sum_{l=1}^{K} w_l \, \phi\left(\|\mathbf{x} - \mathbf{x}_l\|\right) \tag{11.2}$$

where $\phi : \mathbb{R} \to \mathbb{R}$ is a pre-defined radial function, which will be evaluated for all the L_2 distances between each point $\mathbf{x}$ for which we want to estimate $f(\mathbf{x})$ and the known points $\mathbf{x}_k$ of f. Classically, we choose $\phi(r) = r^2 \log(r)$ for an interpolation known as *Thin Plate Spline*.

Equation 11.2 involves real weights w_l determined as follows:
1. by writting the set of the K Equations 11.2 for all the points $\mathbf{x}_k$ whose value $f(\mathbf{x}_k)$ is known, i.e., $f(\mathbf{x}_k) = \sum_{l=1}^{K} w_l \, \phi\left(\|\mathbf{x}_k - \mathbf{x}_l\|\right)$;
2. by formulating this set of equations with K unknowns as a linear system $\mathbf{F} = \mathbf{MW}$, as:

$$\mathbf{F} = \begin{pmatrix} f(\mathbf{x}_1) \\ \vdots \\ f(\mathbf{x}_K) \end{pmatrix}, \quad \mathbf{M} = \begin{pmatrix} \phi(\|X_1 - X_1\|) & \cdots & \phi(\|X_K - X_1\|) \\ \vdots & \phi(\|X_k - X_l\|) & \vdots \\ \phi(\|X_1 - X_K\|) & \cdots & \phi(\|X_K - X_K\|) \end{pmatrix}$$

and $\mathbf{W} = \begin{pmatrix} w_1 \\ \vdots \\ w_K \end{pmatrix}$, the vector of weights that we are looking for;

3. by solving this linear system: $\mathbf{W} = \mathbf{M}^{-1}\,\mathbf{F}$.

The weights w_l being estimated, the function f can then be evaluated at any point $\mathbf{x} \in \mathbb{R}^n$ of the space, with Equation 11.2.

The *RBF* interpolation works the same for any dimension n of the definition space of f in that it interpolates the known values in a continuous way, and that these values do not have to be located on a regular grid in $\mathbb{R}^n$. From an algorithmic point of view, the method relies mainly on the inversion of a $K \times K$ symmetric matrix, for which there exists an algorithm in $o(K^3)$. This means that the computation time increases very quickly with the number of known samples K.

Figure 11.15 shows the application of the *RBF* interpolation for the reconstruction of an gray-level image, of size 224×171, from a small selection of 1187 value samples (representing 3% of the total image data).

a) Input image 224×171 b) Selection of 1187 samples   c) *RBF* interpolation

Figure 11.15 – Example of reconstruction of a 2D image from a set of sparse samples, using *RBF* interpolation.

When the function $f : \mathbb{R}^n \rightarrow \mathbb{R}^P$ is vector-valued (e.g., color images), we can estimate the $K \times P$ required weights w_k^p at once, by solving the linear system $\mathbf{F} = \mathbf{M}\,\mathbf{W}$, where $\mathbf{F}$ and $\mathbf{W}$ have P columns rather than a single one, one column for each vector component of the function f to interpolate.

In practice, *RBFs* allow to build very generic interpolation methods, adaptable to many types of data, as long as the number of keypoints K remains reasonable. This will be the case here (at most a few dozens).

11.4.3 *RBF* for image warping

Rather than interpolating scalar values (pixel intensities), as in Fig. 11.15, we will here use *RBFs* to interpolate the 2D displacement vectors 2D $(\Delta x_k, \Delta y_k)$, associated with each keypoint (x_k, y_k). These vectors will represent the difference between the original coordinates of the keypoint (its coordinates when it was added) and its current coordinates, after it was moved by the user.

In practice, the set of keypoints is stored as a list `CImgList<float>`, each element of this list being a `CImg<float>` image of size 1×4, containing the values (x_k, y_k, X_k, Y_k) in that order. The (x_k, y_k) are the current keypoint coordinates in the image, and the (X_k, Y_k) are the original keypoint coordinates. The displacement vectors to be interpolated are therefore $(\Delta x_k = X_k - x_k, \Delta y_k = Y_k - y_k)$. To be independent from the size of the images, the coordinates are normalized between 0 and 100 (which is equivalent to consider that we are working on displacement fields of size 100×100).

We first initialize this set of keypoints with four points, corresponding to the four corners of the image:

```
CImgList<> keypoints;
CImg<>::vector(0,0,0,0).move_to(keypoints);
CImg<>::vector(100,0,100,0).move_to(keypoints);
CImg<>::vector(100,100,100,100).move_to(keypoints);
CImg<>::vector(0,100,0,100).move_to(keypoints);
```

RBF interpolation requires the construction of two matrices: $\mathbf{M}$ (of size $K \times K$) and $\mathbf{F}$ (of size $2 \times K$). The matrix $\mathbf{F}$ has two columns, and thus will be stored as an image of size $2 \times K$, because two displacement values $(\Delta x, \Delta y)$ are to be interpolated:

Code 11.19 – Construct of matrices M and F for the RBF interpolation.

```
CImg<> M(keypoints.size(),keypoints.size());
cimg_forXY(M,p,q) { // Filling the matrix M
  float
    xp = keypoints(p,0)*(img.width()-1)/100,
    yp = keypoints(p,1)*(img.height()-1)/100,
    xq = keypoints(q,0)*(img.width()-1)/100,
    yq = keypoints(q,1)*(img.height()-1)/100,
    r = cimg::hypot(xq - xp,yq - yp);
  M(p,q) = phi(r);
}

CImg<> F(2,keypoints.size());
cimg_forY(F,p) { // Filling the matrix F
  float
    xp = (keypoints(p,0) - keypoints(p,2))*(img.width()-1)/100,
    yp = (keypoints(p,1) - keypoints(p,3))*(img.height()-1)/100;
  F(0,p) = xp;
  F(1,p) = yp;
}
```

We shall have previously defined the function $\phi(r)$ by:

```
double phi(double r) {
  return r*r*std::log(1e-9 + r);
}
```

The variable `img` is a `CImg<unsigned char>` containing the image from the *webcam*. The function `cimg::hypoth(a,b)`, used to calculate `r`, simply returns

$\sqrt{a^2 + b^2}$. With these two matrices defined, the system $\mathbf{MW} = \mathbf{F}$ can be solved using the method `CImg<T>::solve()`, which returns the $2 \times N$ image that contains the weights $\mathbf{W}$:

```
CImg<> W = B.get_solve(A); // Get the RBF weights
```

The dense displacement field `warp` can then be computed, by implementing the formula (11.2). For the sake of speed, we compute it for an image resolution four times smaller, and then linearly re-interpolate the resulting dense field to the size of the *webcam* image. This ensures that our application works in real time.

Code 11.20 – Compute the dense field of motion vectors.

```
CImg<> warp(img.width()/4,img.height()/4,1,2);
cimg_forXY(warp,x,y) {
  float u = 0, v = 0;
  cimglist_for(keypoints,p) {
    float
      xp = keypoints(p,0)*(img.width()-1)/100,
      yp = keypoints(p,1)*(img.height()-1)/100,
      r = cimg::hypot(4*x - xp,4*y - yp),
      phi_r = phi(r);
    u += W(0,p)*phi_r;
    v += W(1,p)*phi_r;
  }
  warp(x,y,0) = 4*x - u;
  warp(x,y,1) = 4*y - v;
}
warp.resize(img.width(),img.height(),1,2,3);
```

The desired image warp is then obtained by applying the displacement field `warp` to the original image `img`, using the method `CImg<T>::warp()`:

```
img.warp(warp,0,1,1);
```

11.4.4 User interface for keypoint management

We give here the keys to implement a simple interface for managing keypoints, allowing a user to put them over the *webcam* image, move them or delete them. As for any task related to image display and event management, we use the features offered by the `CImgDisplay` class. We therefore start the program by initializing an instance `disp`:

```
CImgDisplay disp;
```

The creation of an empty `CImgDisplay` instance does not directly display a window on the screen. It will only appear when an image is displayed for the first time. We can then write this first simple event loop associated to the display `disp`:

Code 11.21 – Event loop for the display of the image and its keypoints.

```
do {
  // Get the webcam image.
  img.load_camera(0,640,480,0,false);

  // Estimate the displacement map by RBF.
  CImg<> warp = get_RBF(img,keypoints);

  // Display the image in the window.
  if (!disp) disp.assign(img,"RBF-Based Deformation",0);
  CImg<unsigned char> visu = img.get_resize(disp,1);
  cimglist_for(keypoints,l) { // Draw keypoints
    int
      x = (int)cimg::round(keypoints(l,0)*(visu.width()-1)/100),
      y = (int)cimg::round(keypoints(l,1)*(visu.height()-1)/100);
    visu.draw_circle(x,y,8,black,0.75f).draw_circle(x,y,6,white,0.75
      f);
  }
  disp.display(visu).wait(40);
  if (disp.is_resized()) disp.resize();
} while (!disp.is_closed() && !disp.is_keyESC());
```

This event loop simply displays in a window the image stream from the webcam (in 640×480 resolution). It also displays the keypoints defined in the keypoints list (so for the moment, only the four corners of the image).

The user management of these keypoints (adding, moving, deleting) is not very difficult to implement, as shown in Code 11.22, to be added at the end of the loop.

Code 11.22 – Keypoint management.

```
// Get mouse coordinates and state of the mouse button.
int xm = disp.mouse_x(), ym = disp.mouse_y(), bm = disp.button();

if (xm>=0 && bm) { // The user has clicked in the window.
  float // Mouse coordinates in percent.
    xmp = xm*100.0f/(disp.width()-1),
    ymp = ym*100.0f/(disp.height()-1);

  // Determine if an existing keypoint has been selected
  // by the user.
  if (selected<0) cimglist_for(keypoints,l) {
    int
      x = (int)cimg::round(keypoints(l,0)),
      y = (int)cimg::round(keypoints(l,1));
    if (cimg::hypot(x - xmp,y - ymp)<15) { selected = l; break; }
  }
```

```
if (selected<0 && bm&1) {
  // No selection + left button -> Add a new keypoint.
  int
    xw = (int)(xmp*(img.width()-1)/100),
    yw = (int)(ymp*(img.height()-1)/100);
  CImg<>::vector(xmp,ymp,
                 warp.atXY(xw,yw,0,0)*100/(img.width()-1),
                 warp.atXY(xw,yw,0,1)*100/(img.height()-1)).
                 move_to(keypoints);
  selected = (int)keypoints.size() - 1; // Keep it as a selection

} else if (selected>=0 && bm&1) {
  // Selection + left button -> Move the keypoint.
  keypoints(selected,0) = xmp;
  keypoints(selected,1) = ymp;

} else if (selected>=0 && bm&2) {
  // Selection + right button -> Suppress the keypoint.
  keypoints.remove(selected);
  selected = -1;
  disp.set_button(); // Flush event 'button pressed'
}
} else if (!bm) selected = -1; // No button -> no selection
```

where

```
int selected = -1;
```

is a variable that will be defined at the beginning of the program (outside the event loop), which gives the index of a selected keypoint (if any), or -1 is no keypoint has been selected.

All these blocks of code, put together, make it possible to build a fun and interactive distorting mirror application.

List of *CImg* Codes

Chapter 7

Chapter 8

Chapter 9

Bibliography

[1] R. Achanta et al. "SLIC superpixels compared to state-of-the-art superpixel methods". In: *IEEE transactions on pattern analysis and machine intelligence* 34.11 (2012), pages 2274–2282 (cited on page 176).

[2] T. Ahonen, A. Hadid, and M. Pietikäinen. "Face Description with Local Binary Patterns: Application to Face Recognition." In: *IEEE Trans. Pattern Anal. Mach. Intell.* 28.12 (2006), pages 2037–2041 (cited on page 148).

[3] V. Barra, A. Cornuejols, and L. Miclet. *Apprentissage artificiel - 4e édition: De Bayes et Hume au Deep Learning*. Eds. Eyrolles, 2021 (cited on page 167).

[4] J. Bernsen. "Dynamic thresholding of gray-level images". In: 1986 (cited on page 167).

[5] J. Canny. "A Computational Approach to Edge Detection". In: *IEEE Trans. Pattern Anal. Mach. Intell.* 8.6 (June 1986), pages 679–698. ISSN: 0162-8828 (cited on page 84).

[6] V. Caselles, R. Kimmel, and G. Sapiro. "Geodesic Active Contours". In: *Int. J. Comput. Vision* 22.1 (Feb. 1997), pages 61–79. ISSN: 0920-5691 (cited on pages 151, 153, 154, 156).

[7] V. Caselles et al. "A geometric model for active Contours in image processing". In: *Numerische Mathematik* 66 (Jan. 1993), pages 1–31 (cited on page 153).

[8] L. D. Cohen. "On Active Contour Models and Balloons". In: *CVGIP: Image Underst.* 53.2 (Mar. 1991), pages 211–218. ISSN: 1049-9660 (cited on page 155).

[9] J Cousty et al. *The 4D Heart Database*. Accessed: 2020-06-22. 2006 (cited on page 236).

[10] R. Deriche. "Using Canny's criteria to derive a recursively implemented optimal edge detector." In: *Int. J. Comput. Vis.* 1.2 (1987), pages 167–187 (cited on pages 84, 86).

[11] R. Deriche. "Recursively implementating the Gaussian and its derivatives". In: (1993) (cited on page 88).

[12] S. Di Zenzo. "A note on the gradient of a multi-image". In: *Computer Vision, Graphics, and Image Processing* 33 (1986), pages 116–125 (cited on page 221).

[13] C. Galambos, J. Kittler, and J. Matas. "Progressive Probabilistic Hough Transform for Line Detection". In: *1999 Conference on Computer Vision and Pattern Recognition (CVPR '99), 23-25 June 1999, Ft. Collins, CO, USA*. IEEE Computer Society, 1999, pages 1554–1560 (cited on page 131).

[14] J. Gomes and O. Faugeras. "Reconciling Distance Functions and Level Sets". In: *Journal of Visual Communication and Image Representation* 11.2 (2000), pages 209–223. ISSN: 1047-3203 (cited on page 157).

[15] R. C. Gonzalez and R. E. Woods. *Digital image processing*. Upper Saddle River, N.J.: Prentice Hall, 2008 (cited on pages 43, 59).

[16] C. Harris and M. Stephens. "A Combined Corner and Edge Detector". In: *Proceedings of the 4th Alvey Vision Conference*. 1988, pages 147–151 (cited on pages 122, 123).

[17] D.C He and L Wang. "Texture classification using texture spectrum." In: *Pattern Recognit.* 23.8 (1990), pages 905–910 (cited on pages 138, 140).

[18] B. K. P. Horn and B.; G. Schunck. "Determining Optical Flow". In: *Artificial Intelligence* 17 (1981), pages 185–203 (cited on pages 184, 185).

[19] H. Hotelling. "Analysis of a complex of statistical variables into principal components". In: *J. Educ. Psych.* 24 (1933) (cited on page 210).

[20] J. Illingworth and J. Kittler. "A survey of the Hough transform". In: *Computer Vision, Graphics and Image Processing* (1988), pages 280–280 (cited on page 137).

[21] R.E Kalman. "A New Approach to Linear Filtering and Prediction Problems". In: *Transactions of the ASME–Journal of Basic Engineering* 82.Series D (1960), pages 35–45 (cited on page 205).

[22] M. Kass, A. Witkin, and D. Terzopoulos. "Snakes: Active contour models". In: *International Journal of Computer Vision* 1.4 (1988), pages 321–331 (cited on page 153).

[23] A. Koschan and M.A. Abidi. *Digital Color Image Processing*. USA: Wiley-Interscience, 2008. ISBN: 0470147083 (cited on page 213).

[24] B. D. Lucas and T. Kanade. "An iterative image registration technique with an application to stereo vision". In: *Proceedings of the 7th international joint conference on Artificial intelligence - Volume 2*. IJCAI'81. Vancouver, BC, Canada: Morgan Kaufmann Publishers Inc., 1981, pages 674–679 (cited on pages 185, 189).

[25] Y. Ma and Y. Fu. *Manifold Learning Theory and Applications*. CRC Press, 2012 (cited on page 210).

[26] J. Macqueen. "Some methods for classification and analysis of multivariate observations". In: *In 5-th Berkeley Symposium on Mathematical Statistics and Probability*. 1967, pages 281–297 (cited on page 170).

[27] L. Maddalena and A. Petrosino. "Towards Benchmarking Scene Background Initialization". In: *New Trends in Image Analysis and Processing – ICIAP 2015 Workshops*. Edited by Vittorio Murino et al. Cham: Springer International Publishing, 2015, pages 469–476 (cited on page 119).

[28] T. Ojala, M. Pietikäinen, and T. Mäenpää. "Multiresolution Gray-Scale and Rotation Invariant Texture Classification with Local Binary Patterns". In: *IEEE Transactions on Pattern Analysis and Machine Intelligence* 24.7 (2002), pages 971–987. ISSN: 0162-8828 (cited on pages 145, 146).

[29] S. Osher and J. A. Sethian. "Fronts Propagating with Curvature-Dependent Speed: Algorithms Based on Hamilton-Jacobi Formulations". In: *J. Comput. Phys.* 79.1 (Nov. 1988), pages 12–49. ISSN: 0021-9991 (cited on pages 153, 157).

[30] N. Otsu. "A Threshold Selection Method from Gray-Level Histograms". In: *IEEE Transactions on Systems, Man and Cybernetics* 9.1 (1979), pages 62–66 (cited on page 164).

[31] P. V. C. Hough. *A Method and Means for Recognizing Complex Patterns*. US Patent: 3,069,654. Dec. 1962 (cited on page 128).

[32] P. Perona and J. Malik. "Scale-Space and Edge Detection Using Anisotropic Diffusion". In: *IEEE Trans. Pattern Anal. Mach. Intell.* 12.7 (July 1990), pages 629–639. ISSN: 0162-8828 (cited on page 114).

[33] W. Pesnell, B. Thompson, and P. Chamberlin. "The Solar Dynamics Observatory (SDO)". In: *Solar Physics* 275 (Nov. 2012), pages 3–15 (cited on page 213).

[34] D. Scharstein and R. Szeliski. "A Taxonomy and Evaluation of Dense Two-Frame Stereo Correspondence Algorithms". In: *International Journal of Computer Vision* 47.1/2/3 (Apr. 2002), pages 7–42 (cited on pages 269, 272).

[35] C. Schmid, R. Mohr, and C. Bauckhage. "Evaluation of Interest Point Detectors". In: *Int. J. Comput. Vis.* 37.2 (2000), pages 151–172 (cited on page 122).

[36] J. Serra. *Image Analysis and Mathematical Morphology*. USA: Academic Press, Inc., 1983. ISBN: 0126372403 (cited on pages 53, 58, 59).

[37]   J.A. Sethian. *Level Set Methods and Fast Marching Methods: Evolving Inter-faces in Computational Geometry, Fluid Mechanics, Computer Vision, and Materials Science*. Cambridge Monographs on Applied and Computational Mathematics. Cambridge University Press, 1999. ISBN: 9780521645577 (cited on pages 156, 158–160).

[38]   C. E. Shannon. "A Mathematical Theory of Communication". In: *The Bell System Technical Journal* 27 (July 1948), pages 379–423, 623– (cited on pages 4, 244).

[39]   J. Shi and C. Tomasi. "Good Features to Track". In: *IEEE Conference on Computer Vision and Pattern Recognition* (1994), pages 593–600 (cited on page 126).

[40]   H. Tamura, S. Mori, and T. Yamawaki. "Texture features corresponding to visual perception". In: *IEEE Transactions on Systems, Man and Cybernetics* 8.6 (1978) (cited on page 140).

[41]   B. Triggs and M. Sdika. "Boundary conditions for Young-van Vliet recursive filtering". In: *IEEE Transactions on Signal Processing* 54.6 (2006), pages 2365–2367 (cited on page 88).

[42]   D. Tschumperlé and B. Besserer. "High Quality Deinterlacing Using Inpainting and Shutter-Model Directed Temporal Interpolation". In: *Computer Vision and Graphics: International Conference, ICCVG 2004, Warsaw, Poland, September 2004, Proceedings*. Edited by K Wojciechowski et al. Dordrecht: Springer Netherlands, 2006, pages 301–307 (cited on page 111).

[43]   I.T. Young and L.J. Van Vliet. "Recursive implementation of the Gaussian filter". In: *Signal processing* 44.2 (1995), pages 139–151 (cited on page 88).

[44]   T. Y. Zhang and Ching Y. Suen. "A Fast Parallel Algorithm for Thinning Digital Patterns." In: *Commun. ACM* 27.3 (1984), pages 236–239 (cited on page 64).

Index